Reformed America

Reformed America

The Middle and Southern States, 1783-1837

FRED J. HOOD

The University of Alabama Press
University, Alabama

Library of Congress Cataloging in Publication Data

Hood, Fred J.
  Reformed America.

  Bibliography: p.
  Includes index.
  1. Reformed (Reformed Church) in the Middle States—
History. 2. Presbyterians—Middle States—History.
3. Reformed (Reformed Church) in the Southern States.
4. Presbyterians—Southern States—History. 5. Middle
States—Church history. 6. Southern States—Church
history. I. Title.
BX9496.M53H66   285.7′75   79-28834
ISBN 0-8173-0034-1

To My Parents

Contents

Acknowledgments

My indebtedness to others is incalculable. Many scholars whose names do not appear in footnotes have contributed insight and understanding at some point, but the rivulets have become so mixed in the stream that to give appropriate credit would be impossible. I have attempted to give references primarily to source materials and those scholars contributing most directly to my efforts. I am deeply grateful to a number of librarians. The staffs of Speer Library of Princeton Theological Seminary, Gardner A. Sage Library of the New Brunswick Theological Seminary, Free Library of Philadelphia, City Library of New York, and the American Bible Society were most helpful. I am especially indebted to the staff of the Presbyterian Historical Society and to Virginia Covington of the Cooke Memorial Library of Georgetown College. I also wish to thank the National Endowment for the Humanities, the American Philosophical Society, and Georgetown College for grants that made this study possible. I am deeply indebted to John F. Wilson, Robert T. Handy, Theodore L. Agnew, John Ellis, Martin E. Marty, John M. Mulder, and Donald G. Mathews for help and encouragement at various stages. My sincerest appreciation goes to Susan M. Chapman, whose assistance in the final phases of manuscript preparation was invaluable.

Publication of this book was made possible, in part, by financial assistance from the Andrew W. Mellon Foundation and the American Council of Learned Societies.

Reformed America

Introduction

A perceived relationship between religion and national welfare has been a constant feature of American history. It has been widely recognized as one of the most fundamental aspects of colonial America and some scholars, Carl Bridenbaugh and Alan Heimert in particular,[1] have understood it to be one of the major issues in the American Revolution. While this latter point is a matter of dispute, the significance of religion in American national life is even more vaguely understood. Religion as a significant motivating force appears in discussions of abolitionism and the Civil War, the Social Gospel and late nineteenth- and early twentieth-century liberalism, and the world wars and the mid-twentieth-century anti-Communist crusade, but an adequate explanation of the interrelatedness of these has eluded the community of historians. This significant gap in understanding the nature of the American experience has derived from a concentration on what would probably be inadequately labeled as the religious extremes. The study of religion in America has focused on the obviously conservative, rational, and community-oriented tradition of New England on the one hand and on emotional, revivalistic, and allegedly individualistic pietism on the other hand. The more significant contribution to an ongoing belief that American national welfare was directly related to the religious practice of its citizens was made by adherents to the Reformed tradition in the middle and southern states.

The contributions of the Reformed of the middle and southern states to national developments in religion have not been apparent because to an amazing degree these Reformed have been largely overlooked by critical historians as a subject for investigation. Even for the largest of the Reformed denominations, the Presbyterians, historiography is sparse. One searches in vain for a recent critical history of Presbyterianism in the United States. The most recent attempt was that of Robert Ellis Thompson in 1895. More recent histories have been restricted in chronological or geographic terms. Leonard J. Trinterud wrote an excellent study of colonial Presbyterianism that traced developments to 1788. Lefferts A. Loetscher wrote a history of theological developments within the Presbyterian Church in the United States of America since 1869. More recently, George M. Marsden produced a study of New School Presbyterianism. These latter two studies were strongly influenced by the Presbyterian tradition, but there is no such treatment of the period from 1789 to 1837. This period has received some attention in the regional studies of William Warren Sweet, Walter Brownlow Posey, Ernest Trice Thompson, L. C. Rudolph, and Robert Hastings Nichols. These studies, however, focus predominantly on the southern and western regions of the nation, thus leaving the major centers of Presbyterian strength untouched by modern critical scholarship.[2]

This lacuna in historiography would be deplorable if for no other reason than because the Reformed denominations of the middle and southern states collectively formed the largest religious sector of the United States in 1780. The Presbyterians, Reformed Dutch, and German Reformed alone had 785 churches, almost all of them in the middle and southern states, as compared to 749 Congregational churches. By 1820 these Reformed denominations had twice as many churches as the Congregationalists but claimed fewer churches than either the Methodists or Baptists.[3] In terms of social prestige, however, the highly educated Reformed clergy stood far above the Methodists and Baptists and few contemporaries doubted their greater national significance. Charles Beecher called the General Assembly of the Presbyterian Church "one of the most impressive as well as powerful bodies in the world." Beecher believed that the assembly "swayed a power rivaling, if not really surpassing that of the Congress," and was sure that it affected "not merely the religious, but the civil interests of the nation."[4]

Although more numerous than the New England Congregationalists, the Reformed of the middle and southern states have received inadequate attention in the more general interpretative histories of religion in America. Theological similarity to the more thoroughly investigated Congregationalists has led to interpretation of the Reformed tradition of the middle and southern states as a Congregationalist appendage. The discussion by Winthrop Hudson is illustrative. At the beginning of the national era, according to Hudson, the Presbyterians and Congregationalists "had come to regard themselves as a single phalanx, with a regional allocation of territory." While this seems accurate enough, Hudson later discusses the "Protestant counter offensive" of the early nineteenth century, about which he said, "The Protestant America that the several denominations sought to fashion was defined in what may roughly be described as New England terms."[5]

This study questions such often repeated generalizations. Not only did the Reformed of the middle and southern states follow a theological course that differentiated their reflection on the nation from that of New England, but their total situation was vastly different and evoked different responses. While at least some of the New England Congregationalists enjoyed legal preferment well into the nineteenth century, the Reformed of the middle and southern states came into the national era with a heritage that varied from a position of legal equality in the middle states to that of a recently emerged dissenting sect in many of the southern states. Given national aspirations at least as well defined as those of New England, the Reformed of the middle and southern states were forced to develop means of implementation in the face of governmental disengagement from religion long before the New Englanders found themselves in a similar legal environment. On the basis of chronology alone, then, it would seem probable that the Reformed of the middle and southern states tutored the New Englanders in the ways and means of promoting religion in the wake of disestablishment.

Not only has the essentially conservative contribution of the Reformed of the middle and southern states been concealed by a concentration on New England, it has also been deemphasized by a misunderstanding of the nature of Reformed evangelicalism. A consistent feature of the historiography of religion in America has been the equation of all revivalism with emotionalism and an emphasis on the salvation of individuals. Since the Reformed, especially the Presbyterians, experienced a number of revivals, there has been a tendency to interpret these as having similarity to the pietistic tradition most often described in terms of Methodism. The Reformed of the middle and southern states, however, promoted a tradition of revivalism that was both rational and community-oriented and that was fundamentally consistent with their conservative national aspirations. Some members of the Reformed tradition succeeded in adjusting this tradition to accommodate the more popular emotional revivalism while retaining the community-oriented functions that promoted the national aspirations of the Reformed.

The Reformed of the middle and southern states have thus been interpreted as adjuncts to other important and, significantly, functionally dissimilar religious groups when in reality they developed their own patterns of thought and action with regard to the American nation. While the New England Congregationalists were still favored by their state governments and could still fancy that God ruled nations through a contractual or covenantal relationship, the Reformed of the middle and southern states developed the idea that God ruled through the means of natural and unchanging moral laws that could be determined through rational inquiry. Incorporated into Reformed theology and conveyed through their understanding of American history, this gave the Reformed the leverage to insist that the only road to national prosperity and happiness was Reformed Christianity. This same ideology propelled them to associated activity designed to indoctrinate Americans, especially underprivileged groups, to comply with the Reformed way. In the 1820s and 1830s some of these Reformed tired of the slowness of such an approach and turned to revivalism as a more efficient means of promoting religion among Americans and thereby securing national prosperity.

In this study I have used the terms "Reformed" and "Reformed tradition" to refer to those persons and groups in the theological tradition of John Calvin. On a denominational level I have confined the study to those bodies with the most obvious Reformed heritage, the most significant of which were the Presbyterians and the Reformed Dutch. The German Reformed were numerically large but because of less homogeneity within the denomination, which was only reflected in the language problems, it was of lesser national significance. The smaller Reformed bodies, such as the Associate Reformed church, the Reformed Presbyterian church, and the Associate Synod of North America, were vigorous proponents of the Reformed tradition, furnished some significant leaders, and supported the national aspirations of the larger denominations. The Reformed tradition, however, was not confined to these denominations. As Edwin Scott Gaustad has noted, "Of the colonial religious bodies, only the Quakers and Roman Catholics stood distinctly outside the Reformed tradition."[6] On an individual basis, many Baptists (especially those of the Philadelphia Baptist Association), Episcopalians, and even a few Methodists shared the Reformed national aspirations and cooperated with them in national endeavors. Although I have confined this study primarily to persons from the major Reformed denominations, when these other individuals became involved in predominantly Reformed associations they are quite properly considered as part of the Reformed tradition.

This is not a history of the "church" or of the Reformed denominations. It is a study that intends an analysis of the Reformed tradition of the middle and southern states in relation to the American nation. As such, it ignores large areas of development that were of vital concern to the Reformed and possibly to their descendants of the present day. Those aspects of the tradition related to the internal development of the denomination, for example, have been considered only when they were intimately related, or thought to be related, to the total life of the nation. Thus, while the Reformed tradition of the middle and southern states, as one expression of American religious life, is the subject of investigation, the lines of inquiry are controlled by the concept of the American nation.

Many of the older secondary sources, as well as many of the more recent accounts of various aspects of this period, have been written as instances of "denominational historiography," with the result that their focus has been on areas of development affecting the denomination itself. Emphasis has been given to manifestations of divisions within the church that have been interpreted as critical. Although Presbyterians, for example, were united in a single denomination between 1758 and 1837, denominational historians have relentlessly sought to distinguish between parties throughout that period. During this time several generations of leaders came and departed and the issues actually varied considerably. No single vote taken in the Presbyterian General Assembly prior to the mid-1820s really discloses much about the impending Old School and New School fissure. The alignments in every case were substantially different from the lines of division that occurred in 1838.

From a broader perspective it is the striking degree of continuity and homogeneity that is more significant. The period from 1783 to 1826 was one of the most harmonious in Presbyterian history, and on matters of national life the unity was even more striking. It was in fact the degree of conformity that made minor variations the subject of often bitter controversy. The large areas of agreement among the Reformed were of far greater importance, from the national perspective, than the shades of differences within these areas. The presbyterian form of government, with presbyterial control over ministerial education, ordination, and appointment, was designed to promote uniformity, and the efficiency with which any variation was detected and brought to trial further tended to produce conformity.

At the same time, this is a study of the Reformed leadership and as such largely ignores the rank and file, or the common man. This is, of course, often the case with historical literature. The elites are simply easier to study because they are the ones who have left the volumes of written materials that still form the basis for most history. This approach leaves many intriguing questions unanswered. To what extent did the masses of Americans, Reformed churchgoers and others, agree with the Reformed understanding of the relationship between religion and national prosperity? What percentage of the population actively supported Reformed endeavors? To these and other equally interesting questions I have had to be content with an occasional meager insight. These questions, however, could not be properly posed without first having acquired some basic understanding of the aspirations of this long-neglected Reformed leadership.

There is also the question of relative influence in terms of the total national development. Were the Reformed of the middle and southern states more influential than the New Englanders in developing national patterns of thought and action regarding the relationship between religion and the nation? Was the Reformed version of Enlightenment philosophy more pervasive and influential than that of the Jeffersonians? Was religion of greater significance in the total life of the nation than politics or economics? While there has been a constant temptation to draw conclusions on these broader issues, I am well aware that historians most frequently err in interpretation by drawing conclusions of greater magnitude than warranted by the scope of their research.

At the same time, intensive study of any phenomenon can provide possibly valid insight into broader subjects. I am convinced, for example, that Reformed Protestantism was a dominant element in the American world view for at least fifty years beyond the signing of the Declaration of Independence—and maybe for longer. If this is the case, those historians who have emphasized the influence of "liberal" or Enlightenment philosophy on American institutions have basically misunderstood the

intellectual forces that were most powerful. It is entirely possible that
"liberal" philosophy provided the conceptual basis for the thought of a
few American leaders, however influential, but that these same ideas
were of greater consequence as understood and interpreted by more
conservative and orthodox Americans. Another conclusion implied in
this conviction is that the significance of political and economic developments has been overemphasized. Political and economic conflict
may have occurred in a context of a more fundamental consensus that
was more medieval than modern, more conservative than liberal, more
religious than political or economic. My research suggests these as viable
hypotheses, but does not lend itself to arguing them. The thoughtful
reader will certainly want to consider the possibilities.

One further word of explanation. The preponderance of Reformed
strength was in the middle states and the most influential Reformed
institutions were located in that region. It is inevitable, therefore, that
the middle states receive greater attention. At the same time, and in spite
of a recent argument to the contrary,[7] for most of the period under
consideration the Reformed of the middle and southern states were a
distinctive entity. I have not concentrated, however, on the noticeable
divergence of the sections in the 1820s. As the sections drifted apart the
common philosophy of the relationship between religion and national
welfare came to serve them both and was expounded with equal fervor
and conviction during the Civil War.[8]

Chapter 1

An American Philosophy of the Connection between Religion and National Prosperity

By the time George Washington presented his Farewell Address in 1796, twenty years after the signing of the Declaration of Independence, Americans were fully engaged in the process of self-government. All the energy that had transformed a basically conservative colonial American elite into a revolutionary force bent on overthrowing British rule was now directed toward the perpetuation of the government resulting from that revolution. In the Farewell Address Washington urged Americans to "resist with care the spirit of innovation" in principles of government and declared the "continuance of the union" to be a "primary object of patriotic desire."[1] There was no need now for a Thomas Paine or for natural rights propaganda. America had secured its liberties, a term used most frequently to describe home rule. What was now deemed necessary was something to insure political and economic stability. In many ways the personality of Washington had been the single greatest factor working toward that end, and for that reason he had delayed his retirement. In 1796 he was bent on leaving active political life and he strongly desired to use his influence to secure the stability and prosperity of the nation. In this context Washington was solicitous to remind Americans that their future was intimately connected with God's providential government of the world.

While historians have devoted pages to Washington's admonitions against party spirit and foreign alignments, his strong statements on the necessity of religion to national prosperity have been essentially neglected. This is understandable because of the fascination of partisan politics to American historians, but nevertheless unfortunate because it has obscured a point of more significance for an understanding of the nature of the American experience. That religion was necessary for national prosperity was an American maxim, denied by only a few of the nation's elite. Washington gave expression to this national conviction with the rhetorical question, "Can it be that Providence has not connected the permanent felicity of a nation with its virtue?"[2]

Washington's statement of the relationship of religion to national prosperity was so significant as to warrant extensive quotation. He voiced the popular opinion that "of all the dispositions and habits which lead to political prosperity, religion and morality are indispensable supports." No one could claim to be patriotic if they attempted to subvert "these firmest props," and politicians as well as religious persons should respect and cherish them. Without the support of religion, oaths in the courtroom could not be dependable and there would be no "security for property, for reputation, for life." Morality could not be maintained without religion and "morality is a necessary spring of popular government." Indeed religion was the "fabric" of society.[3]

These statements were not only significant as a display of Washington's respect for religion as a means of social control, but also for the manner in which he made them. The whole of Washington's literary legacy, both public and private, demonstrated his firm belief in providence. In his operation of Mount Vernon, Washington consistently acquiesced in what he believed to be acts of providence. Of a drought he declared, "At disappointments and losses which are the effects of Providential acts, I never repine; because I am sure the alwise disposer of events knows better than we do, what is best for us, or what we deserve."[4] Beyond this, Washington strongly believed in providence as the supreme power controlling the destinies of nations. As a military commander he ordered "all officers, and soldiers . . . to implore the blessings of heaven upon the means used for our safety and defence."[5] During the course of the Revolution and afterwards, he consistently ascribed America's good fortunes to the beneficial work of "Heaven."[6]

Therefore, when Washington spoke of the necessity of religion to national prosperity in his Farewell Address, he was voicing a conviction of long standing. Although the final version does not make it evident, Washington's first draft, which was submitted to Alexander Hamilton for revision, placed the religious appeal in an extremely prominent position. After quoting his retirement address prepared for use in 1792, Washington indicated a need to make certain additions since "considerable changes" had taken place in the intervening four years. The first of his "ardent wishes" was that "party disputes . . . may subside, . . . as the wisdom of Providence has ordained that men on the same subjects shall not always think alike. . . ." The second wish was that Americans not squander the beneficence of providence that had "favored no nation on earth with more abundant and substantial means of happiness than United America."[7]

In the Hamilton version adopted by Washington, both the order and the language were considerably changed. Because of Hamilton's concern for pressing political problems, the religious appeal lost its place of prominence. It was pressed into the middle, rather than coming both first and last as in Washington's draft. More significant, however, was the change in the language. Washington's draft was consistent with a hundred other of his statements over the previous twenty years.

Washington's generalizations about providence could have applied to any nation in the world and could have been penned by any number of European heads of state. The final published version was something entirely different and represented what had become an unmistakably American conception of providence.

The essential feature of the philosophy was that virtue and morality were necessary to the existence and prosperity of all governments but especially and emphatically to "free government" or "popular government," and that national virtue and morality could not be "maintained without religion." A central concern of the doctrine, however, was never far removed from the "security of property." Washington detracted from the full force of the American doctrine by deleting the third paragraph, which began with the admonition and comment, "Cultivate, also, industry and frugality. They are auxiliaries of good morals, and great sources of private and national prosperity."[8]

This statement of the doctrine of providence reflected an American intellectual development that had taken place primarily at the College of New Jersey and was rapidly spreading throughout the middle and southern states. It was based on the Reformed theological tradition, reflected the strong influence of the Age of Reason, and, of greater significance, it was firmly rooted in American political development.

Because of these factors, this conception of providence was peculiarly successful as a basis for forging an alliance in American society between religious and political leaders. For conservative members of the clergy, the matrix of ideas associated with this conception of providence required very little alteration of the language of orthodox Calvinism. On the other hand its apparent reasonableness and practical utility as an effective means of social control commanded support from political figures, many of whom were neither pious nor orthodox. This view of providence therefore came to serve as a "higher law" than the American Constitution.

Through this process the American upper classes were able to develop an informal establishment with most of the characteristics of European establishments. The clergy remained the primary disseminators of the world view to the population at large, and therefore the bulwark of the establishment, while the politicians were substantially freed to follow the personal and secondary pursuits associated with the acquisition and maintenance of political power. Thus this peculiarly American conception of the government of God was the dominant world view and served as the basis for a consensus among the American elite. Political parties, sectional disputes, opposing economic interests, and even sectarian religious differences all occurred within this broader and overriding consensus.

Washington's Farewell Address easily could have been penned by any student at the College of New Jersey for a full generation prior to 1796, but by the time the sentiments appeared in this nationally public way they were already gaining widespread acceptance. At Princeton John Witherspoon and his son-in-law, Samuel Stanhope Smith, had been the primary architects of this view of the relationship between religion and national prosperity that was a synthesis of Reformed theology, the rational legacy of the Enlightenment, and American social and political development. Hamilton's draft represented a highly condensed but accurate reflection of what Witherspoon and Smith had taught in their courses in moral philosophy. This is not to claim direct dependence, although the amazing similarity of Hamilton's language with Witherspoon's published lectures strongly suggests that as a possibility. Hamilton moved in the "Presbyterian circle" in New York and New Jersey from the time of his arrival in America until his untimely death. He certainly had every opportunity to become familiar with the main line of thought emanating from Princeton.[9]

Ideas, it is presumed, have a life of their own. Similar thought patterns can emerge independently in approximate circumstances. They can change rapidly or with imperceptible slowness according to different needs. But generally there are some persons more intellectually capable of giving dynamic and systematic statement to those ideas, which then inevitably become associated with the names of those mental giants. But, for ideas to have an impact on the actions of men, to have an active and productive life of their own, they must be widely disseminated and satisfy certain deep-seated social and psychological needs. In this regard Witherspoon and Smith were ideally situated. Possessing the intellectual vigor to process and systematize the matrix of ideas and philosophies circulating in revolutionary America, they produced from these a relatively simple formula for the necessity of religion to national prosperity that met the social and psychological needs of the American elite. At the same time, they dominated the most significant and most truly national intellectual center in the middle and southern states. Through their students to the second and third generations, Witherspoon and Smith exerted a powerful influence on American development. Therefore, without making any claims for the uniqueness or solidarity of their ideas concerning the relationship between religion and national life, the development of those concepts in America can best be comprehended through their work.

In tracing the development of this uniquely American view of the relation of religion to national prosperity, it would be fruitless to attempt to weigh the relative influence of John Witherspoon and Samuel Stanhope Smith. Their lives were so intimately connected and their mutual dependence so strong that their thought, as well as their careers, meshed into a single unit. Smith was Witherspoon's student, son-in-law, and successor as president of the College of New Jersey. Witherspoon's active participation in the Revolution and the fact that he was a signer of the Declaration of Independence has given him a historical reputation far greater than that of his more studious but by comparison politically inactive son-in-law. Yet, because of these very differences, Smith may in fact have made a more powerful impression on national patterns of thought and action.

Witherspoon was president of the College of New Jersey from 1768 until 1794, but much of that time was spent in affairs of state, and during his last years he was blind. On the other hand, Smith moved into the president's house on campus in 1779, when he assumed the important chair of moral philosophy, and lived there until 1812—a total of thirty-three years. Most of the time between 1779 and 1796, when he became president, he carried the responsibility of the office without bearing the title, although he did draw half of the president's salary. During much of that time he was the only person fully engaged in the affairs of the college and in providing instruction. He was generally regarded as the official representative of the college.[10] His own lectures in moral philosophy, which espoused the rational Reformed view of the necessity of religion to national prosperity, replaced those of Witherspoon as the basic text. Both sets of lectures enjoyed a remarkable circulation prior to their being printed, since all students at the college were required to transcribe them and these copies were used as texts and copied by students in schools under the direction of graduates from Princeton.[11] Smith's thirty-three years were partly concurrent with and an extension of the twenty-six years of Witherspoon's tenure at Princeton. The Witherspoon-Smith era was of forty-four years' duration. This much time devoted to molding the minds of prospective statesmen and the future Reformed clergy in an institution with "a more truly national constituency than any other American college" cannot be taken lightly.[12]

Perhaps the most fundamental feature of the Witherspoon-Smith tradition was its American character. Although a mature forty-six years of age when leaving his Scottish home to come to America in 1768, Witherspoon's patriotism enabled an early biographer to exaggerate that he "became an American the moment he landed on our shores."[13] Varnum Lansing Collins was perhaps more accurate when he wrote that after three months Witherspoon "was learning what an American was, and unconsciously but none the less surely his own metamorphosis had begun."[14] The process required less than six years, for when he penned the essay "Thoughts on American Liberty" "his transformation into an American" was complete.[15]

Witherspoon became active in the American cause and spent much of the last twenty years of his life in American politics. He served on local committees of correspondence and participated in the movement to have the royalist governor of New Jersey imprisoned. On May 17, 1776, he preached a sermon, "The Dominion of Providence over the Passions of Men,"[16] which marked his full entrance into the American political tradition and dramatically symbolized his conception of the relationship between religion and American national aspirations. As a Scotsman, he had been decidedly against ministers participating in politics.[17] As an American his first avowedly political sermon ended with the prayer, "God grant that in America true religion and civil liberty may be inseparable and that unjust attempts to destroy the one may in the issue tend to the support and establishment of both."[18] Thereafter there could be no fundamental distinction between his religious and national endeavors. Working either to establish American government or the Presbyterian denomination, he was promoting the cause of "true religion and civil liberty."

Witherspoon was named a delegate to the Continental Congress in June 1776, where he argued for and signed the Declaration of Independence. His support of the Revolution was such that British soldiers burned his effigy, posed as if haranguing the American generals. He served in the Congress with some intermission until November 1782. An English officer attending commencement ceremonies at Princeton in 1783 said that Witherspoon "had not a less share in the Revolution than Washington himself. He poisons the minds of his students, and through them, the Continent."[19] Witherspoon took an active part in the debates surrounding the adoption of the Articles of Confederation and was a member of the New Jersey convention that ratified the federal Constitution in 1787. He served in the New Jersey state legislature in 1783 and 1789. Brought to America to be a leader of Presbyterians, Witherspoon became a truly national leader, but he would not have considered that ironic.[20]

If Witherspoon's "Americanism"—and, significantly, Witherspoon himself coined that phrase in 1781[21]—was apparent in his political and religious career, that of Samuel Stanhope Smith was almost wholly confined to his role as a teacher. Although Smith was a strong Federalist, his active political participation was limited to serving as a New Jersey elector for John Adams in 1801. Smith was consciously a teacher and trainer of American statesmen. Witherspoon started a trend in this direction at the College of New Jersey when he added graduate courses to the curriculum to "fit young Gentlemen for serving their Country in public Stations."[22] Under the direction of Smith the trend was accentuated, even at the expense of ministerial training, as an increasingly larger proportion of Princeton's graduates went into public positions other than the ministry. Smith held that colleges and academies should serve "as so many elementary schools for training a constant succession of wise and enlightened statesmen for the republic."[23] As the College of New

Jersey had been, under Witherspoon, the most forward of all American institutions of learning in promoting the American Revolution, under Smith it easily assumed a commanding position as trainer of American statesmen.[24]

Although thoroughly grounded in the Reformed tradition, both Witherspoon and Smith were as much products of the Enlightenment as their more illustrious contemporary Thomas Jefferson. However, because of their ability to reconcile the use of reason to the Reformed heritage, the theology to which most Americans subscribed, they ultimately exercised greater influence in establishing American cultural patterns in the area of the relationship between religion and national life.

When Witherspoon was invited to America his religious credentials were considered far more important than his academic qualifications. Indeed, having spent his whole Scottish career in the ministry engaged in theological disputes, his suitableness as administrator and professor was questionable. His American career, however, demonstrated that he was flexible and certainly a man of learning. Most important for the future of America, Witherspoon was a vigorous exponent of the Scottish philosophy of common sense, a product of the Enlightenment that elevated the use of reason and at the same time served as a loyal ally to religion.

The name most frequently associated with that philosophy is Thomas Reid, a contemporary of Witherspoon. The philosophy of common sense was primarily a rejection of the skepticism of Hume and the subjective idealism of Berkeley. Reid held that man could come to a knowledge of truth through intuition and the power of reason that all men held in common. In this way, according to Reid, "the learned and the unlearned, the philosopher and the day-labourer, are upon a level."[25] Reid held that truth could not be made evident by deductive proofs, but that false conceptions and ideas were usually patently absurd. Many of his followers, however, adopted a method of investigation consisting of observation and induction of facts.[26]

In many ways the philosophy was well suited to America. Its emphasis on natural laws that could be known simply through the observation of human history and its emphasis on the use of common sense made it particularly attractive to the basically pragmatic Americans. Moreover, of all the philosophies emerging during the Enlightenment, it appeared most congenial to traditional beliefs. Entering American life at a time when Puritanism no longer seemed functional, the philosophy of common sense served as a basic intellectual framework until absorbed and adjusted by Social Darwinism and Pragmatism.

Witherspoon forcefully introduced this rational philosophy into America. When he came to the College of New Jersey he found it "infected" with the idealism of Berkeley. It was said that he attacked these

ideas vigorously, with reason when possible and ridicule when necessary.[27] The significance of this for the development of the Reformed
tradition in America could hardly be overestimated, for it provided the
philosophical framework for a century of Presbyterian theology and the
context in which developed a distinctively American and Reformed
mode of thinking about the relationship between religion and national
prosperity.[28]

Witherspoon not only introduced this aspect of the Enlightenment
into American thought, but also served as a conservative influence on
theological developments. The result was that the Reformed tradition in
the middle and southern states diverged sharply from and developed
independently of that of New England. In contrast to the dynamic
theological evolution in New England, thought in the middle and southern states was static. Most changes merely reflected New England developments and had divisive tendencies. After the Great Awakening, the
Presbyterians were divided into "New Light" and "Old Light" factions.
Witherspoon was brought to the College of New Jersey as a candidate
acceptable to both sides. His theological stance, however, reflected none
of the American innovations and served to strengthen the faction resist-
ing ideas from New England. Witherspoon was a vigorous leader and his
adherence to traditional Reformed theology helped fashion theological
conservatism among the Reformed in the middle and southern states.[29]

It would be interesting to speculate on the probable development of
Reformed theology had Jonathan Edwards, Witherspoon's elder by only
twenty years, lived to a ripe old age as president of the College of New
Jersey. Influenced by Edwards, New England ministers were susceptible
to daring ventures in theology that produced a wide range of opinion
and dynamic developments. The New England Unitarians made exponents of all shades of opinion in the middle and southern states seem
perfectly orthodox by comparison. It may not be too far astray to say that
Edwards used philosophical idealism to illumine theology, and in the
process altered it, while Witherspoon used reason largely independent
of the received opinion but strengthened it by so doing. Long before
Charles Hodge became the "assailant par excellence" of New England
theology, Reformed ministers to the south followed a theological course
that differentiated their reflection on the nation from that of New England.[30]

The blending of American experience, common sense philosophy,
and Reformed theology that produced the American conception of the
relationship between national prosperity and religion occurred in the
context of the study of moral philosophy. In the late eighteenth century
this subject included ethics, international law, and political science. In his
courses in moral philosophy at Princeton, Witherspoon operated on the
assumption that there could be no conflict between the truth of revela-

tion and that of reason or common sense. The methodology of moral philosophy, however, demanded that truth be pursued solely by the use of reason. Edwards had dismissed this enterprise as "reducing infidelity to a system," but Witherspoon was convinced that "if the Scripture is true, the discoveries of reason cannot be contrary to it."[31]

As Witherspoon conceived the situation, all men were endowed with a "moral sense" or conscience that was a "law which our Maker has written upon our hearts." Reflecting the Scottish philosophy of common sense, Witherspoon held that the "moral sense," or that part of common sense operative in ethical decisions, encouraged virtuous conduct "previous to all reasoning."[32] However, this innate, God-given foundation of virtue was to be supplemented by reason. This faculty was constant and unchanging through time and space and unrelated to Revelation. Witherspoon held that by taking "conscience enlightened by reason [and] experience" man could ultimately arrive at a "rule of duty" that was but a "transcript" of the moral excellence of God.[33]

Although Witherspoon thus emphasized the harmony of "piety and science," he did not, at least in his published writings, synthesize his philosophical conclusions and his theology. James L. McAllister, a recent investigator of Witherspoon's political philosophy, concluded that the biblical contribution to Witherspoon's political thought was "almost nothing." McAllister further noted, "When one probes yet deeper into the prevailing character of Witherspoon's views he discovers a background conflict between conservative theology and Enlightenment philosophy which the Princeton professor never synthesized."[34]

It remained for Smith to form a synthesis of the philosophy of common sense and Reformed theology. When Witherspoon came to Princeton, Smith was already in the advanced stages of the program and was one of the students that Witherspoon "saved" from philosophical idealism. His indebtedness to his father-in-law is obvious. Definitions of the "moral sense" and "virtue," for example, he adopted wholly from Witherspoon.[35] But Smith went beyond his mentor in two significant ways. First, he adopted a rigorous "scientific" methodology that elevated reason and experience over conscience as a guide to truth. Second, maintaining that there was no difference in the validity of truth demonstrated by rational processes than truth revealed in Scripture, he followed this maxim to its logical conclusions and incorporated his philosophical findings into his theology.

As a philosopher Smith was much more rigorous and carried on more intensive investigation than Witherspoon.[36] Smith was primarily concerned with the investigation and delineation of the "laws of nature." If they could be identified mankind would have an unerring guide to proper behavior. While he acknowledged that the "weakness of the human understanding" prevented man from knowing the "essential nature of things in which the laws of their action are founded," the laws themselves could be understood. This was possible because nature was constant and the "uniformity of a multitude of facts" would allow the careful observer to discern the natural law.[37]

In locating and defining natural laws, Smith insisted that "the same rules ought to be observed which have been followed in natural philosophy ever since the age of the great Newton." He insisted first that no untested hypothesis should be considered a natural law, but only those resting "solely on an induction of facts." Laws thus derived should be considered universal until invalidated by conflicting facts. A third rule was that "laws founded on a partial induction of facts should not be extended beyond the limits to which they are certainly known to apply. . . ." Things that appeared to be similar should be ascribed to the same cause. Finally, the philosophy of common sense was reflected in his scientific methodology. Smith firmly believed that "the testimony of our senses, and of all our simple perceptions, ought to be admitted as true" when verifying fact.[38]

History, the record of man's activity, was the subject to which this methodology was to be applied and from which the moral laws of nature were to be derived. Witherspoon had introduced the study of history into the curriculum of the College of New Jersey. He felt that history was "necessary for providing the truths of natural, and confirming those of revealed religion." Witherspoon's lectures were scanty and have survived in a single, fragmentary manuscript of a student's notes.[39] Smith continued and strengthened the study of history, believing that "history may be regarded as a volume of moral experiment."[40]

Having developed this rather sophisticated methodology, Smith was prepared to incorporate his philosophical conclusions into his theology. He stated his position in the *Lectures on the Evidences of the Christian Religion*. "Truth," he maintained, "is always consistent with itself, and with all other truths." Error may appear to "bear a semblance of truth." One may expect that the Scriptures, having been compiled when the development of science was limited and covering such a wide range of knowledge, would contain numerous errors. "But improvements in genuine science have hitherto only more clearly elucidated and confirmed the doctrines of the scriptures, and especially the facts of sacred history."[41]

Smith's first encounter with the intellectual world was an example of his integration of science and the Scriptures and won him the reputation as a true son of the Enlightenment. Elected to the American Philosophical Society in 1785, he delivered an oration before that organization two years later which was expanded and published as *An Essay on the Causes of the Variety of Complexion and Figure in the Human Species*. The purpose of this work was "to establish the unity of the human species, by tracing its varieties to their natural causes," thereby "bringing in science to confirm the verity of the Mosaic history." Renouncing any intention of "introducing the authority of religion to silence enquiry" or to make it a "substitute for proof," Smith confined his investigation to a study of the effects of natural forces, climate, and manner of living on the body.[42] This ability to lay aside all traditional religious arguments to defend inherited traditions in a way acceptable to the exponents of the Enlightenment was of vast significance for the future of America.

The most influential product of this merger of rational philosophy with Reformed theology and the American experience was the concept of the necessity of religion to national prosperity that Washington announced in his Farewell Address. While consistent with the theocratic tradition of Calvinism, this philosophy was developed by Witherspoon and elaborated by Smith and presented in a form that commanded respect even from those who would not be inclined to accept the authority of the Christian Scriptures. Witherspoon's *Lectures on Moral Philosophy* and Smith's *Lectures . . . on the Subjects of Moral and Political Philosophy*, which represented the clearest statement of the concept, were the latest and best volumes on political science in early nineteenth-century America.

Witherspoon's *Lectures* were extremely sketchy and were never intended for publication. His statement of the necessity of religion to national prosperity occupied a mere three pages, and most of that was concerned with specific application, but the outline was unmistakably clear. As a fundamental principle, Witherspoon held that "virtue" was necessary to the prosperity of a nation. It followed then that any government desiring to secure national happiness would have to be concerned with the morality of its people. In this view, the various forms of government—monarchy, aristocracy, or democracy—had no inherent qualities that made one superior or inferior to another. Any form of government could promote national prosperity if it tended to "make man good." Witherspoon believed certain moral characteristics to be more essential to the promotion of national prosperity than others. Without going into detail, Witherspoon listed these as "sobriety, industry and public spirit." In another place Witherspoon listed "piety, order, industry, [and] frugality" as the essential virtues.[43] At this point Witherspoon announced another fundamental principle, which he believed to be verified in human history, that "virtue and piety are inseparably connected." That being the case, "then *to promote true religion is the best and most effectual way of making a virtuous and regular people*" and thereby secure national prosperity. Although Witherspoon's *Lectures* did not appear in print until the first edition of his works in 1800, they were widely circulated prior to that time and their influence on Washington's Farewell Address is immediately apparent.

Witherspoon did not shrink from the full implications of his reasoning. If national prosperity depended on religion, then it was clearly the duty of the government to support "true religion." While the "magistrate" was "to defend the rights of conscience," his support of "true religion" could not be considered a violation of that "natural right." In fact, Witherspoon believed that a policy of toleration could have adverse effects if not offset by active state support of Protestant Christianity. Specifically, Witherspoon discerned three functions within the scope of government policy toward religion. First, the magistrates "ought to encourage piety" by example and "discountenance those whom it would be improper to punish." Second, "The magistrate may enact laws for the punishment of acts of profanity and impiety." Although men may differ in religious opinion, the rights of conscience were not to be used as sanctions for acts that any of the "sects" counted profane. Finally, Witherspoon felt that there was "a good deal of reason" for the opinion that "the magistrate ought to make public provision for the worship of God, in such manner as is agreeable to the great body of the society." Although all dissenters ought to be fully tolerated, government should do this "so instruction may be provided for the bulk of the common people, who would, many of them, neither support nor employ teachers, unless they were obliged." Witherspoon explained that "the magistrate's right in this case, seems to be something like that of a parent, they have a right to instruct, but not to constrain."[44]

What Witherspoon outlined Smith expounded at length and in considerable detail. Smith's rigid adherence to the exposition of natural laws led to a rational understanding of cause and effect that in the extreme denied the necessity of divine intervention in the government of the world. Concerning moral philosophy, Smith contended that "the prosperity of nations . . . [is] intimately connected with the practical knowledge of those truths at the cultivation and improvement of which this science aims."[45] There were certain courses of collective behavior that would, in the nature of things, produce national prosperity, and others that would precipitate ruin. The practice of religion was the most basic requirement for national prosperity, not so much because it secured the favor of a capricious God but because it provided the basis of social order and social control. Smith's conception of national prosperity was of great significance because it was ultimately incorporated into the Reformed doctrine of God's providential government of the world.

While the suggestions of Smith were at no point brought together in a single discussion, there emerged from the whole certain virtues that would, in the nature of things, provide for national happiness. In a discussion of public spirit as a virtue he pointed to those qualities that combine to insure the prosperity of nations. Public spirit was not only a virtue in and of itself, he said, but "it is intimately associated with frugality, temperance, justice, piety, respect for religion, and all those noble qualities, most immediately related to the great interests of the community." These virtues supported public spirit, and, if they declined, public spirit would disappear along with "national glory and happiness."[46]

While piety and respect for religion appeared last in this list, it is clear that religion was considered to be the foundation of the prosperity and happiness of states. Smith believed that nations could flourish under any kind of government, even a despotism, but for a despotism to survive he thought that it must encourage and have the support of religion,[47] which was the only force powerful enough to form the basis for the other virtues necessary to hold society together. While Smith, like Witherspoon, listed conscience, general interest, and religion as the sanctions for virtue, he concluded that without religion the others would be feeble.[48] Religion was natural to all men. From the sense of morality there rose notions of the natural law and its creator. While these perceptions of divinity needed to be cultivated, and varied in their correctness from one society to another, they exerted the most powerful incentive to morality. Reason or conscience alone were too weak to check man's "unlawful passions." Smith conceded that it was possible for an atheist to live a life of "decent morality," but only when held within bounds by a religious community. If a general atheism prevailed, "That useful influence which public opinion now creates in favor of virtuous manners, would . . . cease to exist, and the bonds of society, which are effectually maintained only by the public morals, would hasten to be dissolved."[49]

One of the principle doctrines of religious belief that Smith believed to be most effective in promoting morality was a belief in a future life with rewards and punishments. Smith acknowledged some difficulties in arriving at this belief solely on the basis of the moral sense and reason, but he was convinced that it was at least "strongly implied." This belief motivated good people to continue their virtuous living even though they could see no immediate benefit to themselves. Likewise it constrained the vicious. Disbelief in a state of future retribution was "among the principle symptoms and causes of that depravity, which generally precedes the ruin of states and empires." The decline of the Roman republic, Smith reminded his readers, was accompanied by the spread of the Epicurean philosophy that held that the soul became extinct at death.[50]

Consistent with his belief about the universality of the moral sense in man and in the uniformity of moral law, Smith at no point attempted to discuss the diversity of non-Christian religions and any consequent variation in their moral tendency. Religions were for him essentially equivalent to each other. While apprehensions of religion are at no time perfect and vary according to time and place, "when the customs, and manners and sentiments of different nations are explained with true philosophic

candor, we shall find a striking uniformity of moral sentiment."[51] On these grounds Smith dismissed as a "pious conjecture" the notion that the variation of religion among different nations resulted from a more or less accurate tradition of an original revelation.[52]

Sentiments like these brought Smith into conflict with more narrow-minded leaders of his denomination, but he was too much the Presbyterian not to recognize the superiority of Christianity. In his understanding, ancient philosophers found it necessary to spend a great deal of time discussing and teaching moral precepts because ceremonial religions placed little emphasis on behavior. The Romans introduced public censorship to maintain the purity of morals. Nevertheless, the religions to which they adhered produced morals. The ancient legislators relied primarily on religion "to lay the foundations of society most securely" because "the rites with which the people continually approached its altars, impressed the public mind with a salutary reverence for those divine powers which were believed to preside over the world, and were avengers of crimes." But the "Christian religion" was superior to all of these because it "adds principle to ceremony, and instruction to the rites of devotion, and seizes on the soul by the double power of religious illumination, and religious awe."[53]

At a number of points in his system Smith indicated that the general diffusion of Christianity in America made it unnecessary for him to elaborate particulars. In a discussion of social duties, for example, he said, "From the general information which prevails in a country like ours, continually enlightened by the pulpit on the practical duties of society, it would be wholly unnecessary, in this place, to go into an extensive detail of our social offices."[54] Throughout the work, Smith diligently attempted to rely on the evidence of the moral sense and reason. But since he thought that there was no difference between true science and true religion he felt it useless to expand what was well known and accepted on the basis of revelation.

Another instance was his treatment of those "essential parts of a rational worship" that were "so generally understood as not to require any further illustration." Smith felt, however, that two plausible objections against the duty of divine worship in general required some attention. In meeting these objections he illustrated the connection of religion and morality and the consequent effect on the doctrine of providence. The first objection was that it was an unworthy idea of God to believe that he received pleasure from hearing his own "praises extolled by mortals," or from listening to "humiliating confessions" from persons whose errors were already known and for whom God already had pity. Smith answered this objection by saying that it was a "law of our nature" to express strong affections and that repeated expression strengthened them. The "infinite mind" did not require worship for his own

virtuousness of their national character. Virtuous national character could only be created and sustained by constant and widely diffused religious and moral education.

There were other elements in Smith's thought about the prosperity of nations that found their way into the Reformed idea of providence. The first appeared in a discussion of ways to increase population, which Smith considered an indication of national prosperity. In the presentation of an advanced economy based on agriculture and commerce, using money for transactions, featuring individual ownership of land, and flourishing under a system of government that secured the rights of individuals "whether consisting in the property of the soil, or in the free and entire use of the fruits of his own labor," Smith repeatedly referred to two moral principles that tended to increase population.[64] These were the related pinciples of industry and frugality. The government and economy that encouraged these would promote the greater population and thereby the greater national prosperity.

Industry for Smith was, like all moral qualities, of intrinsic value. In a different context, Smith sought to explain the presence of certain evils in the world on the basis that "the wants of man contribute to rouse that industry and habitual exertion of all his faculties of body and mind, on which their vigor and perfection depend." Industry was an essential part of man's nature. Since virtue was conformity to that nature, "The happiness, no less than the improvement of our nature, lies chiefly in constant and useful employment, stimulated by these necessary wants." Without these incentives to industry, man would degenerate into "a lazy, torpid, and vicious animal."[65] Smith was convinced that one of the most important duties of parents of the lower classes was to train their children in "habits of prudent industry" so that they would not become a "burden on society." In the "middling and superior classes" it was "still more necessary to awaken a generous ambition of becoming useful, or of rising to distinction in it by their virtues and their talents."[66]

The related principle of frugality was the opposite of luxury, ostentation, voluptuousness, and effeminacy and included simplicity and elegance. Luxury tended to waste the natural resources of a country and make it difficult to sustain a large population. It would not be too bad if luxury were confined to a small portion of the population, but when it invaded "the body of the people," they tended to think of former luxuries as necessities and as a result delay or abstain from marriage and reproduction, which would deprive them of such "necessities." Thus luxury inevitably discouraged a large population.[67]

The principle of frugality did not oppose the acquisition of wealth but controlled the use of it. The emphasis on industry demanded remunerative labor and Smith found commerce the most beneficial pursuit because "in the midst of wealth, and a certain magnificence which accompanies it, [commerce] is always frugal."[68] Smith found some difficulty in drawing the line between elegance and extravagance. He was certain that elegance required more than the "necessaries of life," and that a demand for "elegancies of art" tended to promote "new demands on industry," but he came up with no criteria to indicate when this had degenerated into "effeminacy and voluptuousness."[69] He was sure, however, that any wealth not gained by industry was bad. Smith contended that when "regular industry is no longer requisite in its acquisition, we see only a tasteless ostentation planted by the side of poverty and wretchedness, the unfailing symptoms of a declining population."[70] For this reason he favored heavy taxation on inherited wealth, but opposed sumptuary laws as restraints on industry.[71]

When the principles of frugality and industry were combined with a system of government that encouraged them, national prosperity was the inevitable result. Even large-scale war, natural calamities, or emigration could not diminish the population of a nation characterized by industry and frugality. "The true causes of a deficient, or declining population can only be found in the imperfection of the government, or the corruption of the public morals." Industry and frugality were intimately connected with morality and therefore religion. Smith felt that these virtues must be ingrained into the national character through religious instruction before the nation could prosper.[72]

The other element of Smith's thought that worked its way into the prevailing view of providence was "that the forms of civil government ought to be varied according to the character and manners of the people for whom they are designed."[73] It should be noted that Smith rejected the social-contract theory of government. In this he clearly demonstrated his independence from Witherspoon.[74] The social contract provided a leverage for revolution; Smith's whole system was designed to promote stability. In Smith's understanding civil government had grown out of domestic society and most political associations were "more the result of accident than design."[75] No single form of government was better than another. The important thing for national stability was that a government agree with the "manners" of the people. While his instruction on this matter became an important item in Reformed preaching, the ministers were more inclined to favor a republican form of government and so reversed Smith's dictum, holding that the "manners" of the people must agree with the form of government.

There was a tension in Smith's thought between the idea that man possessed certain natural rights that ought to be protected against the encroachments of governments and the notion that governments were necessary to control the passions of man. The former was faithful to the teaching of Witherspoon; the latter was more integral to Smith's own thought. Smith favored "equal liberty" and believed that some political institutions were more favorable to that ideal than others, but that they could only be "prudently adopted" when the people had been previously prepared to receive such government. The freedom fostered by a democracy or a republic, both of which terms Smith used to refer to the United States, required a virtuous people. As long as a people remained virtuous their freedom was insured. "A well informed people, moulded in the habits of virtue, cannot easily be enslaved." But Smith held that if that virtue degenerated the government should exercise more control to insure national survival. "The state ought, in such case, if possible, to possess some means of revolving easily into another form of government."[76]

Within the framework of public "manners" Smith identified frugality, public spirit, and respect for law as particular virtues requisite for the maintenance of a republic. Frugality has been discussed in another context and requires no further elaboration. Smith defined public spirit as "the general preference of the public, to private interest" that required "the love, and strong attachment of the people to the democracy itself."[77] In the discussion of public spirit Smith's distrust of the masses became obvious. They simply could not possess such unselfishness. "Universal suffrage," he argued, "is always dangerous . . . to the tranquility of the state" because "the mass of the populace is necessarily ignorant" and would tend to choose "men who are deeply tinctured with their own prejudices." The best way to insure that the electorate had public spirit was "to place the elective powers of the community in the hands of those who, by their property, have the most ample means of information, and the deepest interest in the public welfare."[78] As one would expect from Smith's emphasis on industry and frugality, he believed that there was a direct connection between wealth and virtue.

Even by restricting the franchise, however, there was no guarantee that the elected officials would have the interest of the public at heart, for factions (political parties), which Smith believed to be inevitably opposed to the general good, could arise. For this purpose it was wise to have a senate that was appointed rather than chosen in "popular elections." The resulting conflict of interest would "hardly leave them any other point of union but the public good."[79]

Smith considered public spirit or patriotism one of the chief virtues and saw it intimately connected with frugality and piety. He was sure that an irreligious man could never have the good of the society at heart and that "luxury, and genuine patriotism in the spirit of a country, are forever incompatible."[80] In Smith's discussion of politics was the seed of an orthodoxy that identified patriotism and Christianity. Even party politics, which denied the priority of religious considerations over political philosophy, was viewed as a danger to the favor of providence.

Finally, Smith emphasized obedience to the laws of the nation as necessary to the continuance of republics. While this was an overriding concern throughout Smith's work, it came out most pointedly in connection with a discussion of the corruption of the principle of equality, the "spring" of democratic republics. All men were by nature equal, Smith believed, but in the course of time there appeared an inequality of property among citizens. As the fruits of industry, this property should be protected by law. "It is essential to the peace and prosperity of the state that property should be respected, that the citizens should be obedient to the laws, and should reverence the magistrate as their interpreter, and the organ of their justice."[81] If the people became envious of the rich and thwarted the authority of the law, or if political demagogues stirred up the passions of the poor against the rich, all respect for the law would disappear and corruption and anarchy follow. The result would be that "popular favorites starting up, and aiming to enslave the people by means of the people themselves, they are all, at length, superceded by one more fortunate than the rest; who becomes the tyrant of a new dynasty.—Thus perished the liberty of Rome."[82]

The moral philosophy of John Witherspoon and Samuel Stanhope Smith gave considerable strength to the emerging American philosophy of the relationship between religion and national welfare. Smith moved away from the ancient and unpopular idea of religious establishment, but in so doing presented a rational case for the absolute necessity of religion to social order and national prosperity. This philosophy commanded much respect and was accepted and promoted by Washington in the Farewell Address. These sentiments were often quoted in support of religion. The Witherspoon-Smith tradition was particularly viable in America, however, because it could be accepted as truth in a scientific sense and because it proved to be basically compatible with orthodox Reformed theology.

Chapter 2

The Transformation of Theology: An American Doctrine of Providence

The rational philosophy that construed religion to be the primary and only effective instrument of social control was utilized and disseminated as an integral part of orthodox Reformed theology. This gave the ideas a force and influence far beyond what they could have enjoyed if retained in philosophical form. Theology, after all, was still a primary, if not *the* primary, mode of communication in America just as "religion . . . was the backbone . . . of the whole American Enlightenment."[1] Sermons with heavy theological content formed a steady diet for American church-goers, and laymen spent hours discussing each week's production. Probably one of the most difficult things to comprehend for the twentieth-century American, who is almost theologically illiterate even if religiously pious, is the sophistication and keen interest with which his counterparts of the late eighteenth or early nineteenth century discussed theology. It was not ministerial vanity but consumer demand that made sermons and other religious materials dominate the production of American presses during this period.[2] Persons with such far-reaching political, social, and scientific interests as John Adams and Thomas Jefferson spent a great amount of time reading and reflecting on religious subjects.[3] For many Americans religious writings formed the major part of the literary diet. The most influential ideas, the ideas that elicited response and became symbols for action, were conveyed through sermons. Often lay members of a congregation would request the printing of a sermon they believed to be of particular social benefit. Thus, while one finds the rudiments of the Witherspoon-Smith philosophy in all sorts of social and political statements, the ideas about the relationship between religion and national prosperity were most fully developed and disseminated through the theological media.

In the Christian theological tradition the doctrine of providence encompassed thought about God's government of the world. This doctrine thus served naturally as a model conception through which members of Reformed groups interpreted America's past and the unfolding present, and, more importantly, as an intellectual framework in which they sought to give direction to the nation's future. After the American Revolution the doctrine of providence underwent a marked development from a dynamic concept of God's personal activity in history toward a static belief that God worked primarily through natural, moral laws that could be discovered by man. This development, which came about primarily from the incorporation of the moral philosophy of John Witherspoon and Samuel Stanhope Smith into the doctrine, also entailed a shift in emphasis in the subject matter of providence. The changed content of the doctrine of providence confirmed that the development went beyond the pattern of Christian thought that traditionally viewed God's activity in history as a demand for human response in the present. As God's activity seemed to be less capricious, and more predictable on the basis of human behavior, providence became more concerned with the social, political, and moral activity of man than the movement of God in nature. Thus man rather than God became the controlling focus in the emerging doctrine of providence.

The development of the doctrine of providence among the Reformed groups in the middle and southern states was in marked contrast to that of New England. This factor is of great significance for an understanding of the relationship of religion to American national life. In the New England states the doctrine of providence evolved during the colonial period within covenantal or federal theology. In this context it was believed that God entered into a compact with a nation or political unit and then governed in accordance with the terms of the agreement. Fulfillment of the covenant obligations secured to that nation the blessings of God while violation of the covenant—sin—brought about "declining times" and the disfavor of God.[4] This type of thinking was well suited to the religiously and socially homogeneous colonies of New England because it could reasonably be assumed to be true.

To the more heterogeneous Reformed of the middle and southern states, however, covenantal thinking would have strained credulity. It was difficult for persons living in a highly diversified religious environment, with Presbyterians and Dutch Reformed competing with Friends, Anglicans, and even Baptists and Catholics for religious hegemony, to conceive of themselves as a unique national group chosen by God for a special covenantal relationship. For this reason the doctrine of providence among the denominationally diverse Reformed groups in the middle and southern states remained essentially conservative during the colonial era. That is, the doctrine of providence was more nearly like that of Calvin than the notions of a national covenant held by the orthodox of New England.[5] The theology of the Westminster Confession of Faith, which emphasized the distinction between a covenant of works and a covenant of grace, flourished as it did among all Reformed groups, but this did not necessarily contain the notion of a national covenant. In the middle and southern states the conception of the providential government of nations retained primary emphasis on the sovereignty of God, who was thought to govern the world for his own glory through a variety of means. God could work within established means, or laws of nature, or contrary to them, and it was not within the power of man to fully comprehend and explain God's actions.

In many ways, this combination of religious diversity and theological conservatism gave to the Reformed groups of the middle and southern states a distinct advantage over their counterparts in New England in developing a national American theology of providence. Unlike the New Englanders, they were not embarrassed with reshaping a theology that was blatantly out of step with the national experience, and their years of trial in religiously diverse colonies helped prepare them for rapid adjustment once America emerged as an independent nation subject, in their view, to God's providential government. The nationalism created or expressed in the American Revolution and the availability of a philosophy connecting religion, not a particular established denomination, with national prosperity were the only ingredients needed to produce an American doctrine of providence.

The most perceptive analysis of the development of covenant theology in America is that of Perry Miller. According to Miller, the New England idea that the colonists were in a contractual relationship with God had permeated America so that prior to the war British oppression was nearly universally viewed as punishment for America's failure to fulfill its contractual obligations. During the Revolution the jeremiad, "a threatening of further visitation upon the covenanted people until they returned to their bond by confession and reformation," had been focused exclusively on the evils of British rule. Complete victory in the Revolution nearly destroyed the concept that had been admirably suited to invigorating the rebelling colonists. Victory thus rendered the device ineffective as a means of unifying American Protestantism. According to Miller, demoralization produced by the morally degenerate nature of American life in the 1790s, a period coincident with the French Revolution, and the fear of latent barbarism produced by the expanding frontier combined to force the American churches "to recognize that in fact they now dealt with the Deity only as particular individuals gathered for historical, capricious reasons into this or that communion." In this situation, "They had to realize, at first painfully, that as a united people they had no contractual relationship with the Creator, and that consequently a national controversy with Him could no longer exist." The churches were forced to "yield government to the secular concept of the social compact, accept the First Amendment, and so to concentrate, in order to resist Deism and to save their souls, upon that other mechanism of cohesion developed out of their colonial experience, the revival."[6]

Whatever the merits of Miller's analysis of this alleged metamorphosis of American Protestantism, most emphatically it failed to take account of the marked diversity within Protestantism in the colonial and early national period. The presumption of cultural coherence that served Miller so well in his studies of New England Puritanism cannot be transferred to the more pluralistic Protestantism of the middle and southern states either before or after the American Revolution. Miller, like so many before and after him, has erred by fashioning general interpretations about America while saturated only in New England sources.[7]

At the time of the Revolution Americans of all descriptions, and the exceptions were few, believed in some way that the deity controlled the movement and destiny of nations. This fact alone was of greater significance than the diversified ways of expressing that belief. That very diversity, even among persons adhering basically to the Reformed tradition, makes a general characterization of the doctrine of providence in that era difficult. Certainly the most frequent models or illustrations for God's activity in history came from the Old Testament, but even within that context there was a wide range of conceptual variations of the common notion. The favorite examples of American ministers necessarily and unavoidably came from the Biblical history of Israel. Since the Old Testament was written by a people believing themselves to enjoy a special covenantal relationship to Yahweh, it was only natural that sermons based on that model should have covenantal overtones. But ministers in the middle and southern states rarely made an identification of America with Israel in that regard. By no means was there an explicit acknowledgment of a national covenant between America and God. Even the Associate Reformed ministers, who continued to emphasize the practice of public covenanting, did not contend for this position. They believed America's covenant obligations stemmed from the fact that most Americans descended from English and Scottish origins. In fact, during the early part of the period members of this denomination refused to take loyalty oaths to the United States because the Constitution did not recognize the existence and providence of God.[8] Beyond this, the Old Testament itself provided a variety of models for understanding God's government of nations. The Old Testament writers presupposed that Yahweh controlled the destinies of other nations in accordance with his purposes. God's "chastisement of Nebuchadnezzar" was as real to American ministers as his deliverance of the children of Israel from Egypt.[9]

Within this diversity, however, there was one rather obvious point of agreement among adherents of the Reformed tradition. God was believed to be an active participant in the affairs of men and nations. This dynamic view of providence was prominent in the sermons delivered on December 11, 1783, a day recommended by the Congress as a "day of public thanksgiving" for victory in the Revolution. It was a common conviction that God had been instrumental in the American cause. The congressional proclamation reflected this by declaring that "the interposition of Divine Providence in our favour hath been abundantly and most graciously manifested."[10] In response to this proclamation few ministers felt it necessary to explain the doctrine of providence in the abstract. Only John Witherspoon prefaced his description of the providential nature of the Revolution with a brief statement of "these known and general truths."[11]

According to the ministerial descriptions of the events of the Revolution, God rather than man was the primary actor. It was God who had unified the American people and given harmony to their public councils. It was God who had raised up a powerful ally in France. Washington, that "Joshua of the day," had been "inspired from above with every military endowment."[12] According to John Rodgers, collegiate pastor of the Brick Street Presbyterian Church in New York, the successes of the American armies at the Battle of Trenton and in the following campaigns so clearly pointed "to the finger of God, that it would be unpardonable stupidity not to notice it, and the basest ingratitude not to acknowledge it."[13] God not only strengthened and supported the Americans but also confused the British and was directly responsible for their errors of judgment that allowed an inferior power to gain military victory.[14]

Why God did all of this was a question that the clergymen largely ignored. Presumably it was a display of his sovereignty and a part of his total plan for mankind. According to George Duffield, pastor of the Third Presbyterian Church in Philadelphia, the Revolution afforded "an irrefragable argument (to convince even an *Atheist*) that the MOST HIGH ruleth over the affairs of men, and raiseth up, and casteth down at his pleasure."[15]

In the course of a few years this dynamic understanding of God's role in national affairs evolved into the much more static concept that God worked through established laws. In this new understanding the destruction or prosperity of nations followed naturally in response to specific kinds of human behavior. In essence, the doctrine of providence was changed to accommodate the newly developed and highly applicable philosophy of Witherspoon and Smith. Throughout the early national period that philosophy became the most common ingredient in the doctrine of providence, which otherwise continued to receive diversified expression.

Witherspoon's thanksgiving sermon of 1783 represented a stage in the transition of the doctrine of providence that took place under his influence. The sermon was made up of two parts. The first and longest portion was a development of the traditional doctrine of providence, very much like the other sermons of the day, in which Witherspoon reviewed the events of the Revolution that indicated to him that American victory should be interpreted as a favor of providence. In the second section, or the "improvement of the subject," Witherspoon dropped the theme of providence and offered the congregation some "instruction and direction" based upon the conclusions that he had derived from his study of moral philosophy. He declared that the prosperity of the new nation depended on the promotion of "religion and good morals," and he admonished his hearers to "cherish a love of piety, order, industry, [and] frugality." In conclusion, Witherspoon, who had not envisioned the emergence of a single nation, predicted that "whatsoever state among us shall continue to make piety and virtue the standard of public honor, will enjoy the greatest inward peace, the greatest national happiness, and in every outward conflict will discover the greatest constitutional strength."[16]

Witherspoon made no attempt to integrate the two parts of the sermon. He was convinced that "piety, order, industry, [and] frugality" were beneficial to the health and prosperity of nations, but he did not seek to make the activity of God toward the nation dependent on adherence to these principles. Any nation would prosper as the natural result of the operation of these moral qualities, but Witherspoon had a special talent for keeping orthodox theology and philosophy in their respective spheres.

It was Smith who more than any one else thoroughly integrated the rational philosophy of the necessity of religion as an agent of social control, and therefore national prosperity, with the doctrine of providence. While the development could be illustrated through a number of his sermons,[17] the best example appeared in a sermon with the title, unsurprisingly, "Religion Necessary to National Prosperity." The text of the sermon was Exodus 20:5-6, "I the Lord thy God, am a jealous God, visiting the iniquities of the fathers upon the children, unto the third and fourth generation of them that hate me, and showing mercy to thousands of those that love me and keep my commandments."

In this sermon Smith pointed out that God's government of the people of Israel served as a model for "all the nations of the earth," thus making the whole question of covenant irrelevant. The text, he declared, "discloses one of the most certain and invariable rules" of providence, "that the prevalence of virtuous manners among any people, and their respect to the institutions of religion, is usually connected with national prosperity." On the other hand, irreligion and "a general dissolution of public manners" prepared a nation for "some disastrous and fatal revolution." This was the case because religion formed the "firmest basis of civil government," and impiety naturally produced "voluptuousness and effeminacy, avarice and prodigality, a restless ambition, dark treacheries, and a universal disregard of justice." Such was not only "the course of divine Providence," but also "a principle immutably ingrafted into the system of nature."

Religion was necessary to the maintenance of "civil society" because morality was indispensable and the two could not be separated. The conservative nature of Smith's reasoning was apparent. Religion alone was powerful enough to force obedience to "the laws already existing." If it were not for the religious teaching of "a future state of being" men would be "absorbed in private interest" and law would be powerless. There would be nothing to insure that "the poor man permit the rich to enjoy unmolested all the benefits of society." But if members of a society were influenced by religion, "the state, strong in the virtue of its citizens and purity and innocence of the public manners, will continue to flourish for ages." This demanded at no time the "interposition" of God because he had "so laid the plans of his providence over the world, that the course of nature shall avenge the violated majesty of his law and become itself, the minister of his justice."[18]

The doctrine of providence that flourished in the early national period held in tension the dynamic God of revolutionary America and the deity of the Witherspoon-Smith legacy who was self-contained to the operation of natural laws. The inherited concept of a God who controlled human events at his pleasure and according to a plan not entirely known to man was too strong to completely succumb to the idea of God in the thought of Smith. The traditional idea of a dynamic God persevered, however, more as a rhetorical premise that was neither necessary nor consistent with the content of thought on providence. The diversity that was characteristic of the earlier period was confined primarily to this rhetorical framework of the sermons. Within this diversity there was a remarkable consistency. The Reformed adopted the moral philosophy of Witherspoon and Smith as the authentic interpretation of Scripture.

This development was saturated with irony because Smith was discredited as a religious leader. His rationalism and compelling desire for consistency were not palatable to the Presbyterian taste. In seeking to defend the Old Testament patriarchs, for example, Smith attempted to justify polygamy and was severely criticized. His departure from accepted Presbyterian thinking nearly resulted in a trial before the General Assembly.[19] Smith was ultimately forced to resign from the presidency of the College of New Jersey. As early as 1808 Archibald Alexander raised questions openly before the General Assembly about the suitability of the college to train ministers. Under Witherspoon a trend had started toward the training of statesmen as well as ministers. Under Smith the process of "secularization" had spread to the point that some men were allowed to pursue only physical sciences, although they could obtain no degree. Alexander believed this to be detrimental to the training of ministers, which had been the original purpose of the institution. In the same year Ashbel Green began to question the orthodoxy of Smith's sermons. This combination of events, together with the excessive disciplinary problems of the college, foreshadowed both the retirement of Smith and the erection of a theological seminary to replace the college as the primary center for training Presbyterian ministers. In 1810 the trustees of the college, led by Samuel Miller and Green, set up an inquisitiorial committee of visitors to replace Smith as head disciplinarian and to attempt to find someone else to teach theology. Two years later, in the same year Princeton Theological Seminary opened, the trustees secured Smith's resignation.[20] The irony was that the majority of the Reformed clergy reflected to a remarkable extent the thought of this discredited leader, and most of the clergy of the smaller Reformed denominations were theologically more conservative than the Presbyterians who questioned Smith's orthodoxy.

Hundreds of sermons on the doctrine of providence testify to the impact of the moral philosophy of Witherspoon and Smith on that conception. From whatever starting point, the Reformed ministers invariably turned to the theme of a natural connection between religion and national prosperity. The rhetorical premise of the sermons often mirrored the particular text, but when the ministers made demands of the American people, national prosperity or destruction was depicted as flowing naturally from the operation of fixed laws. Increasingly, illustrations from non-Biblical history served to demonstrate God's way of governing the world. While preached with the authority generally reserved for revealed truth, the notion that the doctrine could be proven from man's experience in history was maintained, and it was put forward as truth to be received on both counts.

Illustrations of this tension between the rhetorical framework and the content of the doctrine of providence were abundant. On July 4, 1798, William Linn, pastor of the Reformed Dutch Church in New York City and formerly a Presbyterian minister and chaplain in the American Revolution, addressed the Tammany Society. In an extended discussion of the Revolution, Linn reviewed the events in a fashion almost identical to that of the sermons of 1783. However, when he turned to "improve" the subject he expressed neither a dynamic nor covenantal view of providence. Rather he declared that "virtue is highly necessary for the support of order and good government." Americans should devote themselves to the service of God because the Christian religion led "to the exercise of this virtue." "Let us," he continued, "comply with its precepts, and pray for its universal spread and influence. Nothing would so conduce to our national prosperity and happiness."[21]

The following year another Dutch Reformed minister, John B. Johnson of Albany, developed a similar pattern. Johnson spoke of the "providential interference in those measures which lead to the establishment of our INDEPENDENCE" and the "wonderful interposition of the God of Battles, in our behalf." But when he contemplated the future he did not consider the possibility of divine "interference." If Americans were to continue to be prosperous they should "cultivate wisdom, and practice virtue and religion" because these were "the best security and essential supports of republican governments."[22]

Eliphalet Nott, the Presbyterian president of Union College, similarly admonished his Albany audience in 1801. In a highly rhetorical mood, Nott compared the American Revolution with the deliverance of the children of Israel from Egypt. "The arm of Omnipotence *stretched down from heaven,* smote the wave that was overwhelming us: it divided; and we passed into a new world . . . ." In the course of the sermon, Nott moved to a more rational position. About the achievements of Washington he noted that "if nothing was miraculous, everything was providential." Toward the end of the sermon God completely disappeared from consideration and the laws of nature and nations became dominant. The safety of the nation depended on religion because "without this no people can long be prosperous and happy." Religion was the "cement of society," for without it "the sanctions of an oath have no validity; contracts cannot be supported; crimes cannot be investigated; and courts of justice must cease." Religion alone, not civil law, was a sufficiently powerful agent of social control. Infidelity undermined "the very *foundations of society*" by "taking all restraint from the wicked." Nott reminded his hearers that "A DEPARTURE from the pure principles of religion has been, in *all ages,* and in *every country,* the sad prelude to destruction." Obviously, to remind a people of a covenant that few would have recognized would have been ineffective, but a "law" of such magnitude carried weight.[23]

Although some aspects of the theology at times appeared to be particularly suited to America, it could also be applied to other nations. John M. Bradford addressed himself in 1814 to the Dutch efforts to achieve independence, which Americans considered to be an essential element of national prosperity. The whole issue, he contended, was "in the hands of the Most High," but it soon became clear that any activity on the part of God was unnecessary. Holland seemed to be a perfect example of the alleged natural connection between religion and national prosperity. That nation had lost its independence because it had been "enervated by riches and luxury" and had become "polluted and debased by infidel principles." Having lost "that virtuous attachment to truth and religion," the nation became morally degenerate and declined. Noting that "God has evidently arisen," Bradford concluded that "God helps them that help themselves."[24]

More reflective ministers were aware of the tension between statements about the free activity of God and those indicating that national prosperity or punishment came as a result of the working out of natural laws, and they attempted to harmonize the two notions. Ashbel Green as a young pastor in Philadelphia reflected this position in a sermon, *Obedience to the Laws of God, the Sure and Indispensable Defense of Nations.* This sermon was interesting because it illustrated precisely how the moral philosophy of Witherspoon and Smith entered orthodox theology. Green was chosen as the successor to Smith at the College of New Jersey to restore that institution to orthodoxy. But Green, a graduate from Princeton in 1783, had been taught by both Witherspoon and Smith, and their instruction left an indelible mark that was clearly discernible even through such an "orthodox" and authoritarian personality.

In this sermon Green developed the then-fashionable doctrine of providence at some length. He emphasized the doctrine of natural law because he was concerned that his hearers might deny the necessity of a deity. "But remember," he reminded, "that this natural connexion between piety and prosperity, vice and ruin, is still the appointment of God, and even, on this plan, is as much his order as if it had been made for every particular case in which its effects are felt."[25]

Almost as an afterthought Green added, "Scripture and experience, however, do, I think, concur in teaching, that *beside* this natural connexion, God does often and especially *interfere* by his providence, both to preserve and bless those who obey him, and to destroy those who reject and despise his laws." The cautious way in which Green approached this statement indicated the uneasiness that the concept of God's interference in the order of nature remained in the doctrine of providence. This statement was in fact inconsistent with the whole of Green's sermon, for he had already informed the congregation that the "miraculous exertion of [God's] power" was no longer necessary in the government of the world. Green explained that God used miracle in the early days of man's existence to preserve or destroy nations because man had not yet had sufficient time to understand God's method of governing the world. In using miracles to save those nations that served him, or to destroy those that did not, God furnished examples for the instruction of those who followed. In the present, "abundant experience has shewn what is the settled order of the divine dispensation" so that "miracle is not to be expected, because it is not necessary."[26]

Alexander McClelland, foremost of the Associate Reformed ministers and professor at Rutgers College, attempted to resolve the dilemma by making a subtle change in the meanings of "interposition" and "interference." Maintaining the sovereignty of God to the fullest, McClelland declared that "human actors are, with all their bravery and strut, mere fantoccini or dancing puppets, acting their little part on the stage according to the will of the great Mechanician, who holds within his fingers every one of the strings that give them play and movement." This characterization of the relationship between divine and human action only seemed to be in contradiction to the prevailing doctrine of providence as "simply the regular operation of certain general laws, which are either eternal or were impressed on matter at the creation." There was, after all, observed order in the universe. The doctrine of God's interference was not the "unphilosophical hypothesis of a constant arbitrary interference with the regular and beautiful course of nature established at the beginning." To speak of man as a puppet was not to advocate "violent interposition nor miraculous introduction of a discord into the established order of things." Man's inability to perceive this seeming contradiction came as a result of his feeble attempts to force God into "his own image and superscription." The truly "beautiful feature" of God's government was that miracles happened "*in the most natural* and apparently spontaneous manner."[27]

The ministers insisted that miracles, or "immediate interference" of God with the order of nature, were no longer to be expected[28] but that God nevertheless controlled the rise and fall of nations. This apparently caused some confusion on the part of laymen. Those not quite so philosophically astute had difficulty in discerning the difference between the "orthodox" doctrine of providence and the theory espoused by the "infidel" deists. In addressing the Kentucky legislature in 1815, James M'Chord complained of the "humiliating necessity" of taking so much time to explain the doctrine of providence, but he felt that the "tone of public sentiment" demanded it. Because God worked through "his own established order," M'Chord explained, many people failed to understand that God constantly exercised his power. It would be easier for people to comprehend the doctrine if God interrupted the order of things and started a new chain of second causes. In any case, M'Chord, in a somewhat authoritarian tone, insisted that his influential audience acknowledge God's superintendence of the world through the regularity of "second causes."[29]

If the modified version of the doctrine of providence presented some difficulties and inconsistencies in interpreting the activity of God in social and political phenomena, it created even more in the area of natural phenomena. In colonial America famine, pestilence, earthquakes and the like played a significant role in the conception and explanation of providence. Inevitably these were considered to be indicators of God's anger and evidence of his "interposition" in the order of nature. These notions were basically incompatible with the early nineteenth-century predominant idea that God controlled the prosperity or decline of nations according to established laws. It had become almost impossible to speak of God's anger. According to the new understanding of providence, natural occurrences had to be taken into account separately, explained inconsistently, or altogether dropped from consideration.

James Wilson, for example, explained the doctrine of providence as it related to the prosperity of nations and concluded that "no immediate divine agency" was required to punish the wicked because "this proceeds according to the settled course of moral law." But when Wilson, a graduate of the College of New Jersey, entertained ideas of natural catastrophe he was forced to contradict himself. These matters, he believed, pointed to another "important truth," which could be known only through "pure revelation." This was that "the moral laws, of themselves, are not sufficient to restrain or punish the wickedness of man while living in society on earth." God's purposes could not be defeated and he would "employ the most effectual means to accomplish them." This, Wilson claimed, accounted for "wars, famines, pestilential diseases, and all the long train of calamities which so afflict our race."[30]

Samuel Miller, who is best remembered as professor of church history at Princeton Theological Seminary, faced the problem of interpreting the doctrine of providence as a young minister in New York. Two opportunities appeared in the course of 1798. The first was a traditional fast day and the second came when over two thousand residents of the city died with yellow fever in just over a hundred days. In the earlier sermon, Miller pointed out that the judgments of providence could be either "the ordinary operation of what are called natural laws" or the "result of more immediate and supernatural interferences," but that "God is to be equally acknowledged as the author of both." The content of the sermon, however, was primarily of the political nature by then common in sermons based on the doctrine of providence, and Miller emphasized solely the natural law arguments.[31] After the epidemic of yellow fever, Miller again went before his congregation with a providential interpretation. But the principle of natural law as a way of understanding providence had become too strong in Miller's mind for him to designate the passing of the pestilence as the "more immediate and supernatural interference" of God. Miller understood the ecological and medical reasons for epidemics much better than most of his contemporaries, and he emphasized the necessity of eliminating these causes to prevent future outbreaks. With some difficulty, however, he maintained the coincidence of natural causes with the operation of providence. "Let none say, that placing *moral reformation* among the principal preventives of future calamities . . . is discarding the agency of second causes." Miller did not want to be misunderstood for having stressed the natural causes because "God, no doubt, in general, acts both in the natural and moral world, through the instrumentality of means." He concluded his statement with the rhetorical question, "But is it inconsistent with this acknowledgment to believe, that He disposes natural means in such a manner as to accomplish moral purposes?"[32] The total impact of the sermon was such that one could seriously doubt if the question were more rhetorical than real.

This tension in the doctrine of providence between natural law and the extraordinary activity of God was symptomatic of a transition in the conception of that doctrine. As the doctrine developed further in the direction of natural law the tension was largely removed by a parallel transition in content. The acts of nature became decidedly secondary to those political and social themes contained in the moral philosophy of Witherspoon and Smith. Only some extremely terrifying natural event such as the recurring epidemics of yellow fever, outbreaks of cholera, or particularly devastating fires called for providential interpretation at the national level. These events were too convenient not "to improve," but the traditional providential interpretation was often strained. Then too, these and similar events[33] were absorbed to a large extent through another element of Reformed thought, the millennium.

The response to the fire in a Richmond theater in 1812, which resulted in the death of a number of Virginia's leading citizens, illustrated this transition. The theater was uniformly condemned by Presbyterians and members of other Reformed denominations, and this catastrophe would seem to have offered a perfect opportunity "to improve" the event by describing it as the judgment of providence. Yet, to an amazing degree, providence as a category of explanation was noticeably secondary in the sermonic accounts of the fire. Samuel Miller used the occasion to sustain an attack on the theater. Although he felt the fire to be an indication of providential disfavor of the theater, he made no application on a national level.[34] Archibald Alexander, a Philadelphia Presbyterian, was extremely hesitant to broach the subject of providence. His sermon was primarily a discourse on the nature of grief. When first addressing himself to the implications of the fire, he chose a natural law approach, without mentioning providence. The theater was bad for morals and its popularity was "a certain indication of a people ripe for ruin." That is, the theater would produce adverse effects without any action on the part of the deity. Only near the end of the sermon did Alexander remind his congregation that "a righteous Providence sounded loudly in our ears."[35]

At the time of the Richmond fire, Reformed ministers were intensely interested in the prospects of an imminent millennium. Since most of them associated natural disorders with the introduction of that golden era, the Richmond disaster was generally interpreted as one of the "signs" of the approaching millennium. Providence had by then become almost exclusively interpreted with reference to social and political events that could be construed as the operation of natural laws.[36]

Even when a minister considered these natural events, it was often only for a passing reference in the context of natural law arguments. Andrew Wylie, president of Washington College, noted that "wars, famines, pestilence, are some of those plagues with which the Almighty

scourges the nations." Not wishing to dwell on these things, Wylie
pushed toward more familiar ground. "And, if we could trace these
calamities to their moral causes, we should see that religion, or the want
of it, has always been the true reason why nations have flourished or
declined." In these cases he thought that the connection could only be
discerned "in the pages of inspiration," but political consequences of
moral behavior were readily discernible. Wylie declared that "vice, in its
own nature tends to national ruin," and he proceeded to show how
religion made possible social control and therefore national prosperity.[37]

The subjects that became conventional in the explications of the doctrine of providence were those emphasized in the teaching of Witherspoon and Smith. The necessity of religion to morality and morality to the
welfare of the nation formed a congenial framework for the Reformed
to make their demands on the nation. In this context the Reformed
emphasized the necessity of Christian rulers, wholesome laws, and obedient citizens. The phrases "national character," "public manners," and
"industry and frugality" became stock ingredients in sermons on providence.

The political themes became integrated with American developments,
particularly republican government and civil and religious liberty, and
will be discussed later. The incorporation of the moral philosophy of
Witherspoon and Smith into the doctrine of providence can be illustrated through the concepts of "industry and frugality." In the period
from the Embargo of 1807 through the War of 1812, Reformed fast
day sermons, which were normally devoted to the discussion of the
doctrine of providence, frequently listed "extravagance" and its synonyms
as one of the grave sins that would, in the nature of things, lead to
national ruin. Although pronounced in the tone of orthodox theology,
the language was more reminiscent of Smith's moral philosophy than
the Bible.

In 1807 the General Assembly of the Presbyterian Church complained of
"the prevalent inordinate attachment . . . to things."[38] The arrival of the
fast day proclaimed by the Assembly brought forth a plethora of statements
on this theme. That of James Inglis of Baltimore was representative. He
proclaimed that the widespread "spirit of Luxury and Dissipation—
pomp and fastidiousness—profuse voluptuousness—prodigality and
debauchery—revelling and wantonness—pride and ambition" was as
hostile "to the genius of our Republican constitutions" as it was to "our
holy Religion."[39]

The same concern was prominent in the sermons preached on a fast
day just before the beginning of the War of 1812. Joseph Clark, who
framed his sermon with talk of a covenant God but followed Smith's
teaching point for point in the body, listed "idleness and extravagance"

as one of the major "abominations" of the nation. He spoke of "the lamentable departure of those industrious, sober habits, frugal and simple manners, so favorable to morals and religion" and the contemporary rage for "those dissipations which corrupt the mind, [and] unhinge the moral order of society."[40] Stephen Rowan, pastor of the Eighth Presbyterian Church in New York and later moderator of the General Assembly, affirmed that one of the most obvious sins for which the nation was suffering the affliction of providence was "luxury and extravagance ... , debauchery and intemperance."[41]

At the close of the war, John Latta of Delaware was convinced that one of the blessings of the war was that it "checked unbounded luxury and extravagance" and the "onslaught of effeminacy which would have ruined the country."[42] The postwar expansion of the economy prompted David M'Conaughy to preach on the duties and dangers of prosperity. According to his understanding, "Seasons of ease and earthly abundance, often produce torpid insensibility and luxurious indolence." This was one of the vices most natural to man, and its avoidance called for great vigilance. If not guarded against it would be a sure prelude to national ruin.[43]

But the emphasis on frugality and industry was not limited to prosperity alone. In 1819 the General Assembly adopted a statement concerning recent "commercial embarrassments" in the United States and sent it to all major newspapers for publication. The financial crisis was not merely the result of poor economics, in the view of the commissioners, but of poor religion. It was their opinion that there was no hope for general prosperity until there was a "return to those habits of industry, temperance, moderation, economy, and general virtue, which our common Christianity inculcates." The members of the General Assembly encouraged the churches "to cultivate in themselves, and to endeavour to promote in others, those simple, frugal, and regular pursuits, which cannot fail to exert a most benign influence on the best interests of society." It was essential that ministers "impose on the minds of their hearers the all important truth, that the religion of Jesus Christ, in its vital power and practical influence, is the best friend of civil society. . . ."[44]

The Reformed continued to apply the concepts of industry and frugality as part of the doctrine of providence throughout the period. "Persons of wealth and rank" who attended the churches were constantly reminded of the dangers in "the spirit of rivalry in gay dissipation, in splendor of style, in the luxury of the table, in extravagance of dress."[45] These themes not only persisted, but became stronger as the restless pursuit of wealth and ostentatious display that characterized Jacksonian America threatened the social order dear to the Reformed.[46]

Of greater social and political significance, however, was the application of these principles to the poor and the alteration of the doctrine of providence as it applied to social classes. The traditional concept depicted a world in which social classes, from the very wealthy to the very poor, existed as a result of the action of God. Perhaps the sentiment was never more tersely expressed than by John Winthrop in a speech delivered before the *Arbella* on the way to America in 1630. According to Winthrop, "God Almightie in his most holy and wise providence hath soe disposed of the Condicion of mankinde, as in all times some must be rich some poore, some highe and eminent in power and dignitie; others meane and in subieccion."[47] This conception had largely disappeared from Reformed thought three hundred years later. To be sure, a conservative minister like Philip Milledoler could still insist in 1806 that "the very great inequalities with respect to earthly advantages" were necessary "to answer the purposes of his [God's] moral government."[48] Few, however, would have gone as far as Jacob Brodhead to declare that "the difference which exists between many of those wretched, pitiable objects . . . and us (however great it may be) is owing, neither to their greater crimes, nor our superior merit."[49]

The new conception emphasized that poverty was the result of human failings or sin rather than the activity of God. Poverty was produced by the lack of industry and frugality. There was a definite parallel between this development and the changing conception of the providential government of nations.[50] Like other aspects of the doctrine of providence, the traditional conception of God-created inequality sometimes remained in certain rhetorical remarks but did not serve as a basis for action. In the view of most of the Reformed, as indeed for most Americans in the middle and southern states, there was a direct connection between poverty and wickedness. Definitions of poverty became more sociological and less theological. Jacob Janeway reflected this conviction when he declared unequivocally that "the poor are vicious" and that it was "a work worthy of a rational creature to endeavour to reclaim them, and make them virtuous and pious."[51] The most rational attempts to categorize the poor placed irreligion as the cause in the majority of cases.[52] If the factors of unemployment, seasonal work shortage, low wages, and illness occasionally entered the thinking of the Reformed, they made very little impact.[53] As Ward Stafford noted, the "respectable poor . . . are mixed with the vicious, are regarded in the same light, and are treated in the same manner."[54]

There had been a kind of religiously sanctioned protection for the poor in the old order. It was, to be sure, noblesse oblige. The new conception of providence, whether applied to the nation or to individuals, tended to leave out environmental considerations, making man both individually and collectively responsible for his own destiny. While saved in the period of transition from its worst consequences by the retention of at least some aspects of noblesse oblige, the way was prepared for the most devastating features of late nineteenth-century Social Darwinism.

In the context of industrialization, urbanization, and the growing numbers of the poor, the Reformed increasingly viewed poverty as a primary threat to political stability and national prosperity. Since poverty was viewed as resulting from moral shortcomings, religious education was believed to be the most effective remedy. According to Archibald Alexander, first professor of Princeton Theological Seminary, the poor needed "religious instruction more than others, because their time is commonly completely occupied and their education defective." Experience had demonstrated that the problem of poverty could not be solved by legal remedies. The only "true remedy" was to change the character of the poor "by instilling into their minds sound religious instruction."[55] The Reformed believed that the growth of poverty could alter the national character and bring providential ruin to the nation. As Alexander put it, "no evil is more threatening in free countries than the increase of pauperism."[56] Thus industry and frugality, which Smith had emphasized in connection with ways to increase population, had become part of "our common Christianity" and was inculcated through the doctrine of providence.

As could be expected in a conception that transferred the primary role in history from God to man, the role of nature and divine activity in the doctrine of providence was replaced by the recorded activity of man—history. Increasingly sermons on the providential government of nations started with Old Testament texts but relied on "profane" history to buttress the primary conclusions regarding the connection between religion and national prosperity. The study of history in America was fostered and encouraged as a handmaid to religion. As noted earlier, Witherspoon first introduced the study of history at the College of New Jersey as a companion to his course in moral philosophy.

Perhaps the best statement about the nature and function of history during the period was made by James Spencer Cannon, Dutch Reformed minister and professor of metaphysics at Rutgers College. Cannon's title was illustrative. In 1830 he published his *Lectures on History and Chronology Introductory to the Reading of Ancient, Sacred, and Profane History,* which he had been giving since 1819. These lectures contained rudimentary methodological considerations and outlined the utilitarian values of the study of history. Among the latter Cannon noted, "In conveying useful moral lessons, History presents herself in the most winning dress." While biography could serve this function admirably for individuals, history could also instruct nations. In this regard Cannon's "history" was almost identical with the "moral philosophy" of Witherspoon and Smith. "Nations, too, are seen in history, to rise by temperance,

industry and regard for religion: and after succeeding in acquiring
power, wealth and fame, to be enervated by luxury: and then to sink,
under the weight of their own depravities." As a guide to the national
behavior that insured national prosperity, "The study of history *is
friendly* to Religion, especially the religion taught in the Bible, or the
Christian Religion."[57]

Of all the examples from history, those of republican Greece and
Rome were most often cited as proof of the natural, providential connection between religion and national prosperity. Following the suggestions
of their tutors, the Reformed ministers viewed the decline of religion in
Greece in the fourth century B.C. as the fundamental cause of civic decay
and military defeat by the Macedonian Philip II. When strong in "religion and virtue," the ministers contended, Athens alone could withstand
"the unnumbered myriads of Persia."[58] Decline in religion was followed
by a decline in virtue and public spirit. Party strife and factionalism
predominated and the Greeks became an easy prey to foreign invasion.

The fall of the Roman republic was alleged to have been the result of
similar causes and was the example most often cited. As understood by
the Reformed ministers, Rome flourished and expanded because of
strong religious convictions, especially those beliefs relating to a divine
providence. "While the Roman people felt the influence of this first
principle of all religion, they were virtuous, free, and invincible."[59] But
when the Roman populace came under the sway of the "atheistic"
philosophy of Epicurus, moral dissipation and corruption followed.
"Luxuriousness," "effemanacy," and "voluptuousness" became prevalent and the Romans surrendered the republic, considered to be the
apex of national prosperity, to tyrants.[60] Although occasionally other
examples from ancient history were cited, Greece and Rome were
deemed most appropriate to the American situation because of their
republican form of government. Ministerial warnings about the fate of
these ancient republics became as frequent as references to the captivity
of Judah and almost completely replaced the destruction of Sodom and
Gomorrah in sermonic rhetoric. Cicero was often quoted as if his
writings had been canonized and placed in the Scriptures after Deu-
teronomy. This could happen because the central thesis in the conception of providence had changed from the idea of a dynamic God who
created or destroyed nations at his pleasure to the conviction that there
was a natural connection between religion and national fate. The traditional Christian idea of God had so far receded into the background
that it made almost no difference that these ancient peoples were pagan.
For most ministers Greece and Rome were prime examples of God's
providential government of the world.

From modern history France became the most often cited example of
the connection between religion, social order, and national prosperity.

In the initial stages of the French Revolution, American clergymen rejoiced. They understood that event to represent a continuation of their own revolution and anticipated a "reign of Righteousness and Peace."[61] But the ensuing violence and destruction caused all but a few to reverse their opinions. The excesses were blamed on the rejection of all religion. Militant American Protestants could not fret over attacks on Roman Catholicism, but they believed that religion even in its most vile form, as they thought Catholicism to be, could help preserve social order. Eliphalet Nott thought the French Revolution to be conclusive evidence that society could not be controlled without religion, and he argued that the French had to restore religion before obtaining stability. If religion were demonstrably essential to organized society, Nott reasoned that it was only a question of what kind of religion a nation would have. He believed Protestantism superior not only as a religion but as an instrument of social control.[62]

Like ancient Greece and Rome, France became a frequent illustration of the doctrine of providence. If the Biblical history taught that God withdrew from his chosen people for their wickedness, the Reformed interpretation of the evolution of France confirmed that "religion, or the fear of God, is the strongest pillar of a state, and of all civil felicity."[63] For most, this alleged natural connection between religion and political stability was of greater significance to America than the Old Testament conception of a chosen and covenanted people. France's political upheavals represented no covenantal violation, but "their atheistical sentiments burst asunder those bonds by which alone a Republic can be held together."[64]

Ultimately the history of the United States itself furnished the prime example of providential prosperity based on religion. Reformed ministers of the middle and southern states appropriated to themselves, and all of America, the tradition of New England Puritanism and ascribed America's success to its religious heritage. If it could be boasted that "God sifted three kingdoms to get the finest wheat,"[65] in the final analysis American glory was believed to be not an unmerited gift of a generous God but a hard-earned achievement flowing naturally from the practice of religion. If America had arrived to the heights of national glory and independence through the practice of religion, and if there were a connection between religion and national prosperity in all nations, then the inevitable conclusion was that America's future could only be assured by adherence to religion.

The emerging doctrine of providence not only provided a congenial ideology for the Reformed of America but also became functional in a way that would have been impossible for the older version. This new interpretation of the divine government of nations maintained the idea of the solidarity of national experience before God without the embarrassment of preaching a covenant to a pluralistic nation that was "too big, too sprawling, too amorphous" to consider itself "somehow all caught up within a special and particular bond" with God.[66] In early nineteenth-century America the natural law, applicable to all nations and supposedly proven by the whole history of the world, was more easily proclaimed as truth. Whether the nation believed or not, the church knew the secret of national prosperity and, if for no other reason, believed that it should retain a dominant position within the society.

In this vein the Reformed met the most serious intellectual challenge to the position of the church in society. The deists, led by Thomas Paine and Elihu Palmer, had attacked revealed religion and its clergy as opponents of equalitarian and republican principles and had urged deism, natural religion, as the basis for a "pure and unadulterated morality."[67] The Reformed, whose own approach was closer to deism than they realized, refused to consider deism as religion and thus presented a caricature of deism as an attempt to separate morality from religion. Then they adopted the arguments that Smith had presented for the necessity of religion and made it apply solely to Christianity. With these adjustments in logic they attacked deism as unsupported by human experience, reason, or revelation.

Ashbel Green's tirade against deism was representative. He characterized it as a "mere Atheistical hypothesis and speculation," which was in conflict with the facts and the experience of all nations. He was sure that "no nation has ever yet existed where this phenomenon of morals without religion has made its appearance; and there is no reason to believe that it is even possible from the very nature of the human mind."[68] On the other hand, Green was convinced that the proposition that "obedience to the divine laws . . . will insure to a nation the protection and blessing of heaven" could be "incontrovertibly supported by fact." There was no need to rely on Scripture for proof because there was sufficient evidence "of the historical kind." In the end Green was convinced that "the doctrine [providence] which I proposed to demonstrate has been shown to be supported by facts, and to be sanctioned by the soundest principles of reason.—It has been proved *to be true;* and *how,* and *why,* it is true, has been explained."[69] While the deists did not succumb to this logic, it was after all an age of reason and this approach to providence commanded intellectual respectability within American society.

The dynamic understanding of God's providence that was expressed in the colonial period, complete with illustrations of God's "warnings," "pleadings," and "mercy," had been transformed into a static concept of a precise natural law of cause and effect. In retrospect this transition seemed as necessary as it was useful. In an age of rationalism, when men of the world were cautious about accepting what was not readily comprehensible on the basis of human experience, the new doctrine presented itself as preeminently reasonable. In an age when men were extremely suspicious of absolute authority, the new conception of providence freed the ministers from reliance on the authority of Scripture. In an age of great religious heterogeneity, the new doctrine made no demands based on presumptions of cultural solidarity. Finally, in an age and country where the state had officially withdrawn its support of religion, the new doctrine maintained the necessity of religion to the very existence of civil government. This conscious and sustained theory that religion was the only force capable of social control made it possible for religion and the clergy to retain the social status that they had held through recorded history. In the transition, the force of mystery and the awe of divine power had largely disappeared. This victory was not without its price. The successful adjustment to the new era, in the final analysis, hastened the advent of societies with nonreligious methods of social control.

Chapter 3

"The Association between Religion and Patriotism": Providence, Civil and Religious Liberty, and Republican Government

Now the fact is that in many material points, *the same names mean things wholly different* in different ages of the world, and even in coeval nations. What do the *rights of man* mean, at Vienna, or St. Petersbury? What does *sovereign* mean in America? ... What does freedom, or liberty of the press, or Christianity mean at Rome, at this day? Our freedom is our peculiarity, as it is our glory.[1]

Analytic clarity in historical interpretation depends on the seemingly simple, but ultimately complex, task of understanding the use of terms with a high degree of precision. American historians, especially of the classically liberal disposition, have long adopted a literal understanding of the terms "religious liberty" and "separation of church and state" to describe the status of religion and the relationship between religious and governmental institutions in America. On the broad spectrum of thought in the early national period, nothing could be much more imprecise and incorrect.

Recent attempts at greater analytic accuracy have effectively questioned the former understanding and provided insight into the difficulty of the problem. John F. Wilson characterized the American situation as "not 'Church' and 'State' but diverse religious institutions and manifold civil governments."[2] James Fulton Maclear attempted to clarify the statement by describing it as "the 'true American union' of church and people."[3] More recently, Sidney E. Mead attempted to revive James Madison's statement regarding "the line of separation between the rights of religion and the civil authority."[4] While all of these are essentially true of some aspect of the situation, they are not comprehensive. They are, respectively, too institutional, too narrow, and too legalistic.

A careful examination of the language of the Reformed ministers of the middle and southern states indicates that for this significant number of the American population, and for those for whom they spoke, Protestant Christianity was deemed not only a necessary support for American republican institutions but was thought to be inseparable from them. As they understood it, America's civil and religious liberty and republican governments were the direct results of the influence of Protestant Christianity and could not be perpetuated without its instrumentality. Thus when the philosophy that religion was necessary to social order and national prosperity in all nations was applied to America it meant precisely that Protestant Christianity was essential to the stability and prosperity of the nation. America itself, but with emphasis on civil and religious liberty and republican government, was believed to be so grounded in Christianity that its continuance and prosperity depended on the strength of its alleged religious base. As the Reformed viewed it, the American religious settlement was not merely institutional, legal, and residual with the people; it was all of these and more. It encompassed every aspect of national life. One Reformed divine described it as "an association between Religion and patriotism."

The Reformed interpretation of American history was indicative of their firm belief in the relatedness of civil and religious liberty and American government. That same tradition of historiography also provides important clues to the basic meanings of those concepts. In the Reformed mind the significance and essence of American history could be demonstrated through three events—the Protestant Reformation, the Puritan migration to and settlement of New England, and the American Revolution and the writing of the federal Constitution. Although widely separated in time and space, covering nearly three centuries and nearly the whole of the Western world, these events ran together in the Reformed mind, eclipsing myriads of other phases of American development, and epitomizing the whole.

According to this interpretation, God providentially prevented the settlement of America until after the Reformation. For America to have been peopled with adherents to Catholicism, allegedly victims of mental tyranny and superstition, would have doomed her to an awful destiny. In the Reformed view, Americans would have been at best ignorant slaves controllable only by the brute force or standing armies of a stern monarch. The Reformation liberated the mind from the domination of Roman Catholicism, more particularly the Roman pope, and prepared in the Old World a people capable of exercising freedom. One of America's greatest blessings was that it had been "discovered by the light of the Reformation."[5] As American Protestants understood it, the most significant legacy of the Reformation was religious liberty, but they thought that it effectively promoted civil liberty as well. As John Breckinridge signified, "it is not speaking too strongly, when we say, that the light of our national liberty dawned in the cell of Luther."[6] But the Reformation was in and of itself quite incomplete. There remained in the Old World state interference in religion and vestiges of religious persecution.

The next material development in Reformed historiography was the
Puritan migration to the New World. In fleeing to America the Puritans
obliterated the most significant scars of the Old World, despotism and
misguided religion, and moved much closer to perfect liberty. Their
attachment to religion, unrivaled in the annals of mankind, perfectly
prepared them for national distinction and glory. Reformed Americans
of the early nineteenth century deemphasized, and some seemed con-
veniently to forget, both the religious bigotry and restrictions on personal liberty that characterized the Puritans. This was accomplished for
the most part without any sacrifice of principle or gross misconception of
history, because their own understanding of civil and religious liberty
was much closer to that of the Puritans than to that of twentieth-century
Americans, or for that matter, to such contemporary figures as Thomas
Jefferson and James Madison. As late as 1828, Edward D. Griffin, pastor
of the Presbyterian Church in Newark, could affirm that the earliest
settlers of New England "came with unconquerable attachments to civil
and religious liberty," without either being accused of misusing the language or of historical ignorance.[7]

If American Puritanism substantially advanced the principles of the
Reformation, the American Revolution and the adoption of the federal
Constitution—these events formed a single unit in Reformed thought—
brought to fruition and embodied both. In the Reformed explication
of American history the whole period from the 1690s to the 1760s,
as well as the diversified religious conditions in the middle and southern states, seemed insignificant. The Revolution was apprehended to
be so intimately associated with New England Puritanism that it could
well have been placed a century earlier without doing violence to the
Reformed historiography. The delineation of Symmes C. Henry was
typical. "The principles of civil and religious liberty which they [the
Puritans] brought with them when driven into exile by the intolerant
spirit of persecution, became generally diffused, were incorporated with
all their institutions, and thus laid the foundations of that national government, which the United States now enjoy; which is the perfection of
ages, and the admiration of the world."[8] In this one sentence Henry
epitomized the Reformed historiography and identified the alleged in-
separableness of civil and religious liberty, American governments, and
Reformed Protestantism.

In this reconstruction of American history it was assumed that the
federal Constitution and the First Amendment embodied the Refor-
mation-Puritan concept of liberty. Ministerial interpretations of that
amendment often contained explicit references to the Reformation.
Eliphalet Nott, president of Union College, expounded eloquently the
view that Reformation principles were enshrined in American political
institutions. "In the worst of times" he admonished, "cling to the institu-

tions of your country," because "these, under God, are your political ARK of safety; the ark that contains the cradle of liberty in which you were rocked; that preserves the vase of Protestant christianity, in which you were baptized."[9]

The consistent emphasis on the interrelatedness of religion and American government was so strong that any use of the term "separation" to describe Reformed thinking seems absurd. As Jedidiah Morse noted in 1799, those things affecting "our religion" and "our government" were "so closely allied that they cannot, with propriety, be separated." This was the case because "the foundations which support the interests of Christianity are also necessary to support a free and equal government like our own." Morse was convinced that any attempts "to destroy the foundations of our holy religion" were also subversive of political freedom. "Whenever the pillars of Christianity shall be overthrown, our present republican forms of government, and all the blessings which flow from them, must fall with them."[10]

In the context of this historiographical tradition the Reformed conceptions of religious and civil liberty emerge with some clarity. Since religious liberty was believed to be antecedent to and a prerequisite for civil liberty, it was the more basic. Fundamentally a religious rather than a legal notion, the primary features of religious liberty were the twin Reformation doctrines of the priesthood of all believers and the supreme authority of the Scriptures. The essence of religious liberty in the Reformed understanding, therefore, was the freedom of each individual to interpret the Bible for himself.

The idea that the Bible was the supreme authority seemed to Reformed ministers a logical, necessary, and just conclusion from the American doctrine, as expressed in various official documents generally associated with Thomas Jefferson and James Madison, that man was responsible solely to his creator in matters of conscience. In 1824 John Holt Rice of Union Theological Seminary in Virginia announced that the principles of religious liberty in America were so well established that they needed no explanation or defense. "We all know that God is the only Lord of conscience; and that Scripture is *authoritative*."[11] Recognition of the Bible as absolute authority was believed effectively to prevent "the horrors of spiritual oppression" and all the ill effects of religious establishments. As Joshua Moore explained to the Michigan legislature, "The light of the truth, beaming from God's word, shall assert triumphantly the rights of conscience, and in vain shall the effort be repeated to warp its dictates to the low purposes of temporal or spiritual domination."[12] In the Reformed understanding the legal provisions for religious liberty made the Bible the "Supreme Law of the Land."[13]

Recognition of the supreme authority of the Scriptures was only part of the Reformation concept that pervaded American thinking about religious liberty. The other aspect was the priesthood of all believers or the right of each individual to interpret the Scriptures for himself. Eliphalet Nott emphasized this facet by explaining that in America "no assuming pontiff dictates to us our faith. . . . Here light without a veil examates from the sun of righteousness, and salvation, without a mixture, flows pure and unrestrained from its sacred source—the gospel."[14] Or, as Asa Hillyer understood the American religious situation, "Here, every one is permitted to think for himself, and to form his religious opinions according to the word of God, and the dictates of his own conscience."[15]

Religious liberty for members of the Reformed tradition in the middle and southern states, then, was a concept with positive religious content rather than an abstract idea of freedom that was neutral to religion. The ordinary formula used in thanksgiving sermons of the era was an expression of gratitude for "civil and religious liberty," but the meaning was not different when James Richards substituted "our republican form of government and our spiritual privileges and hopes."[16] Thus it was no mistake but a common use of the term when Ezra Stiles Ely declared of prison inmates, "Civil liberty may be taken away, but God forbid that six hundred souls should be deprived of the *liberty of hearing the Gospel!*"[17]

As a positive religious dogma, religious liberty did not include the right to be nonreligious. To the Reformed mind, freedom of conscience did not mean that individuals had that right or the right to reject the authority of God as revealed in Scripture. The liberty to worship God according to the dictates of conscience and the instruction of Scripture was not to be confused with the freedom not to worship. Worship was understood as a duty incumbent on all men. Individual liberty was limited only to the mode of worship. Solomon Froeligh, a Dutch Reformed minister who led a conservative schism in 1822, was speaking for the vast majority of the Reformed in 1794 when he postulated, "Religious liberty is carried to licentiousness . . . when it is used as a cloak to vice, an encouragement to open blasphemy, and a daring neglect of all devotion."[18] E. P. Smith was even more precise when he insisted that liberty became licentiousness when used as a "pretext for demolishing all the safeguards of pure religion."[19] This was what John B. Romeyn was thinking when he declared, "No one is a more decided friend of religious liberty: but at the same time a more determined opponent of religious indifference, than I am."[20] It was even deemed incumbent on persons enjoying religious liberty actively to promote the cause of true religion.[21]

Even when the Reformed used Lockean or Enlightenment language to describe religious liberty they had in mind the affirmation of the Protestant religious article of faith rather than an abstract political or social right. The Presbytery of Hanover, for example, explained to the General Assembly of Virginia that the Assembly had no authority in matters of religion since "the only proper objects of civil governments are the happiness and protection of men in the present state of existence, the security of the life, liberty and property of the citizens." To "illustrate and confirm these assertions," however, the presbytery cited religious principle rather than social contract. The presbytery affirmed "that to judge for ourselves and to engage in the exercise of religion agreeable to the dictates of our own consciences is an unalienable right, which, upon the principles that the gospel was first propagated and the reformation from popery carried on, can never be transferred to another."[22]

Another illustration of this was the use of the section in the Westminster Confession called "Christian Liberty, and Liberty of Conscience." In this seventeenth-century document "Christian liberty" was defined as "freedom from the guilt of sin, the condemning wrath of God, the curse of the moral law" and freedom from "bondage to Satan." In this context, it was affirmed that "God alone is Lord of the conscience." To believe anything "contrary to his word . . . is to betray true liberty of conscience." In setting forth their intentions at the time of the reorganization of Presbyterianism in 1788, the Synod of New York and Philadelphia quoted this section of the confession and concluded that "therefore, they consider the rights of private judgment, in all matters that respect religion as universal and unalienable."[23] Thus in Reformed usage the language of the Enlightenment was saturated with conservative theological content.

When Reformed ministers did stray from the dominating religious statement of the idea of freedom of conscience to consider the more obviously legal aspects of the concept, their interpretation still demanded basic consent to Protestant Christianity. The ministers generally understood religious liberty to exclude those things that would affect the rights of others or disturb the peace and order of society. Any open denial of Christianity was presumed to undermine the social fabric and prevent the maintenance of social order. Therefore, almost any anti-Christian act was thought to be punishable. Sabbath breaking, profane swearing, blasphemy, and other forms of irreligion were believed to be subversive of social order and not legally allowable under the provisions for freedom of religion. While this line of thought was in no way encouraged by American constitutional law, it was totally consistent with Reformed thinking and found support in the common law tradition. If freedom of conscience was allowable only within the limits of social control, and Christianity was the only effective means for securing that control, then it followed that religious liberty should be restricted within the limits of Protestant dogma.[24]

The full consequences of the Reformed understanding of religious liberty were not made manifest until the Irish Catholic immigration of the 1820s and 1830s. The basic story of American Protestant reaction is well known.[25] Part of the significance of the episode was that it provided valuable insight into the precise understanding of Reformed views on religious liberty. The Reformed resisted the rapidly growing number of Catholics because they believed them to be a threat to the freedom of religion and therefore to the existence of the nation. As they understood the situation it was not a matter of bigotry but of national survival.

In the late eighteenth century the relationship of Catholicism to religious liberty in America was an academic question. When Witherspoon considered the problem he did so in abstract fashion. He felt that the reasoning may be "just" that denied toleration to "Popery" on the basis that its tenets were "subversive of society and inconsistent with the rights of others." However, in his lifetime there were but few Catholics in America and he could safely suggest that "toleration" was the best policy, and he could dismiss a Catholic threat with the caustic remark that "such as hold absurd tenets are seldom dangerous."[26] A generation later the tides of Irish Catholic immigration removed the discussion from an abstract basis to the level of social and political reality.

Because of their obviously Protestant interpretation of religious liberty and their conviction that the American constitutional settlement embodied that conception, the Reformed naturally believed that a Catholic population threatened the survival of both religious and civil liberty. It seems paradoxical to the twentieth-century mind, but the Protestant anti-Catholic "crusade" of the 1830s was fought in the name of religious liberty.

One of the most vehement opponents of Catholicism was William Craig Brownlee. Although more outspoken and less moderate than most Reformed ministers, Brownlee was no oddity or radical in Reformed circles. Educated at the University of Glasgow, he served as a pastor in the Associate Reformed, Presbyterian, Associate Scotch, and Reformed Dutch denominations. He held various teaching positions, including a professorship at Rutgers College, and was editor of the official Dutch Reformed magazine.[27] Brownlee's ideas were perhaps most tersely expressed in the title of one of his books, *Popery, an Enemy to Civil and Religious Liberty; and Dangerous to our Republic,* published in 1834. A consistent theme in Brownlee's anti-Catholic publications was that Catholicism was a threat to American religious liberty because it prohibited the laity the free use of the Bible, "the very fountain of religious liberty," and that it interfered with "man's right to know, and think, and act for himself." Because of their denial of the Reformation religious principles, Catholics were viewed as subversive of America's civil government and therefore subject to civil penalities. According to Brownlee, any person who supported Catholicism was "to all intents and purposes, a conspirator against the liberties of this republic" because Catholicism "tends to deprive the humblest citizen of his religious liberty." Such a person could "neither claim nor enjoy civil liberty" and should be considered a "pest of civil society, and a dangerous traitor to our country."[28]

Perhaps the most detailed, and somewhat restrained, discussion of this topic from the Reformed point of view came from John Breckinridge, a Philadelphia Presbyterian. This ensued from a debate with John Hughes, a Catholic priest also located in Philadelphia. The debate, which occurred in 1836 and was extended over fifteen separate sessions, was later published under the title, *A Discussion on the Question, Is the Roman Catholic Religion, in Any or All Its Principles or Doctrines, Inimical to Civil or Religious Liberty? And of the Question, is the Presbyterian Religion in Any or All of Its Principles or Doctrines, Inimical to Civil or Religious Liberty?* The first part of the question was the original topic of the nonsectarian debating society in Philadelphia. Hughes would agree to debate the Catholic question, however, only on the condition that Breckinridge debate an equal amount of time on the same question as applied to Presbyterianism. As could be expected, the debate was inconclusive, but the published account demonstrated rather substantially that the arguments were not far removed from the Reformation era, American liberalism notwithstanding. The contestants agreed on a definition of religious liberty that was essentially confined to the context of Christian tradition and reflected but little interest in personal liberty. They concurred that religious liberty was "the right of each individual to worship God according to the dictates of his own conscience, without injury or invading the rights of others." At bottom, Breckinridge's argument was reflective of the twin Reformation doctrines that characterized Reformed thinking on the subject. He noted, "It is 'according to the dictates of his own conscience;' not that of the priesthood; and therefore each has a right to *inform* his conscience, by all means in his power; by reading the Bible. . . ."[29]

Another distinctively American feature of the meaning of religious liberty, in addition to the amalgamation with civil liberty and republican governments, was the incorporation of legal disestablishment into the concept. Initially religious liberty and disestablishment were related but at the same time entirely different concepts in the Reformed mind. In the period during and immediately after the American Revolution, the Reformed idea of religious liberty would have allowed, if not demanded, some kind of establishment. The only acceptable establishment at that time would have been one giving equal treatment to all Protestant denominations and one under which the state exercised no direct controls over religious doctrine or church government. Unlike the perceptions of religious liberty, which remained relatively consistent, ideas about establishments changed significantly in the late eighteenth century. This came about largely as a result of the American experience in which the diversity of religious sects and their mutual jealousy made any thoughts of a plural establishment untenable. In the final analysis, disestablishment came to be identified as a basic component of religious liberty and as such a positive benefit to religion.

The most logical conclusion from the dominant idea that religion was absolutely essential to social order and civil government was that the government should support, or establish, religion as a means of its own preservation. This was in no way considered as a threat to religious liberty. It should be recalled that John Witherspoon presupposed that the state should support religion and that he entertained a discussion of religious liberty in that context; Witherspoon believed that the state could reduce the risks involved in a policy of "toleration" by supporting the Protestant "sects."[30] Nor did the Presbytery of Hanover, long celebrated for its petition of 1776 on religious liberty, believe some form of government support of religion to be inconsistent with religious liberty. In October 1784, the presbytery sent another, and perhaps more significant, memorial to the General Assembly of Virginia. In this communication they reasoned that since religion was "absolutely necessary to the existence and welfare of every political combination of men in society," it was "wise policy" for the state to seek the aid of religion. It was "upon this principle alone," declared the presbytery, "that a legislative body has a right to interfere in religion at all. . . ."[31] As the Presbyterians of Virginia soon came to realize, a pluralistic Protestant establishment could not be made a reality. Their own jealousy and fear of Episcopal dominance plus other difficulties precluded the possibility of legislating and implementing such an establishment.[32] The Virginia experience was incorporated into the Reformed mind and, by the time the idea of any formal establishment on a national basis was rejected by the adoption of the First Amendment, the Reformed on the whole acquiesced in and supported that decision. After that time, however, the Reformed idea of disestablishment was identified with religious liberty. In this way legal disestablishment itself came to be part of religious dogma.

The assessment made by William Linn in 1794 seems to have been an accurate description of the attitude among the Reformed of the middle and southern states: "In this country there are still a few advocates for establishments of some kind; but the most rejoice. . . ." This characterization would have been incomplete and incorrect if Linn had not gone on to say, "We believe that religion will flourish more than ever, and that the old establishments in Europe are a great impediment to its progress, and a part of the anti-christian system."[33]

In effect, if it seemed that the Reformation secured the authority of the Bible and the right of individual interpretation from ecclesiastical domination, disestablishment in America was conceived to have achieved that same status in relation to civil government. In retrospect, it appeared to the Reformed that "true religion" had suffered as much from governmental support, and the resulting governmental control, as it had under the domination of the Roman popes. As an instrument of the state, religion had become perverted and a source of human political ambition and greed. The "church" was prevented from exercising the influence believed inherent in the purity of Biblical religion. Disestablishment freed religion from the stagnation inherent in state interference, restored the Scripture to its rightful place of authority, and became a necessary ingredient of religious liberty.[34]

In the final analysis disestablishment as part of the expanded concept of religious liberty was believed to be necessary to the ultimate success of Protestant Christianity. Unlike James Madison, who assumed that the sects would remain divided and unpowerful, the Reformed believed that disestablishment would be the prelude to greater uniformity and greater influence. This conviction was, of course, grounded in the belief of a universal acknowledgment of the authority of Scripture. This was joined with a further optimistic assumption that "truth needs only an equal advantage with error, to gain an eternal victory over it."[35] Armed with these convictions, the Reformed anticipated that disestablishment would provide the background for massive surrender to the overpowering influence of the gospel. United under the authority of the Scripture, Protestants would reign in America.[36]

As in the case of religious liberty generally, disestablishment in the Reformed mind was not understood as a separation of church and state, nor was it understood that the state would remain indifferent in its attitude toward religion. Disestablishment was often viewed as nothing more than the government's promise of neutrality toward the various Protestant denominations.[37] Religion was believed to have been freed from the control of the state so that it, understood as Protestant Christianity, could have a greater impact on the common life of the nation than was possible with an establishment. Paradoxical as it may seem, the Reformed held that disestablishment brought religion and civil government closer together rather than separating them. It was, in fact, the legal provisions for disestablishment that made America "a truly Christian country and nation," for in this way America professed the religion "revealed in the Scriptures."[38]

It followed from the Reformed understanding of religious liberty that the only means to preserve this particular feature of American society was the extension of the influence of Protestant Christianity. A basic ingredient of all Reformed literature of the period, this concept was given classic statement by John Holt Rice in a work with the title *Historical and Philosophical Considerations on Religion*. In many ways Rice was admirably suited to this task. Although he was more active than reflective and often did not understand clearly the distinctions between his and other positions, he stated his own convictions unambiguously and without hesitation. Archibald Alexander, a lifelong friend, observed that even as a young man Rice abstained from philosophical and theological arguments and read little in these areas. The effect of this was, according to Alexander, that "it rendered him less acute in minute discrimination, than he otherwise might have been." On the other hand, Alexander believed this allowed Rice "to seize the great and prominent points of a subject with a larger grasp."[39]

This was certainly the case with *Historical and Philosophical Considerations on Religion.* Rice's lack of "minute discrimination" was seen in the dedication of this work to James Madison, "enlightened, and dignified friend of rational liberty." The purpose of the volume was to "show how the freedom" that Madison had labored to win "may be perpetuated."[40] Although Madison would have been horrified at Rice's directions, Alexander, himself a master of the fine distinction, testified to Rice's ability "to seize the great and prominent points" by expressing his own agreement.[41]

After having argued that religious liberty was necessary before "true religion" could "produce its appropriate effects on the community," Rice sought to show how religious liberty could be perpetuated by preserving those things which led to its initial acceptance. His historical interpretation was "that we owe all our ideas of religious liberty to the Bible." According to Rice, the early Christians were exponents of religious liberty and "every martyr . . . was a fearless advocate." After Constantine turned from his initial support of toleration, the ideas of religious liberty were gradually lost except among the "Waldensees" and several reformers before Luther. The Reformation brought a renewal of emphasis on religious liberty. The basis of this, according to Rice, was a belief in "the sufficiency of the Scriptures and the right of private judgment." He affirmed that "in all cases the men who stood forward as champions of religious liberty, *derived their principles FROM THE BIBLE*." This was so much the case, Rice believed, that one could discover "a remarkably exact proportion between zeal for freedom of conscience, and conformity of religious doctrine to the simple truths of the Bible."[42]

By relying on the power of the state, the Reformers stopped short of their own principles "and the contest was brought to a close before the work was rendered complete." The work begun during the Reformation was completed in America. "The settlement of this country, chiefly by men, who fled from religious intolerance in the old world, was the most important event, except the Reformation, after the establishment of the *great spiritual tyranny*." While Rice admitted that the first settlers possessed something of "the spirit of their age," he believed them to be in advance of that age with regard to religious liberty. Prior to the American Revolution many Christians had resolved upon complete religious liberty and Rice contended that when the various states established governments, the "*forms of political government* were framed in conformity to principles received by the most numerous classes of christians among us." Rice alleged that the support for disestablishment among "infidels" was an attempt to secure the collapse of Christianity altogether. For Rice their participation could not have come under the category of a struggle for religious liberty because it would imply that that term could have a negative meaning that Rice did not allow. "By *religious freedom*," he asserted, "our modern reformers mean, *freedom from all religion*. And thus their liberty is the slavery of sin, and a state of war against the best principles of human virtue." Religious liberty for Rice was a religious concept and it could only come from the Bible.[43]

When Rice turned to discuss means by which religious liberty could be preserved, the emphasis remained on the sufficiency of the Scriptures and the right of private judgment. He held as a cardinal principle that "FOR THE PRESERVATION OF RELIGIOUS LIBERTY, THE SUFFICIENCY OF THE SCRIPTURES OUGHT TO BE ADMITTED: AND THE BIBLE TO BE UNIVERSALLY DISTRIBUTED," and this "does most clearly imply the *right of private judgment*." It is quite clear that Rice maintained this position in opposition to Catholicism. That there could be no religious freedom if laymen were forced to receive the opinions of priests was a proposition that Rice declared to be "considered as settled . . . among protestants." Thus to be "free" in this sense, it was imperative that every citizen possess a Bible. Referring to Madison again, Rice emphasized "*that the Bible is the most efficient support of that liberty, which his labors so materially aided, in procuring for the people of this country.*"[44]

But Rice was not satisfied with this alone. Like all Presbyterians of his time, he considered the way the Bible was interpreted to be extremely important. Therefore he concluded that "*correct views of christian doctrine; and especially the terms of a sinner's acceptance with his Maker, are all important for the preservation of religious liberty.*" Rice held justification by faith to be the central doctrine necessary to religious liberty, which again illustrated the Protestant orientation of his whole concept of religious liberty. The doctrines of penance, extreme unction, and purgatory he alleged to be "suited to extend priestly influence: and therefore to deny religious freedom."[45]

Beyond this, Rice reflected his Calvinistic roots by declaring that simplicity of worship was necessary to the preservation of religious liberty. Elegant temples, he believed, had been used to keep the mind in bondage and ignorance. Freedom of choice demanded knowledge and this could best be attained through a mode of worship that aimed at impressing truth on the mind rather than exciting the passions through ceremony.[46]

Rice applied the same principles to church polity and concluded that it was necessary for the "government of the church" to be "in the hands of the people." At this point Rice hedged by stating his position in a way that he thought would appeal to a majority of American Protestants. In a less public declaration, however, he declared unhesitatingly, "One reason of no small weight why I prefer the form of government of the Presbyterian church, is because the great principles laid down in the Gospel, are accurately drawn out, and reduced to practice with a precise application of all the checks and balances which give security to religious liberty." The "checks and balances" as he conceived them were the power of the church to regulate and discipline ministers; the representation of laymen in ecclesiastical judicatories; the power of the laity in the choice of a minister; the possession of the Scriptures by laymen, which enabled them to judge the performance of the minister; and the marriage of ministers, which gave them an interest in the common destiny of the community. For Rice the conclusion was inescapable that Presbyterianism was the best means of preserving religious liberty.[47]

As to the best method of promoting adherence to these means of preserving religious liberty, Rice was in agreement with Witherspoon and Smith: *"The prevalence of a sound, intellectual and religious education is to be regarded among the most important means of preserving our religious liberty."* Rice believed that anyone not instructed in the Scriptures and brought up under a system of moral education could easily fall prey to enthusiasm, fanaticism, or superstition, all of which could lead to a loss of religious liberty. Rice concluded that the Sunday school system, which was already flourishing, was an "efficient instrument in perpetuating the religious liberty of the United States."[48]

At this point Rice had reached the same conclusions with regard to religious liberty that Smith had with regard to the general prosperity of the nation. Perpetuation of the nation, of religious liberty as understood by the Reformed, could be accomplished in America by nothing short of the domination in fact if not in law of Reformed Christianity. The coming together of these two themes was apparent when Rice declared that "parents and teachers of youth, are committing a species of treason against their country, by neglecting the moral and religious discipline of the young."[49]

If religious liberty was understood by the Reformed of the early national period as the product of Protestant influence on society that demanded the dominance of Protestantism for its survival, no less was true of civil liberty. The Reformed did not search through the annals of political, social, or technological development to explain the emergence of civil liberty, nor did they consider the intellectual influence of the Enlightenment. Theirs was a holistic approach to reality, and religion was the core from which radiated all that was either good, true, or beautiful. Civil liberty they deemed to be one of their most precious possessions. Could it have had any other source but Christianity? According to George Washington Bethune, Dutch Reformed minister in Washington, D.C., "This liberty, like every other blessing, we derive from Christ; and had I time, it could be shown that it is peculiarly the result of Christian principles: for the history of the world demonstrates that civil liberty has ever been in proportion to the prevalence of pure Christianity."[50]

That civil liberty was a product of Protestant Christianity was so widely assumed among the Reformed that most, as in the case of Bethune, did not feel compelled to attempt to prove it. David M'Conaughy was convinced that "such enlightened and liberal views of civil policy as Americans then had, and such a wise system of government as they now enjoy, could be suggested and sustained only by the light, the spirit and authority of revealed truth."[51] Thus in response to the question "Whence has our civil liberty been derived?" he sounded the affirmation, "Christ hath made us free."

This view of the origin of civil liberty was shared by Reformed laymen as well as the clergy. Theodore Frelinghuysen, a profoundly religious senator from New Jersey, gave an entire address at Rutgers College on the connection between the Bible and liberty.[52] Perhaps some insight into the popularity of this idea can be derived from a Fourth of July speech by the layman Daniel D. Barnard. Commenting on the uniqueness of the principle of the equality of all men stated in the Declaration of Independence, Barnard was temporarily diverted by the observation that this was, however, not a new truth. It resulted from "the order of the creation" and "it was proclaimed by Moses and the prophets, and authoritatively taught in the mission of Jesus Christ." Only "as a political truth" was the Declaration of Independence a new announcement.[53]

As basically rationalists, however, some of the Reformed clergy attempted to demonstrate the validity of the common assumption. One such effort was made by Samuel Miller in a sermon with the informative title, *Christianity the Grand Source, and the Surest Basis, of Political Liberty.* Reasoning from the text of 2 Corinthians 3:17, "And where the spirit of the Lord is, there is Liberty," Miller pointed out that the Scripture spoke of a different kind of liberty but that the text was equally applicable to political liberty. The major thesis of the sermon was "that the general prevalence of real Christianity, in any government, has a direct and immediate tendency to promote, and to confirm therein, political liberty." True liberty was not bound with any form of government but existed in the "hearts and dispositions" of citizens, and Miller believed that Christianity promoted the disposition essential to liberty. Christianity taught that all men were by nature equal so that "citizens, of every rank" were considered as brothers, even though their possession of power and rights might be unequal. Christianity promoted the happi-

ness of the community and taught each citizen not to "resign his conscience . . . to the capricious will of men." Justice and benevolence, temperance and moderation were necessary to liberty and inculcated by
Christianity. Christianity taught men the proper duties in all relations of
life and rendered men "contented with those rights which the God of
nature gave them." Appealing to history as his authority, Miller concluded that "with few exceptions . . . there never was a regularly organized government . . . where the true religion was not received, in
which political slavery did not hold a gloomy reign."[54]

Miller came to the same conclusion as Samuel Stanhope Smith when
he considered providence, as John Holt Rice when he surveyed religious
liberty: The best way to insure the continuance of political liberty in the
United States was to insure the dominance of Protestant Christianity.
"Those are the truest and the wisest patriots, who study to increase its
[Christianity's] influence in society." If America wished to "stand fast in
that liberty, wherewith the Governor of the universe" had made it free, it
must remain Christian. And if political liberty were to continue in
America, Christianity would have to be taught to the rising generations:
"Teach them to be Christians and they will ever be free."[55]

The identification of American civil liberty with the "liberty" spoken
of in the Scriptures occurred frequently in Reformed sermons and indicated to what extent civil liberty was believed to be grounded in Christianity. It also indicated the fundamentally conservative nature of civil
liberty in the Reformed understanding. In addition to the text from 2
Corinthians, Reformed ministers frequently cited Galatians 5:1, "Stand
fast in the liberty wherewith Christ hath made us free," as relevant to the
American experience. As a result of their habit of searching the Scriptures for "prophecy," either already or yet to be fulfilled, ministers could
easily identify the first-century religious context of these verses and still
apply them to their own contemporary situation. Solomon Froeligh, for
example, pointed out that the passage in Galatians "no doubt, primarily
alludes to the abolition of that truly cumbersome and expensive train of
Mosaical ceremonies." However, he was convinced that "commentators,
who will not suffer the apostle to have extended his views to more general objects, and looked forward to the success of the gospel in after ages,
are, I conceive, contracted in their sentiments." After a brief panegyric
to liberty, Froeligh went on to discuss liberty, "civil and religious," as
defined by "the best and ablest writers on jurisprudence, and according
to the dictates of common sense," as if these were the ideas of the apostle
Paul.[56]

If the liberty of Galatians 5:1 was deemed identical to American civil
liberty, Galatians 5:13 proscribed the limits of that liberty. The apostle's
warning, "use not liberty for an occasion to the flesh, but by love serve
one another," was considered altogether relevant. In fact, that verse of

Scripture highlighted the two most significant features of Reformed thought about the nature and bounds of civil liberty. The first and most obvious was that civil liberty was in no way to be understood as a negation of order and authority but as a condition requiring responsible, moral, Christian action. In the second place, liberty was basically a community-oriented concept rather than one emphasizing personal freedom. Both aspects tended to make the Reformed understanding of civil liberty more medieval than modern.

Reflecting the first of these features, Gardiner Spring wrote in 1820 that "liberty without godliness, is but another name for anarchy or despotism," because "the religion of the Gospel is the rock on which civil liberty rests."[57] George Washington Bethune agreed that liberty was essentially the right to pursue happiness but that it was "perfectly harmonious with our obligations to obey the laws of God." The truest liberty was obedience to the divine law. To refrain from such vices as drunkenness, sexual promiscuity, and "idleness" was not a loss of liberty because these things were inconsistent with true happiness.[58] If morality was essential to true liberty, vice destroyed it. As John Matthews noted, "let us strongly associate, in our minds, the idea of vice, in all its forms and degrees, with the subversion of our liberties." On the positive side he reminded, "let us, then, measure our attachment to the blessings of freedom by no other scale than that of our morals."[59]

Reflecting this point of view, James Muir, one of the most active Presbyterian ministers of the South, surveyed the American scene in 1798 and concluded that "liberty, in our day, has been a name greatly abused, it has been the rallying point for anarchy and irreligion." If liberty could in any way be used against religion, Muir did not hesitate to affirm that he could not "recommend such a spirit in any manner, or to any degree."[60] The Reformed, then, agreed with Elisha Swift that a "dangerous and fatal licentiousness" that served as a "pretext for demolishing all the safeguards of pure religion" was not liberty but a perversion of it.[61]

This idea of liberty as something less than an absolute right unless accompanied by responsible Christian practice was best illustrated in the Presbyterian position of gradual emancipation for American Negro slaves. That slaves were not capable of becoming "freemen" until they had attained a Christian education was a common sentiment of Presbyterians prior to 1826 and one that was consistent with their total view of liberty.[62] Samuel Miller enunciated this point of view in a sermon before the Synod of New Jersey that was directed toward raising funds for the African School sponsored by that body. Miller declared, "One of the most serious obstacles to the immediate emancipation of slaves, in this or any other country, is that they are not *prepared* for the enjoyment of freedom." Only after they were "taught to read God's holy word" and "instructed in the doctrines and duties of our holy Religion" did Miller think that they could "possess the mental vigour and acuteness, the high sense of character, and the moral restraints and regularity of freemen." Miller believed that in their present "degraded" state the slaves could have nothing but a degrading influence on society: "They could never be trusted as faithful citizens." Christ alone could "prepare those who are in thraldom to be 'free, and not to use their liberty as a cloak of maliciousness, but as the servants of Jesus Christ.'"[63]

A second aspect of Reformed thought about civil liberty was that it was fundamentally a concept applicable to the total community rather than the individual. This factor was obviously present in and inseparable from the notion that liberty required responsible action. Yet its significance requires emphasis. To an amazing degree the only consistently expressed ingredient of personal liberty in Reformed literature was the right to ownership and protection of property. The Reformed thought primarily in terms of the social unit and their goals and ambitions were social. In view of this overriding concern, conformity of the individual was deemed essential. Individualism was as alien to the Reformed as irreligion. "Hence, civil liberty owns authority, submits to restraints, makes sacrifices, uses self-denial, and holds possessions, and even life itself pledged for the public good."[64]

The centrality of the social nature of liberty was apparent in the Reformed interpretation of the American Revolution. The most significant feature of that event was believed to be the securing of liberty *as a people*. It was the collective attainment of national independence, which the Reformed contrasted with national slavery, more than the acquisition of personal liberty that was understood to be the end result of the American Revolution. That event was celebrated as analogous to the Hebrew Exodus. The Fourth of July was remembered not as a day of victory for personal liberty but as "that day, in particular, which gives them a political existence, rescues them from a state of dependence and oppression, restores to them the enjoyment of liberty, and elevates them to the rank of free and independent nations."[65] It was the community connotation of civil liberty that allowed the Reformed to assume the possibility of civil liberty and slavery, or otherwise unequal rights for individuals, in the same society. In this context there was no fundamental conflict, or even paradox, in the system of slavery in a free nation.

If religion was deemed necessary to maintain the level of morality demanded before liberty could be earned, it was also thought necessary to promote unselfish commitment to the general welfare of the community.[66] In Reformed thought Christianity and patriotism were inseparable. This segment of the Reformed mind was illustrative of the whole. They considered patriotism as unqualifiedly good and therefore felt that it must be based on Protestant Christianity.

The Reformed were somewhat embarrassed by the poverty of New

Testament support for patriotism. Samuel Stanhope Smith devoted a whole sermon to refute those who "ignorantly objected" to Christianity because it did not inculcate patriotism. He concluded that while it was not in the New Testament because it would have been "pernicious" in that historical situation, it was everywhere in the Old Testament and congenial to the spirit of benevolence in the New. Patriotism was in fact "the sublimest impulse of our nature," and only the religious man could be patriotic.[67] Other ministers were not quite so cautious in exegesis as Smith. George Washington Bethune boldly began a sermon with the assertion, "Jesus Christ was a patriot," and for evidence Bethune explained that Christ loved his countrymen.[68] Hooper Cumming insisted that Jesus recommended patriotism, that the Old Testament prophets exemplified it, and that the apostle Paul wrote "one of the sublimest examples of patriotism ever exhibited to the world."[69]

Albert Barnes argued the point on different grounds. He contended that America was the only nation in which patriotism required "as an essential constituent, the love of Christianity." This resulted from the fact, as Barnes understood it, that "the Christian scheme has been laid at the foundation of all our acts of government." Since Christianity was "imbedded" in all American civil institutions, they could be sustained only by "the lofty principles of Christian faith." American constitutions and laws without the Scriptures were "a lifeless corpse without the soul." According to Barnes, "He that loves his country, will therefore love the religion that has done more than all other things to give us a name and an exalted standing among the nations of the earth."[70]

Thus, from whatever perspective the Reformed viewed America, the conclusions were the same. From the point of view of the doctrine of providence, America had come to be an independent and promising nation because her early settlers and colonists were dedicated to establishing a Christian society in the new land. If that prosperity were to continue it would be because of the continuing influence of Christianity. While this was believed to be a natural law binding on all nations, America's civil and religious liberty was something peculiar, something special. According to the Reformed interpretation of history, these too were products of Christianity, and if the new nation were to preserve that which it held most dear it could only be done by the perpetuation of Protestant Christianity.

In the Reformed mind, liberty combined with the doctrine of providence at the point of Samuel Stanhope Smith's teaching concerning republics. As John D. Blair of Virginia phrased this insight in defending the general proposition that virtue was necessary to national prosperity, "This, in a greater or lesser degree, is true of all nations; but to those which, like ours, are blessed with free republican forms of government, of which virtue is the leading principle, it is of the greater usefulness and the most indispensable necessity."[71] The thought about liberty and providence interacted at this point so that the strands often became indistinguishable, resulting in the American corollary.

Sometimes the statement of the American corollary sounded like a recitation of the doctrine of providence with an emphasis on liberty. This was the case when John McKnight recommended to his congregation "such manners, and such modes of living, as become republicans and free men, and as will tend to preserve the liberty and privileges which you enjoy." Those things to avoid were "idleness, prodigality, dissipation, and luxury," since these were the "bane of republicanism and of liberty."[72] In other cases there was a greater incorporation of more traditional Christian instruction. John B. Romeyn, who defined "righteousness" as adherence to "the whole system of revealed truth," announced to his congregation that "Where righteousness prevails, there civil freedom is enjoyed." This was not to be confused with "that licentiousness for which irreligious theorists have pled." It was "a freedom which originates in efficient faith and sound literature."[73] In still other instances the statement emphasized the practice of Christianity with only a hint of providence. Jacob Janeway insisted that Americans enjoyed civil and religious liberty because of the teaching of the Bible. "Shut up the Bible; abolish our Christian assemblies for reading and preaching its sacred contents; and in a few years these blessings would be lost."[74] In whatever way the American corollary was stated, it always carried the message that America could preserve neither its existence as a nation or its special features of civil and religious liberty and republican government without adherence to Christianity.

In this way, the question of a formal establishment of religion in the Old World sense had become irrelevant. The Reformed, while expressing full agreement with the American settlement, called for an informal establishment based on public opinion rather than law. George Potts articulated the Reformed position in a sermon on July 4, 1826. According to Potts, "genuine Religion, with all its moral influences, and all its awful sanctions, is the chief, if not the only security we can have, for the preservation of our free institutions." While recognizing that infidels might suspect the strength of his convictions, Potts declared once again "that an established union between church and state, ever has been and ever will be,—while man continues to be, what he now is,—the prolific parent of corruption in both church and state." These seemingly contradictory assertions were reconcilable because "the preservation of our constitutional rights, from the very nature of our government, must be entirely dependent upon the sound character of public opinion." Potts was convinced that only Christianity could so inform public opinion as to provide the morality needed to "hold society together." This informal establishment of Christianity as the basis of the national life through the power of public opinion Potts called "an association between Religion and Patriotism."[75] When Potts, pastor of the First Presbyterian Church of Natchez, Mississippi, delivered this discourse in Philadelphia, he so well expressed the sentiments of the local Reformed clergy that the sermon was printed at their request and with their endorsement. The American corollary demanded the "association between Religion and Patriotism."[76]

Chapter 4

The Millennium:
Scenario for an
American Theocracy

The American expression of the doctrine of providence provided a structural framework through which the Reformed could voice their interpretation and seek to give direction to the new American nation. While this mode of conceptualization provided an outlet for various social, economic, and political directives, it was ultimately subsumed by the religious vision of the Kingdom of God on earth—the millennium. The millennium represented an idealized society completely subservient to the will of the deity as understood and enforced by the Reformed churches. It was believed that the existence of such a society was assured by the promise of God but that its realization required the cooperation and labor of man. While the millennial goal was ultimately universal, an emphasis on a special American role in producing the millennium tended to make the vision intensely nationalistic. The ideals of the millennial state became a pattern for an attempted reconstruction or "renovation" of American society. The millennium complemented and reinforced the ideas contained in the American corollary but added dimensions of its own which pointed to methods of operation and formed a dynamic incentive to action.

Ideas about an imminent millennium were pervasive in American society in the late eighteenth and early nineteenth centuries. Thinking about the millennium was vastly stimulated during the Great Awakening, and received powerful support from Jonathan Edwards's *History of the Work of Redemption*.[1] Alan Heimert has perceptibly noted that "the watershed in American history marked by the 1740s can be understood best in terms of the degree to which, after the Great Awakening, the American populace was filled with the notion of an impending millennium."[2] Indeed, in the early part of the nineteenth century, millennialism seems to have been the characteristic American symbol for expressing collective hopes and ambitions for the future. Millennialism encompassed American nationalism, glorified the American social order, and supported the idea of progressive improvement destined to make the world over in the image of an idealized American Kingdom of God.

The Kentucky Presbyterian James M'Chord did not overstate the case in 1813 when he declared, "The commencement of the millennium has been so long the object of the world's expectations, that none of our hearers, not even the most thoughtless, can be at a loss to comprehend the nature of that period."[3] Expectations of a Christian millennium were not confined to a few insignificant ministers. The most learned and powerful of the clergy gave serious attention to ascertaining the "signs of the times" in anticipation that events foretold in the prophetic literature were to be fulfilled in their own times. Pious laymen invested considerable energies in the same pursuit. These ranged from the little remembered Enoch Shepard, deacon of the First Presbyterian Church in Marietta, Ohio, to Elias Boudinot, president of the Continental Congress in 1783, who wrote a massive treatise entitled the *Second Advent, or Coming of the Messiah in Glory, Shown to be a Scripture Doctrine, and Taught by Divine Revelation, from the Beginning of the World, by an American Layman.*[4] Other political figures, from the locally influential Samuel Bayard of Princeton to the nationally prominent John Jay, voiced the common expectations and hopes of an imminent millennium.[5] Perhaps the redundancy of Thomas DeWitt was warranted when he declared, "By common consent it is universally admitted that the prophetic period of twelve hundred and sixty years is drawing to its close; preceding the universal prevalence of Christ's kingdom in the world."[6]

The Reformed universally agreed that the millennium was imminent. The prophetic calendar that dated the introduction of the millennium no later than the year 2000 and possibly as early as the 1840s was so widely accepted that most Reformed ministers believed it necessary only to state that "the most judicious commentators have concluded, that the predicted period is at length nearly arrived."[7] The two commentators read most widely by Americans in the middle and southern states were William Linn and Alexander M'Leod, both of the Reformed Dutch communion. The millennial calculations were based on an interpretation of the 1,200 days of Revelation 11:3 and "a time and times, and half a time" of Revelation 12:13 as meaning that the reign of Antichrist, defined as the Roman pope, would last 1,260 years. As Linn pointed out, "The great difficulty . . . is when to date the commencement of the thousand two hundred and sixty years."[8] If the date were calculated from the year 606 when the pope was declared universal bishop, the millennium would commence in 1866. If the chronology were calculated from Gregory II's acquisition of temporal power in 729, the millennium would be delayed to near the end of the twentieth century. M'Leod supposed that if the Jewish method of dating was intended, the date of the commencement could be as early as 1843.[9] While there were other dates preferred by some, most fell between these extremes. Linn was of the opinion that as the power of the Antichrist had grown gradually it would diminish in the same fashion. Therefore, without attempting to set a precise date, Linn simply affirmed, "It may be near the two thousandth year of Christ, before the church enjoys the greatest prosperity; yet there is reason to believe that preparatory events are much nearer, and that even we may see a day of the Son of man."[10]

Most of the Reformed, like Samuel Miller, refused to discuss in detail the dating of the millennium. While accepting the opinion of the "commentators," Miller reasoned that it was only logical for the history of the world to follow the analogy of creation. Assuming that the world was created during six days in 4000 B.C., Miller then dated the coming of the world's "Sabbath" millennium at around 2000 A.D.[11] The only other Reformed commentary on Revelation to appear during this period was by Henry Kollock, tutor at the College of New Jersey and pastor in Savannah, Georgia. Kollock considered the whole problem of dating the millennium in a few pages. Since he believed the millennium to be imminent, the exact date was of little importance to him. Like most other Presbyterians, Kollock felt it necessary only to declare to his congregation that "in this very house, long, very long before, in the course of nature, it can crumble into ruins, will the millennial glories of the church be displayed."[12] For the Reformed the millennial vision was too dominating to be obscured and lost in a maze of chronological speculation.

The precise nature of Reformed thinking about the millennium was of extreme social significance. The Reformed position was what later would be designated as postmillennialism,[13] meaning that Jesus was expected to return to the earth at the end of the millennium rather than at its beginning. The millennial "reign of Christ" was understood as symbolic rather than actual. The millennial society was therefore expected to display features not unlike those already familiar to the American population. This interpretation of the millennium served to deemphasize rather significantly religious concern about individual salvation and future life. Ideas about the millennium reinforced the this-worldly collective orientation demonstrated in the doctrine of providence. Postmillennialism was a doctrine espoused by men who were confident that they in large part had control over their society and could direct it toward ends desired by themselves. Premillennialism has been the dream of the disestablished and downtrodden who could expect relief and victory only by the direct intervention of the deity. Perhaps the absolute dominance of postmillennialism in the middle and southern states in the early national period indicates more strongly than other data the extent to which religion was the possession of the elite.[14]

The extent to which postmillennialism prevailed among the early nineteenth-century Reformed was illustrated in the works of Amzi Armstrong, a premillennialist who labored constantly but unsuccessfully to convince his colleagues of their errors. In 1815 he published *A Syllabus of Lectures on the Visions of the Revelation* in an attempt to refute the "commonly received opinions."[15] The extent to which Armstrong failed was clearly indicated in a sermon of 1824. An old man returning to his former pulpit, Armstrong made one last attempt to inculcate his favorite doctrine. He reminded his congregation that the doctrine of the millennium had commonly not been taught in the premillennial form because "men aspired to be Lords over God's heritage. . . . It suited their purposes much better," he alleged, "to allegorize and spiritualize the Scriptures on this subject, in such a way as to leave room for them to arrogate to themselves the honour, and the authority, and the power in the Church, which belong to Christ alone." Armstrong complained about postmillennialism: "so entirely has this scheme prevailed" that it had "chained down the minds of men in darkness on this subject."[16]

The opinion that the millennium would precede the second advent of Christ was so firmly established among the Reformed that it was unnecessary to defend it. As late as 1834, when premillennialism had found new champions in England, Archibald Alexander could still dismiss the whole scheme as "destitute of all solid foundation." For Alexander it was simply unreasonable to consider, since Christ would have to live in some particular location, thus depriving the rest of the world of his personal leadership.[17] Even in 1842, when premillennialism had found ardent advocates such as William Miller in America, the Presbytery of New York refused ordination to the premillennialist John Lillie. They feared he would be a "fanatical disturber of the Church's peace."[18] As long as postmillennialism was the "prevalent opinion, both in the religious, and political world,"[19] it served as a significant social symbol. When the nature of the millennium became a subject of violent dispute in the 1830s and 1840s, its power as a social symbol was dissipated.[20]

If postmillennialism emphasized the this-worldly and elite nature of Reformed thinking, their projection of a semicataclysmic introduction of the millennium stimulated an aggressive nationalism. As with the question of the premillennial or postmillennial return of Jesus, there were historically two interpretations about the method in which the millennium would be introduced. One extreme was that the era would be the consummation of a historical evolution characterized by human progress. The other extreme predicted a miraculous reordering of the world featuring a divine cataclysmic destruction of the forces of evil. The former of these positions was generally associated with postmillennialism, while the latter was more compatible with premillennialism.[21] The Reformed, however, harmonized these discordant elements. By confining the cataclysmic elements to the European civilizations, they were able to envision the United States leading the rest of the world into the millennium through progressive human, social, intellectual, and religious improvement. This both heightened American nationalism and committed the Reformed to an implicit theory of progress and an optimistic view of history.

The prerevolutionary American millennial tradition, associated with the Great Awakening and Jonathan Edwards, had removed cataclysmic elements almost entirely from consideration.[22] However, the violent course of events from 1775 to 1825, featuring the American and French revolutions and the wars in Europe, convinced most of the Reformed that the movement toward the millennium would be either interrupted or consummated by a cataclysmic destruction of the Antichristian forces, always defined in relation to Roman Catholicism. Most came to this conclusion relatively early in the period. Others, like Ashbel Green did not reconsider this until after 1823 when the Italy Alliance became active in Europe.[23]

The possibility of a cataclysmic destruction of Roman Catholicism was gratifying to American Protestants. It seemed perfectly consistent with their ideas of justice. John B. Romeyn described the scenes in vivid language: "It will be a period of calamity, distress, impiety, ferocity, tyranny, superstition, and gross ignorance." Romeyn invisioned "a period darker than the middle ages" in which civilization would be replaced by "barbarian rudeness" characterized by "a lawless, unprincipled, and superstitious tyranny, in church and state." What saved Romeyn, and the Reformed, from a totally illogical view of the future was that these conditions would prevail only "throughout the spiritual Sodom and Egypt—the mystical Babylon, among all the ten kingdoms, which have given their power to the beast."[24] The final cataclysm would involve only that portion of the world once dominated by Roman Catholicism. The horror of the cataclysm was somewhat further reduced by the idea that the destruction of the Antichrist would occur by degrees. The battle of Armageddon became symbolic of a series of wars confined to the "Old Latin earth" rather than a single and decisive battle between the forces of light and darkness.[25]

Interpreted in this light, cataclysm became relatively unimportant in the Reformed vision except for two considerations. In the first place, those same events in Europe that from 1790 to 1815 aided the revival of emphasis on cataclysm also increased the millennial expectation. This was especially true of the events in France from the Revolution through the Napoleonic wars. France was viewed as the "tenth part" of the Roman kingdom supposedly referred to in Revelation 11:13, and the constant activity there, whether otherwise favored or opposed, served to feed the belief in an imminent millennium.[26] This emphasis was such that, while the majority of the Reformed thought it only the "beginning of sorrows," some actually thought that the battle of Armageddon, symbolically understood, had begun with the French Revolution. James Blythe declared in 1814 that only "a few random shots may still be exchanged between the adverse parties" before the millennium commenced.[27]

A second result of this interpretation was to stimulate American

nationalism and heighten the expectations of a special American destiny. America would be spared from this destruction. This belief was based on the conviction that the wrath of the deity would be directed only toward those nations that had persecuted the saints and those governments that had through religious establishments perverted Christianity and made it an instrument of the state. America had "never, as a nation, supported the power of the Anti-Christ."[28] While the statement of this position ranged from a cautious hope, or even prayer, to a firm conviction, the Reformed were generally convinced that their efforts to build up the "American Zion" would not be destroyed in the cataclysm.[29]

This belief was amply demonstrated in the sermons of the era. Alexander M'Leod informed his congregation, "I have it in my power, from the sacred text, to assure my hearers, the Christians and the witnesses of this land shall not suffer in the catastrophe which we have considered." Earlier M'Leod had noted, "Our own country, remote from that earth and from the power of the beast of the pit, will remain an asylum to the dispersed saints, at the time the witnesses shall be slain in their native land."[30] When William C. Davis of South Carolina entertained the prospects of cataclysm he concluded, "I feel for mankind, and bless God that I am an American."[31]

While America's exemption from the calamities was sometimes predicated on continuing virtuous behavior, the millennial vision generally allowed a much more optimistic view of America's future than did the doctrine of providence. In the providential view, American prosperity was interpreted as the legacy of pious forefathers and a bright future could only come from a continuation of that mythical tradition.[32] But the view of the millennium was unencumbered by the necessities of adhering to the standards of an ideal "Golden Age" in America's past.

In addition to being spared from the cataclysmic destruction, America was believed to be destined to provide leadership to the other nations of the world who had not been subjects of the Antichrist. These nations were located primarily in Asia, Africa, and South America. Implicit in this thinking was the idea that all nations in these locations would adopt American social, political, and religious characteristics before the beginning of the millennium. Thus millennialism served as a powerful motivation to American imperialism and colonialism. Americans confidently believed that their laws, form of government, and Protestant religion would be universally adopted. In calculating an imminent millennium, Simeon H. Calhoun declared, "I verily believe, the term of half a century would be sufficient to carry freedom and Christianity, in triumph, around the globe."[33]

America was indeed to have a significant hand in bringing the millennium into being. Most of the Reformed would have agreed with James Blythe that "the discovery and civilization of America is one of the grand preliminary events intimately connected with the latter day of glory, and indeed forming quite an essential part of the important plan." Blythe did not hesitate to point out the potential of American agriculture to feed the "myriads of people shortly to fill the earth," but his main concern was of a different nature. In America's "unparalleled form of government" and "her religious institutions" Blythe believed he could see "Jehovah as with his finger designating America to a post the most honourable, in his new kingdom of glory."[34] That this statement came in the midst of war illustrated how far the millennial vision could look beyond the gloom of the moment. In the words of John M. Mason, "From the eminence of scriptural prediction, a humble believer overlooks the molehill of worldly politics, and decries the moving power, and the necessary effect, of the machinery of Providence."[35]

The effect, then, of a diluted apocalyticism was to heighten the millennial expectation and strengthen the ideas of a special American destiny. At the same time, although fraught with certain logical inconsistencies, optimism that man's attempts to extend the gospel and make progress toward the millennial state was not seriously impaired.

The relative unimportance of cataclysm in the millennial vision was well attested in Henry Kollock's commentary on Revelation. Kollock omitted a discussion of chapters sixteen through nineteen, which contained a description of the Antichrist and "a particular account of the mode of his destruction." As these prophecies were to be fulfilled in the very near future, Kollock explained, "It is enough for us to know that these events are certain." While thus eliminating all discussion of the future calamities, Kollock hastened to affirm that "immediately after this, the *millennium* . . . shall bless the church and the world." It was more important to emphasize the millennium because it was better understood, attested to by all of Scripture, and "so associated with the best feelings of the believer."[36] The vision of the "spiritual church" gaining "sovereign power over the nations" was so bright that the calamities appeared dim by comparison. In the long run it was the idea of progress and human improvement rather than the idea of divine calamity that served the Reformed as a significant motivation to action.

The Reformed optimism that the historical process would lead to a thousand years of bliss on earth was grounded in faith in the promises of God and the power of the gospel rather than on any confidence in man. The Reformed of this era held almost to a man the federal doctrines of original sin and total depravity.[37] Having also rejected the idea that the millennium would be ushered in by a miraculous and universal reordering of nature, the Reformed held that the "knowledge of the Lord" would spread over the earth, effecting a moral change in man and bringing in the millennium. Since it was believed that God ordinarily worked through human instruments, the spread of the gospel and consequently the coming of the millennium ultimately depended on the efforts of Christians.

During this era the Reformed extended the doctrine of man's depravity beyond the area of salvation to preclude the possibility of cultural progress for natural man. In its extreme form this doctrine allowed movement from barbarism to any degree of civilization only under the influence of Christianity or of some nation that had better preserved the original revelation given to Adam, with the latter appearing to be very unlikely. In this view the first human society was the most "civilized" in the history of mankind. Under the influence of Christianity, civilization could progress, but where it was not known man and his culture could do nothing but deteriorate. In the millennium civilization would once again regain the heights of the first society.

What the Reformed meant by "civilization" presents a problem. The concept was ambiguous at best and in all probability it was used without a consciously precise definition. In various contexts it included man's intellectual, moral, and social character.[38] In the simplest usage it was merely the opposite of savagery or barbarism and demanded at least a settled agricultural or commercial economy. It certainly indicated a harmonious, well-mannered, and moral society. While the concept always indicated a certain degree of knowledge about those things essential to man's welfare, it sometimes included the fine arts, methods of written communication, and other advanced sciences.[39]

Whatever its exact meaning, the whole idea of civilization was secondary. The function of the concept was to emphasize the tendency of man and society to degenerate when not under the influence of the Christian religion. The Reformed were appalled by the British philosophers, especially Godwin and Condorcet, who taught the perfectibility of man. While they recognized the similarity of the Christian millennium to the "dream" of the philosophers, they violently disagreed with the idea that man could create a perfect society without the aid of Christianity. Samuel Miller thought it utterly inconceivable that philosophy could "purify, tranquilize, and perfect human society," for that was the work of God. "He will bring good out of evil, order out of confusion, light out of darkness, and a kingdom of the greatest glory and blessedness out of materials which are totally depraved."[40]

An incisive statement of the Reformed view concerning the prospects of the natural man was that of Philip Lindsly, pastor in Princeton and later president of Cumberland College. Lindsly contended, against the opinion that man was originally savage and by a gradual development of his own abilities became civilized, that it was "contradicted alike by reason, by revelation and by history." According to Lindsly, Adam was created fully mature and "taught immediately by his Maker every thing necessary for him to know." Adam lived "nearly a thousand years" and instructed future generations in the arts of civilization, but after his death the process of degeneration began to work. "Man is prone to degeneracy; and when sunk to the lowest state of degradation, he remains stationary, until light from abroad dispels the darkness which envelops him." Pointing to history, Lindsly contended that "the world cannot produce an instance of a nation, a tribe, a family—or an individual who has ever emerged from the rudeness of savage life without any foreign or external aid; or without the instruction and example of those who were already civilized." Even after a nation had reached an advanced state of civilization, the greatest problem it faced, according to Lindsly, was "to keep up to the standard of excellence which has been already reached."[41]

Ashbel Green reviewed Lindsly's sermon in the *Christian Advocate* and expressed his complete agreement with these sentiments. The following year Green printed an essay entitled "The Antediluvian Age" by "Eidolon," which argued the same position in much greater detail. Green commented that there was "much truth" in the essay, but he expressed some doubt about all the conjectures made by the author.[42]

Some of the Reformed carried this position to the extreme of denying the possibility of scientific and literary advance by non-Christians. John B. Romeyn was the most vocal in the expression of this idea, but the literary attainments of the Moslems and "Socinians" caused him some concern. He explained that while these seemed to contradict his position, the Moslems only became interested in learning after their contact with the Roman Empire and Catholicism. Even in what Romeyn considered to be a polluted form, Christianity still produced the Moslem improvement. The Moslems, he contended, were unable to make any advance over what they had borrowed and they soon degenerated into profound ignorance. The "Socinians" were only able to be learned because they were raised in Christian countries. Pointing to Copernicus, Bacon, and Newton, Romeyn concluded that "it is under the auspices of revealed religion, that the most important discoveries have been made in the different departments of human knowledge." Under any other influence man had only been able to originate "preposterous and ridiculous theories."[43]

While all of the Reformed would not subscribe to this extreme statement, it was generally believed that there was a direct relationship between Christianity and civilization. Christianity both demanded and promoted a state of civilization. The most obvious point of contemporary interest was in missions to the Indians. It was a deep conviction that the Indians would have to be Christianized before they could be civilized, but in practice the two went hand in hand. This was symbolized in the use of the one building as both schoolhouse and chapel. One Presbyterian missionary reported some Indian "conversions" in the following language.

> George Colbert, a Chickasaw chief, called in a decent dress, and lodged here. He informed me how he and his brother Levi had laboured to further the pious and benevolent designs of the [missionary] society; that he, Levi, and a number of others, wish to learn good things: no get drunk, but work, make corn, cotton, cattle, hogs, etc.[44]

This statement cannot be construed to be that of a lesser figure who imperfectly conceived his task. It represented the Reformed view in action. In his inaugural address at the College of New Jersey, Ashbel Green declared that it was simply impossible to propagate Christianity without at the same time promoting learning.[45] William Brownlee believed Christianity and civilization were so identified that he declared enemies of missions to be "an enemy to true wisdom; an enemy to the progress of science; an enemy to the extension of the blessings of civilized life; an enemy to the feelings of humanity: who would deprave the heathen 'the blessings of polished life.' "[46]

The degree to which a connection between Christianity and all human progress was assumed may be seen in the cautious way that Samuel Miller stated his opposition to that extreme position. In writing his two-volume survey of the developments of science and literature during the eighteenth century, Miller had come to appreciate some of the scientific work of non-Christians. Miller, more flexible in his youth than he was later to become, acknowledged that "a bad Christian may be a very excellent mathematician, astronomer, or chemist." If any should be offended by his praise "of some distinguished abettors of heresy or of infidelity," Miller cautioned that "justice is due to all men."[47] Although Miller was willing to grant far more to the unsanctified abilities of man than any of his colleagues,[48] he agreed wholeheartedly with them about the end result of man's striving. "Science . . . when committed to the hands of depraved men, is liable to be deformed, abused, and converted from a blessing to a curse." Miller believed that it was the very progress of science that was not "regulated and directed by holy principles" that would lead to the state of degeneracy in the Old World that would precede the millennium.[49]

If the millennium would not be introduced by a miraculous reordering of nature or by the gradual improvement of natural man, it would come by man's being changed and regenerated by the Spirit of God. While regeneration was seen to be the exclusive work of the Holy Spirit, the Reformed believed that this act took place under certain predictable

conditions that were suited both to the character of man and God. More
.mportantly, these conditions could be created by teaching man the
"knowledge of the Lord" that was contained in the Bible.

A concise statement of the general understanding of the process of
regeneration was furnished by Archibald Alexander. The Spirit's work
of regeneration was moral in nature but it was affected through the
means of "understanding and choice." It was "the effect of a divine
operation, yet all its exercises take place aggreeably to the common laws
of rational nature."[50]

This understanding of regeneration was based on the notion that man
can be directed either by the passions or by reason. Some of the Reformed further divided the rational nature of man into intellectual and
moral elements, but these worked in harmony against the passions.
While the passions or animal senses were not believed to be wicked in all
forms, they became so if not subjected to the rational nature of man.
Man's point of contact with God was in all cases through his rational
nature.[51]

Eliphalet Nott frequently turned to this theme in addressing the
graduating classes at Union College. "Controul [sic] and subjugate your
passions" was his first advice to the young men. Nott pointed out that
when man was created, reason was at the helm and "the bosom of man
was calm." But when man lost his innocence he became "blind and im-
petuous" under the rule of the passions. The senses provided some
pleasure if properly restrained, but the "richest banquets" of the senses
soon disgust. On the other hand, Nott saw rational endeavor as a "holy
pleasure" that enabled man to know both science and the "invisible creation." In Nott's judgment, "The wretch who does not prefer it to the
mere indulgence of the senses, though free of other crimes, evinces a
depravity which merits eternal reprobation." It may come as a surprise at
this point to note that Nott preferred the threefold division of man's
nature. While affirming that the moral nature was the highest part of
man, he concluded, "Your intellectual and moral nature, are what ally
you to angels and assimilate you to God."[52]

The Reformed agreed that regeneration was "ultimately wrought on
the *heart*," but it was further their conviction that "the *understanding* is
unquestionably the avenue through which the heart is reached."[53] Man
as a rational being must be led to religious experience through reason.
Any attempt to excite or produce religious experience through the
"animal senses" or passions would inevitably lead man away from the
end in view. According to Joseph Clark, "The more we suffer our en-
quiries" on the true and false grounds of religion "to be directed by the
pride and corrupt passions of the heart, the greater will be the danger of
building our hopes on a foundation that must finally be swept away as a
refuge of lies."[54]

If the "avenue" was the understanding, that which was to be understood was the "knowledge of the Lord." This phrase stood as the central expression for the accomplished millennium and as the primary method of reaching that goal. The passage of Scripture most often quoted in connection with the coming millennium was Isaiah 11:9, "For the earth shall be full of the knowledge of the Lord as the waters cover the sea." In direct proportion as this knowledge was extended over the world the millennium would be coming.

In its most general usage the "knowledge of the Lord" meant "an understanding, and reception of the whole scheme, and science of salvation."[55] More specifically it meant the Reformed understanding of God, man, and Christ. While occasionally some other item was listed under this heading, it always included these three. God must be known in all his "perfections." Man must be understood as depraved. The atonement of Christ must be recognized as the method by which God effected reconciliation with man. As used by the majority of the Reformed, the "knowledge of the Lord" was almost a synonym of the "system" of doctrines of the Westminster Confession or the Synod of Dort.[56]

The "knowledge of the Lord" did indeed include a more intimate knowing of the deity, but this "knowledge" could not be attained other than through the intellectual and rational faculties. A representative statement of the relationship between the two aspects of the "knowledge of the Lord" was that of Edward Griffin. Although this "knowledge" included "the speculation of the understanding," it was not limited to it. "It consists in a clear discernment of God's spiritual glory and in a holy intimacy with him." While it could not be gained "without right affections," neither could it be had "without deep and extensive knowledge."[57] Most Reformed would have agreed with Henry Kollock, however, that "it is possible that a person may know the doctrines of Christianity and yet be unholy; but it is impossible that he should be entirely ignorant of them, and yet be holy."[58]

The extent to which the priority of a rational understanding was stressed was illustrated by the way Kollock interpreted several conversion experiences in the New Testament. In the instance of Paul, Kollock was puzzled as to how he could so quickly come to know the "whole system of Christianity," which of course Kollock considered essential to conversion. Kollock concluded that it had been a miracle. Paul's mind had been "instantaneously infused." Kollock hastened to say that since miracle was no longer to be expected, it was now necessary to study in order to acquire that knowledge. He placed the same construction on the mass conversions at Pentecost and affirmed that Christian education now replaced that kind of miracle although it could not guarantee conversion.[59]

Samuel Miller also espoused this view. He insisted that the first ministers of the gospel were not ignorant fishermen. "They were," he was convinced, "put in possession by miracle, and perhaps in a single hour of that information, which, now, can only be gained by years of laborious study."[60] A contributor to the *Presbyterian Magazine* in 1821 argued that "there can be no reasonable doubt" that "the doctrines of Biblical religion are addressed to the understanding of men." For this reason ministers should avoid at all costs exciting the passions of their listeners. "It must be clear," he asserted, "that no very accurate examination can be made into any system of religious doctrine, while the mind is under the violent impulse of agitated feeling." Christianity could be communicated only through "sound, logical reasoning" and "by sound irresistible argument." The objection that this was possible only for the educated was dismissed with the assertion that true religion was based on a "proper knowledge of the perfection of that God whom we profess to worship."[61]

An intellectual understanding of the "doctrines" or "system" of Christianity—the "knowledge of the Lord"—also implied a correctness of sentiment. The Reformed did not hesitate to affirm that what was understood must correspond to the "truth" before it could produce the desired change in man. It was believed that any improper or incorrect intellectual apprehension of Christianity would invariably lead to immoral behavior and incorrect religious practice. The statement of this position by John Chester would have been widely accepted: "As the views which we possess ... must have a governing influence, over all our sentiments, and conduct; it is absolutely essential that those views be correct."[62]

Understood in this fashion, the extension of the "knowledge of the Lord" was to bring about the millennium. This was believed to be "the only effectual cure for moral depravity: the only system of truth that can purify the polluted recesses of the heart, that can curb irregular appetites, and restrain the impetuosity of passion."[63] Since the actual moral change of man was the work of the Holy Spirit, in the Reformed view, the task of Christians in producing the millennial bliss was to instruct man in the "knowledge of the Lord." As Ashbel Green explained it, the Holy Spirit renovates man through the "instrumentality" of revealed truth, which "gains entry into the mind by several modes or methods of introduction." Among those things listed by Green were reading or listening to the Bible, listening to preaching, reading "pious" books, and catechetical instruction.[64]

Of these modes of introducing revealed truth to the mind, the Reformed preferred Bible reading and preaching, and the spread of the Bible and the growth of the ministry became symbols of the approaching millennium. Thus Arthur Stansbury could declare confidently, "If ever our hopes of [the millennium] are to be realized, the Bible must be spread far and wide. From the Bible's light must dawn this jubilee of the world."[65] But before the Bible could make its full impact it was necessary that all men be able to read it. Every advance in popular education, therefore, was viewed as a step toward the millennium. Thomas DeWitt reasoned that the 1,260 prophetic years were nearly ended because "literature, science, and true religion are extending their benign influence."[66] This idea coincided with the emphasis on the connection of Christianity and civilization, thus reinforcing the belief that religion and human culture, especially education, were closely related.[67]

The expectation of an entire populace reading the Bible for themselves, however, did not detract from the necessity of the ministry. Even though Ashbel Green, for example, could encourage his congregation to check his teaching against the Bible, it was his established opinion that "the mass of mankind cannot, and they are sensible that they cannot, decide for themselves on controverted points, which involve facts beyond their power to investigate."[68] In the final analysis the ministry would be the supreme agency in diffusing the "knowledge of the Lord." The Reformed placed a very high premium on the ministry. It seemed only logical to them that if God had used the ministry since the establishment of Christianity he would do so "whenever the whole earth shall be filled with the knowledge of the Lord."[69]

Although the primary figure in bringing about the millennium was to be the minister, the layman was expected to lend his support to the total effort. It was still believed that it was the "prerogative" and "glory" of God "to bring ... a kingdom of the greatest holiness and felicity out of beings totally depraved," but God had chosen to work through man and would do so to produce the millennium.[70] As Eliphalet Nott reminded the General Assembly, "No new method ... is to be expected." The millennium must be produced by the "exertion of believers."[71] In spite of the emphasis on man's inability to better himself, the millennium elicited the full participation of man and served effectively as an incentive to greater action.

The grand function of the vision of the millennium was that the projected features of that utopia served as a model for an attempted "renovation" of American society. If America were to lead the non-Roman world into the millennium by gradual, but accelerating, progress, then the state of American society was of extreme significance. The symbol of the millennium therefore served as a tremendous incentive to concerted social action. As envisioned by one minister, the expectation of an imminent millennium "will necessarily produce a vast, powerful, concentrated and irresistible action."[72]

The central conception of the Reformed vision of the millennium was that the "world" would be dominated, ruled, controlled, and subjugated by the "church." The vision of the millennium then was preeminently social, encompassing politics, economics, religion, personal relation-

ships, science, literature, and the fine arts. Alexander M'Leod declared
with emphasis that "the principle" that gave unity to all prophecy was
"THE CONNECTION BETWEEN THE CHRISTIAN RELIGION AND SOCIAL ORDER
IN THE HUMAN FAMILY." In the millennium it was believed that all aspects
of human existence would be "rendered conformable to the word of
God in spirit and design."[73] Within this context, the Reformed were
primarily concerned about changes in "civil and ecclesiastical government." In all other areas they were for the most part contented with the
status quo. Thus in the final analysis the vision of the millennium promoted a socially conservative bid for absolute power.

It would be somewhat misleading to describe the Reformed views of
the political structure of the millennium as a theocracy without some
clarification. In the strictest sense the Reformed understood themselves
to be the future rulers of the world. By interpreting the millennial "reign
of Christ" figuratively, the church, as the symbolic Christ, would rule the
world. Henry Kollock precisely articulated the Reformed position. In
commenting on Revelation 11:15, "the kingdoms of this world shall
become the kingdoms of our Lord and of his Christ," and Revelation
12:5, "The woman brought forth a man-child, who was to rule all nations with a rod of iron," Kollock declared, "It is then of *Christ mystical,* of
the succession of true converts, of his spiritual church and people, that
the scripture here speaks." It was Kollock's opinion that "these . . . shall
finally obtain sovereign power over the nations."[74] Understood in this
sense, the Reformed vision can be described as theocratic.

The Reformed were not in principle opposed to an integration of
government and religion. They were, however, strongly opposed to government control of religion and preferred to follow a different course
until their ideal could be made a reality. M'Leod expressed this point
with some precision. "Christianity," he contended "has suffered by its
connexion with civil polity." It would continue to do so "until both learning and power are transferred into the hands of godly men, and so made
subservient to piety." Unsanctified power could be used to further those
interests rather than the cause of religion. Given this alternative, M'Leod
felt it best "for the friend of religion to continue like the witnesses
prophesying in sackcloth."[75] Thus it was the theocratic insistence on
absolute control of government that led the Reformed to support what
appeared to be the "blessed" policy of disestablishment.

The emphasis on liberty among the Reformed of the 1790s can only
be properly understood in this light. The Reformed were not interested
in liberty as an abstract right or quality. It was their firm conviction that
"civil and religious establishments" had prevented men from accepting
the truth of the Christian religion and becoming evangelical Protestants.
Under these systems, John B. Romeyn declared, men "are not free to
obey what they know to be good, but forced to obey that which is evil."[76]

The Reformed believed as firmly that once man possessed full freedom he would soon surrender to what they believed to be the overpowering influence of the gospel. Liberty was necessary before the world could become uniformly Christian. Freedom in terms of independence from the control of Christianity was thought to be nothing more than an intermediate step on the road to universal domination of the world by the church.

The best illustration of the Reformed emphasis on liberty as it impinged on the millennial hope was their reaction to the French Revolution. William Linn, whose interpretation of the millennium was widely accepted among Presbyterians, wrote in 1794 that the "most auspicious sign of the time" was the spread of liberty, "first in America, and now in France." Linn noted the significance of this in the rhetorical question, "Is not the prevalence of civil liberty necessary to the reign of Righteousness and peace?" While he recognized the existence of "infidelity" in France, this caused him no particular concern at this date. He was convinced that "soon as the design for which a wise God hath permitted it, is answered, religion will return in primitive purity and power."[77]

When primitive Christianity did not soon appear in France, the Reformed were forced to modify the statement of their position. John McKnight of New York was probably the last to lose hope in the possibilities of the French Revolution. As early as 1795 he had encountered some opposition from his fashionable congregation because of his views on the subject, but in 1802 he was still convinced that France would yield to the "true religion." In that year he reminded his congregation that "God works in ways not altogether conformable to the expectations and views of man." While he personally loathed the contemporary French situation he was confident that God was at work in it.[78] Jonathan Freeman, however, spoke for the majority of Reformed when in 1798 he lamented, "We were attached to the revolution—prayed for and rejoiced in its success. We beheld Antichrist falling like lightning from heaven—we hailed the millenial dawn. But alas! where is that boasted religious liberty?"[79]

Liberty as a central theme of statements about the millennium was replaced after the turn of the century by more overt declarations of the theocratic vision, but the Reformed position did not change substantially. Any removal of enforced religious opinion was still viewed as an opportunity for the advancement of Christianity, but the Reformed had learned that liberty could lead to "licentiousness" as well as primitive Christianity.[80] Samuel Miller, at the time a young pastor in New York and ardent supporter of Jefferson, pointed to the reformulated statement of the position in 1798. Miller continued to argue that all ecclesiastical and civil establishments, those "fabrics of superstition and despotism" and "systems of unnatural domination," would have to be destroyed before the millennium. He did not fail to point out, however, that "all the vain schemes of those who would govern the heart without religion, and regulate society without God" would also have to vanish.[81] Miller's position was as decidedly theocratic as it was violently anti-Erastian. In the millennium the state would not dictate in manners of religion but would give its entire support to the true religion.

The major text for the millennial theocracy came from Isaiah 49:23, "And kings shall be thy nursing fathers, and their queens thy nursing mothers: they shall bow down to thee with their face toward the earth, and lick up the dust of thy feet."[82] In the millennium God would supremely "govern the world for the sake of the church."[83] Such government, of course, could never be oppressive because all would freely submit to its authority. Liberty would be complete because all would seek to do the will of God voluntarily. A typical statement of the Reformed dream was that of Romeyn, who envisioned a "complete and thorough change" in governments in the millennium. Magistrates would then be "a minister of God for good" and would "acknowledge the mediatorial authority of the Lord Jesus Christ." All of the enemies of the church would be "slain" and the state would become the "handmaid of the church."[84]

There was nothing new or radical in this vision. The hope was nothing more or less than an idealized version of a pattern of church-state cooperation that had already been attempted at various times in the past. According to John Holt Rice, when Christianity was established by Constantine "it was thought that the time foretold by the prophet had fully come, 'when kings should be nursing fathers and queens nursing mothers to the church.'" But since Christianity had then been made into an instrument of state it was nothing but "deceitful smiles." The full realization of the ideal would come only in the millennium.[85]

Because of their peculiar understanding of the nature and benefits of liberty, the Reformed had been able to cooperate fully with other Americans of different views in the "Lively Experiment." By the time those differences became apparent in the triumph of other opinions, the Reformed found it necessary to work toward the theocratic vision without the immediate benefit of "nursing fathers."

In the economic and social order as well as in the political order, the Presbyterian ideal of the millennial state was a religious domination of existing structures. In the millennium "religion [would] dwell in the palace as well as in the cottage," but there was no inclination on the part of the Reformed to envision millennial egalitarianism.[86] The general social principles required in the millennium did not differ from what was demanded by the Reformed interpretation of the doctrine of providence. According to Romeyn, "The Spirit of God will, to an extraordinary degree, enlighten the minds of the members of the Millennial

Church; so that they will understand their duty and privilege, in all the relations of life, social as well as religious, and civil or political as well as social." This meant among other things that "persons of rank and influence will not abuse their blessings to gratify pride and vanity; nor the abundance of their tables, to promote gluttony, drunkenness and lust."[87]

In fact, one of the most outstanding features of the Reformed millennium was the stability of social rank over mobility. Subordination and contentment were highly valued by the Reformed. In the millennium, Romeyn projected, "Children will keep their places as children, and *novices* their places as *novices*."[88] William Staughton, president of Georgetown College and one of the most prominent Baptists in Reformed circles, envisioned a millennium in which ordinary folk worked in contentment and children were occupied with "pious instructions."[89] The Reformed, indeed, never anticipated an egalitarian society. Alexander Proudfit asserted that even in heaven there would be "a diversity of rank, some subordinate and others superior," because people differed "in their capacities for occupying exalted stations, and exerting an important influence in controlling the offices of the world."[90]

The only egalitarianism in the millennium would be the common subservience to the deity and equality in his sight. As noted by one Reformed clergyman, all were alike in the estimation of God, "the pious servant is Christ's free-man, and the free-man is Christ's servant."[91] James Blythe expressed this aspect of Reformed thinking about the millennium with some precision. He declared the Bible to be "the great *leveller*." But the equality deriving from its teaching was spiritual rather than social. While it "inspires the sacred name of *brother*," it did not inspire "the peasant with ambition to mount into his master's throne." According to Blythe, "Let every man's cottage, and every prince's palace, be blessed with a Bible, and the work of fraternizing the world is done."[92]

While the Reformed did not conceive of an egalitarian millennium, they were during this period unable to reconcile Negro slavery with the millennial vision. It was believed that emancipation was to be achieved before the millennium began, but the Reformed generally did not think that they should actively crusade for that cause. It was to them a matter of secondary importance. The more immediate concern was for the religious instruction of the Negro that would give him the "liberty of the Gospel." In the meantime, the Negro was advised that patience and subordination were the best ways to hasten the millennium.[93]

The one social change most desirable to the Presbyterians was perfectly consistent with the ideology of religious conquest. In an age when ministerial power and influence seemed to be declining rapidly,[94] they pointed to a millennium in which this would not be the case. Samuel Miller, who probably dwelt on the ministry more than any other Presbyterian of that era, explained that even in the millennium man would be born in sin and in need of the administration of the gospel. Further, all the ordinances of religion would be universally observed. The result would be that "the ministers of religion will be more numerous, more sought after, and more beloved, than in any former period."[95]

While the Reformed view of the millennium could largely incorporate the existing political, social, and economic structures on the assumption that they would be brought under the control of Christianity, there was one existing structure that was intolerable—a divided church. A church divided among parties each claiming a correct understanding of the true religion for itself was totally inconsistent with the view of world domination. If the church was to reign it must be at peace with itself. It must be unified, and the Reformed believed that unity was promised in the Scriptures as a characteristic of the millennial church.

Unlike modern ecumenists, the Reformed of the early national period conceived of church unity solely in the context of Protestantism and that primarily in theological rather than institutional terms. Roman Catholicism was believed to be one with the Antichrist and would be destroyed before the millennium. On the other hand, very little was said about forms of church government, administration of sacraments, or liturgy. Romeyn's treatment of these questions was representative. He felt that divisions in the structures of the church were produced partly through corruption of the true religion and partly by a multiplicity of civil environments. In the millennium "the distinctions of names, of countries, of doctrines, and of government, will be done away." This was all the discussion required on questions of polity and organization. Romeyn's vision of "one visible body" or "one spiritual community" was primarily of another nature that requires explication.[96]

The primary emphasis in the idea of unity was that of theological agreement. According to Romeyn, in the millennium "there will be no diversity of opinion."[97] The same assumptions that led the Reformed to demand liberty also influenced deliberations about Christian unity. The Scriptures were believed to be an infallible source of truth which could be comprehended by those earnestly seeking it. Once man had the complete freedom to study the Bible, truth would triumph. Since religious truth was considered to be "one and the same," it was considered to be only a matter of time, and certainly by the dawn of the millennium, before religious uniformity would prevail.[98] Implicit in this idea of unity was a rigidity of a sectarian nature that in the long run helped prevent any significant formal union. "Philalethes" noted in 1825 that everyone seemed to agree that the millennium was near because Christians were laying aside the distinctive peculiarities of their sect and professing greater unity. However, he insisted, the millennium would not be based either on "ignorance or indifference."[99]

Some of the Reformed despaired of an entire uniformity of opinion and made toleration the focus of millennial unity. Even in this context, however, it was assumed that there would be agreement on major doctrines. The faith of the future would be the "faith once delivered for the saints" and no Reformed divine could envision that as being too different from his own. As Ashbel Green put it, "We do not believe that great discoveries are yet to be made, in regard to the doctrines of the word of God. [100] James Blythe was one of those who felt it unreasonable to expect the millennial unity to be "letter perfect." Speaking before the Synod of Kentucky in 1814, however, he could not refrain from pointing out that in the West, some "theological *knight-errants*" had baptized "the effusions of their personal dislike, or stupid bigotry, with the holy name of a *contention for the faith.*"[101] Continuing the theme of "forbearance," Blythe believed that the solution to the contemporary problem of diversity was a cooperative effort in the work of Christ with a suppression of debate on theological differences. It was clear from his entire sermon, however, that the extent of his cooperation would be circumscribed by basic theological agreement.[102]

Even the most understanding and tolerant of men pressed for theological agreement. Philip Milledoler constantly referred to the different environmental influences that led to varying points of view. "Men differ so much from each other in intellect, education, and early habits, that for them to see, or think perfectly alike, in all things, is, perhaps, without a miracle, impossible." Because of this, Milledoler recommended forbearance "in minor points." "In great and essential matters, however, we must insist upon greater correspondence."[103]

Thus while the ideal of a unified church received constant expression, few of the Reformed gave form or content to the vision. The emphasis was primarily on theological unity and most statements exhibit more than a suspicion that theology during the millennium would closely resemble that of contemporary American Reformed orthodoxy. To expand on the nature of the millennial unity would, in fact, have destroyed the vision. In an age not prone to the opinion that one religious belief was as good as another, it was easier to agree that all would one day comprehend the truth alike than to specify even the barest outlines of the nature of that truth. It was the very illusoriness of the idea of unity that made it a powerful agent in bringing the Reformed together in a system of cooperation at a time when unity seemed to be the essence of survival.[104]

Chapter 5

American Civil Government: The Record of Success and Failure

The totality of Reformed thought ultimately covered every phase of social and personal life, but it had particular significance for the political life of the United States. The conclusion was inescapable. In the Reformed view, if the United States were to prosper as a national unit and serve its vital role in building toward the millennium, then American civil governments had to conform to certain minimal standards. To be sure, these measures were conceived to be only temporary, for in the millennium all civil governments would conform to the more exacting criterion of the millennial theocracy.

Accepting the basic context of governmental disengagement from the oversight of religion, the Reformed demanded at least three things from American civil governments, from the local to the national level. They insisted that these governments should make an explicit avowal, whether formal or informal, of the providential government of God. They believed that elected and appointed officials of these governments should support Protestant Christianity by deed and example in both private and public life. Finally, they thought it imperative that civil law reflect the natural law or divine law as interpreted by the Reformed churches. All of these were thought to be not only desirable, but acceptable and legal in the face of disestablishment, and absolutely necessary if the nation were to prosper and perpetuate its liberties.

Of the variety of governments, the federal or national government received the most attention. This no doubt arose from a combination of factors. There is every indication that the Reformed exercised greater influence in local and state governments where they enjoyed a significant influence over the majority of the "best citizens." They were therefore apt to be better satisfied with the general direction of things at the local more so than at the national level. However, the whole Reformed ideology was oriented toward the national unit, and it would have been astonishing had they not emphasized the national government.

One of the most fundamental requirements of the Reformed "association between Religion and Patriotism" was that the laws of the civil government be in accord with the laws of God. The Reformed principle was precisely stated in Witherspoon's *Lectures* and did not vary substantially throughout the period. Witherspoon listed as the first object of civil law, "To ratify the moral laws by the sanction of the society." Witherspoon recognized that governments had to enact some laws in the interest of the common good that made certain actions "illegal which before were not immoral." He believed, however, that priority should be given to the enforcement of those aspects of divine or moral law, "even such as may fall under the discipline of a religious society." Any act, therefore, deemed immoral by adherents to Protestant Christianity should be made illegal by the civil government. This Witherspoon believed to be essential to the preservation of the state.[1]

American laws, which were formulated largely under the influence of Protestant establishments, were satisfactory to the Reformed during the early years of nationhood and there was thus little need for them to comment. Most states had laws that enforced the Sabbath, protected religion against blasphemy, and made illegal various kinds of activities that were considered immoral by Reformed Christians.[2] The philosophy of law remained closely connected with the thought of the religious community, and American judges generally ruled in ways favorable to the Reformed ideology. The primary emphasis of the Reformed was to secure enforcement of existing laws, and within that context Sabbath laws became the central issue.

To an amazing degree, American legal philosophy supported and complemented the Reformed belief about the connection between religion and national prosperity. Legal thought, unlike constitution making and legislation, remained relatively free of political strife and was more conservative and unified. Like ministers and politicians, the lawyers and judges were concerned with social stability and control. The more narrow professional interest of these men, however, was specifically related to the desire to secure compliance with law, voluntarily if possible. In this pursuit, they deemed nothing more essential than a religious citizenry. They heartily agreed with the Reformed that divine law was to be pursued and implemented by human governments. They also believed that effectiveness of the judicial process depended upon the "sanctions" of religion, and in particular they thought a belief in future rewards and punishment was essential to securing honest testimony in courts of law. Soon after the Revolution it became a widespread legal opinion that Christianity itself was a part of American common law, and in 1844 this opinion was adopted by the United States Supreme Court.

The earliest attempt to delineate and establish an independent American legal tradition was that of James Wilson. In his maiden lecture as professor of law at the College of Philadelphia (later the University of Pennsylvania), Wilson emphasized the American character of his undertaking by posing and answering the "deeply interesting" question, "Should the elements of a law education, particularly as it respects public law, be drawn entirely from another country—or should they be drawn, in part, at least from the constitutions and governments and laws of the United States, and of the several States composing the Union?"[3] A number of considerations compelled him to take the latter course. The "great principle" that distinguished America from England and made an independent legal tradition necessary was "that the supreme or sovereign power of the society resides in the citizens at large."[4]

Because of this principle alone, Wilson found himself obliged to take a course in many respects independent of Sir William Blackstone. Wilson thought that Blackstone's commentaries on English law were "in many respects highly valuable," but he did not consider Blackstone "a zealous friend of republicanism."[5] Other reasons also demanded an American law. In a "free government," persons trained in law frequently became politically active and their education should be "congenial with the principles of government." Further, some aspects of English law simply could not apply in the American environment, particularly those aspects concerning the "ecclesiastical establishment" and the "monarchical and aristocratic branches." All of these factors indicated to Wilson "that the *foundation*, at least, of a separate, and unbiased, and an independent law education should be laid in the United States," and he expressed his intentions of "contributing to lay that foundation."[6]

In many ways Wilson was ideally suited to complement the national religious aspirations of the Reformed. He was born and educated in Scotland. He received training at the University of Saint Andrews and the universities of Glasgow and Edinburgh. Emigrating to the United States in 1765, three years before Witherspoon, he served as a tutor at the College of Philadelphia and studied law with John Dickinson, later a revolutionary statesman and founder of the Presbyterian Dickinson College. Like Witherspoon, Wilson was a member of the Continental Congress and a signer of the Declaration of Independence. He served as an officer in the war and was a member of the Federal Convention in 1787. Like Witherspoon he combined civic responsibility with teaching, serving as an associate justice of the United States Supreme Court from 1789 until his death in 1798, and as professor of law at the College of Philadelphia. Like Witherspoon, Wilson was a close friend to Washington, who, along with many of the nation's leaders, attended Wilson's introductory lectures on law.

Beyond these amazingly similar developments, Wilson was as vigorous an exponent of the Scottish philosophy of common sense as Witherspoon. Wilson was perhaps more dependent on Thomas Reid and quoted freely from his works.[7] While Wilson believed that man had made progress in other sciences, he was convinced that mankind had been led astray in the science of the human mind. Philosophers speculated by means of "hypothesis and analogy" and ignored the use of "common sense." "The noblest work of God" could best be discerned through "proceeding slowly and cautiously by observation and experience." In this way man could discover "the truth [that] is to be found in their own breasts."[8] Of all the senses, the "moral sense, from its very nature, is intended to regulate and control all our other powers." Through this faculty man could know intuitively the difference between right and wrong. The powers of reason could be useful after these "first principles" of moral science were established. On the foundation of self-evident truths it would be possible to deduce other truths through the power of reasoning.[9]

To this point the philosophy of the Philadelphia jurist was consistent with that of the Princeton ministers, Witherspoon and Smith. However, and perhaps surprisingly so, in the context of moral philosophy Wilson placed greater emphasis on the necessity of revealed truth for the perfection of morals and the happiness of society. Reason and conscience, Wilson believed, were "in need of support and assistance," without which "the mass of mankind would resemble a chaos, in which a few sparks, that would diffuse a glimmering light, would serve only to show, in a more striking manner, the thick darkness with which they are surrounded." The primary source of truth was revelation. According to Wilson, "In compassion to the imperfection of our internal powers, our all-gracious Creator, Preserver, and Ruler has been pleased to discover and enforce his laws, by a revelation given to us immediately and directly from himself." The precepts of the Bible formed "a part of the law of nature" and were of "the same origin, and of the same obligation, operating universally and perpetually."[10]

The "Holy Scriptures" were particularly useful in administering affairs of state because their instructions were explicit and "supereminently authentic." They helped enforce existing and known principles of morality but "by a greater certainty, and by new sanctions." In sum, the Scriptures "present the warmest recommendations and the strongest inducements in favor of virtue: they exhibit the most powerful dissuasives from vice." This was more especially the case since the Scriptures added greatly to "natural knowledge" on the "important subjects" of the deity, providence, and a future state. While Wilson did not dwell at length on the "utility and sociability" of these features, it was clear that he considered them to be essential to human happiness and, by implication, to national prosperity. At any rate Wilson noted, "In the order of Providence . . . the progress of societies towards perfection resembles that of an individual."[11]

In attempting to establish a "foundation" for American law, Wilson considered Christianity to be of primary importance. His most influential and often quoted sentiment that Christianity was a part of the common law carried with it extremely significant legal connotations but was perhaps not as precise as some of his other statements. In defining law, Wilson held that there were two different classes, divine and human. Divine law was defined as "that law, which is communicated to us by reason and conscience, the divine monitors within us, and by the social oracles, the divine monitors without us." Thus both "natural law" and "revealed law" were of divine origin. Of great significance for legal development in America was Wilson's contention that "human law must rest its authority, ultimately, upon that authority of that law, which is divine." It was only fitting that Wilson should end his lecture with the following observations: "We perceive a principle of connection between all the learned professions; but especially between the two last mentioned [religion and law]. Far from being rivals or enemies, religion and law are twin sisters, friends and natural assistants. Indeed, these two sciences run into each other. The divine law, as discovered by reason and the moral sense, forms an essential part of both."[12] At another point Wilson spoke of the "intimate connection and reciprocal influence of religion, morality, and law."[13]

Wilson's views were supported by all the most significant theoretical legal writers in America. David Hoffman of the University of Maryland quoted Thomas Reid and Dugald Stewart to illustrate the connection between "metaphysicks" and jurisprudence. Hoffman was convinced that human law should be based on "the great moral law" that was universally present and immediately apparent to human societies.[14] James Kent of New York argued in his *Commentaries on American Law* that the "law of nations" derived "much of its force and dignity from the same principles of right reason, the same views of the nature and constitution of man, and the same sanction of Divine revelation, as those from which the science of morality is deduced." Kent consistently ascribed the improvement of the "law of nations" to the influence of Christianity.[15] In his lectures at Columbia College, Kent insisted that the lawyer "have his passions controlled by the discipline of Christian truth" and gave evidence of the influence of the "common sense" philosophy.[16] Joseph Story publicly declared Christianity "a part of the Common Law" long before his official decision to that effect, and he held that "the precepts of religion" were the "only solid basis of civil society."[17] St. George Tucker, professor of law at William and Mary, took a somewhat different position but one that was ultimately supportive of the Reformed ideology. In his comments on Blackstone, Tucker held that certain parts of the common law, such as blasphemy, were abolished by the federal Bill of Rights. At the same time Tucker held that statesmen should "countenance" religion by their example and encourage "their fellow citizens in doing the same." With Witherspoon, Tucker believed that "an enlightened people, who have once attained the blessing of a free government, can never be enslaved until they abandon virtue and relinquish science."[18]

Reflecting this theoretical support of religion, the American judicial process maintained and in some instances extended legal protection of religion. In many ways, this was more fundamental than constitutional provisions and the passing of new legislation, because judicial decisions represented law in its most effective application. In the Reformed ideology the most essential aspect of religion as a sanction for social control was the belief in a future state of rewards and punishments.[19] American judges accepted this as valid and consistently disallowed the testimony of anyone not so believing.

This was demonstrated in the case *Jackson* v. *Gridley* before the Supreme Court of New York in 1820. In a litigation over interest on a mortgage in the Oneida Circuit Court in June 1819, the defendant offered Amos Gridley as a witness. The plaintiff objected "on the ground that he [the witness] did not believe in a future state of rewards and punishments, or the resurrection of the dead; and that he had declared, that he would as lief be sworn on a spelling book as the Bible; and that he did not believe in the being of a God." Several witnesses testified that Gridley had made those comments, at which point the counsel for the defendant stated that Gridley was now ready to declare his belief in a future state of rewards and punishments. Gridley was sworn in and testified for the defendant. The judge advised the jury that because of his "character and standing" Gridley "ought not to be believed." The jury, however, decided in favor of the defendant.

The plaintiff requested a new trial and appealed the decision to the New York Supreme Court. Chief Justice Ambrose Spencer delivered the opinion that the plaintiff should receive a new trial because Amos Gridley should not have been admitted as a witness. Spencer was against the practice of examining witnesses, except for children, on their religious beliefs previous to their being sworn in, on the grounds that an infidel, having no conscience, would deny "opinions imputed to him, or pretend to a sudden conviction." He felt every witness should be presumed as religious. However, if it was proved that a witness held such opinions, he could not be sworn in to testify. While every man had a right to his own religious opinions, the courts must seek justice "through the medians of testimony entitled to belief; and no testimony is entitled to credit, unless delivered under the solemnity of an oath, which comes home to the conscience of the witness, and will create a tie arising from his belief that false swearing would expose him to punishment in the life to come."[20]

A similar situation occurred in 1823 in the case *Butts* v. *Swartwood*. A person identified only as "one Piper," a universalist, was objected to as a witness. Justice Jacob Sutherland of the New York Supreme Court ruled that he was a competent witness because "he believed in the existence of a God who will punish him if he swears falsely."[21] This formula was not consistently followed. In an Illinois case the previous year, belief in God and a future state, without punishment, was deemed adequate.[22] But in every case judges held that some religious conviction was essential to guarantee the truthfulness of witnesses.[23]

There were several attempts to further erode the legal privilege of atheists. In the case of *Leonard* v. *Manard* before the Superior Court of New York City, Manard attempted to have the plaintiff's affidavit disallowed because he "had no belief in a Superintending Providence, or a state of future rewards and punishments." The judge refused the motion, however, because there could be no opportunity for Leonard to reply or explain his position.[24] In the Supreme Court of Tennessee, Samuel M'Clure, convicted of murder, attempted to secure a new trial on the basis that one of the jurors was an atheist. Judge Robert Whyte fully agreed with the argument "that no one who is not impressed with the belief of a God, almighty and omniscient, to whom all must render an account, can be a proper juror," but decided that the law was silent on the point and therefore "the court cannot act."[25]

It is apparent that the American judicial system adhered to the philosophy that religion was necessary to a proper enforcement of the law. Religious beliefs, especially in God and in future rewards and punishments, were thought to be an essential "sanction" to secure truthful testimony. The more significant judicial opinions, however, were those relating to blasphemy. In a series of cases leading to the Supreme Court decision of 1844 in the case *Vidal* v. *Philadelphia,* judges in the middle and southern states developed the doctrine that Christianity was part of the common law and that any attempts to subvert its doctrines were destructive of the nation. In these cases the judges expressed explicitly the Reformed concept of the connection between religious and national welfare.

The first significant case, *People* v. *Ruggles,* came before the New York Supreme Court with Chief Justice James Kent presiding. Kent was deeply committed to Christianity and believed it essential to the maintenance of public order. Like many American public figures, his religious beliefs were rarely enunciated but were nevertheless basic. Ruggles was tried and convicted in a lower court on the charge that "he did . . . *wickedly, maliciously,* and *blasphemously* utter . . . concerning the Christian religion, and of and concerning Jesus Christ, the false, scandalous, malicious, wicked and blasphemous words following, to wit, '*Jesus Christ* was a bastard, and his mother must be a whore. . . .'" Kent affirmed the judgment of the lower court on the grounds that such "blaspheming" was a violation of the common law and that Christianity was part of the common law. After citing English cases indicating that "whatever strikes at the root of Christianity, tends manifestly to the dissolution of civil government," and that blasphemy "tends to corrupt the morals of the people, and to destroy good order," Kent declared these principles to be equally necessary in America. "No government," Kent asserted, "ever hazarded such a bold experiment upon the solidity of public morals. . . ." The American principle of religious liberty did not allow reviling "the religion professed by almost the whole community." Nor did Kent believe that such protection should be extended to "the religion of *Mohamet* or of the grand *Lama*" because "the case assumes that we are a Christian people, and the morality of the country is deeply engrafted upon Christianity, and not on the doctrines of those imposters." Although America had no "religious establishment," such offenses were "punishable because they strike at the root of moral obligation, and weaken the security of the social ties." The Constitution, according to Kent, "never meant to withdraw religion in general, and with it the best sanctions of moral and social obligations from all consideration and notice of the law." Kent thought that in a number of ways, citing specifically Sunday laws, the state law supported Christianity "as a religion revealed and taught in the Bible." The case was clear. The blasphemy was "an offense against the public peace and safety" and tended to lessen the religious sanction surrounding the oath. Ruggles was sentenced to imprisonment for three months and to pay a fine of $500.[26]

The Pennsylvania Supreme Court ruled in *Updegraph* v. *the Commonwealth* in 1824 that Christianity was part of the common law. Abner Updegraff had been convicted of blasphemy for an attack on the veracity of the Christian Scriptures while arguing religious questions before a Pittsburgh debating society. He appealed to the Pennsylvania Supreme Court in order to get a decision as to whether Christianity was part of the law and if it was consistent with American civil institutions. Updegraff's attorney, Ross Wilkins, submitted a lengthy written argument contending that the Constitution of Pennsylvania allowed every citizen to express his opinion "on all subjects," and that the common law relating to religious matters did not and could not apply in America because it was "inconsistent with the spirit of our government." Justice Thomas Duncan reversed the decision of the lower court because of technical flaws in the prosecution, but in the decision he carefully refuted the Wilkins argument and declared that Christianity was part of the common law of Pennsylvania.

Justice Duncan's opinion, which extended to about 7,000 words, followed substantially the same argument presented by James Kent. In fact, he cited Kent's decision in *People* v. *Ruggles,* and the writings of James Wilson. According to Duncan, it was "irrefragably proved, that the laws and institutions of this state are built on the foundation of reverence for Christianity," and that Christianity was part of the common law. To be sure, Duncan affirmed, it was Christianity "with liberty of conscience to all men," but punishment for blasphemy was not "to force conscience" but "to preserve the peace of the country." Blasphemy, as well as "profane swearing" and "breach of the Sabbath," were not punished as sins against God but as "crimes injurious to, and having a malignant influence on society."

Duncan not only denied that Christianity was inconsistent with American institutions, he insisted that the existence and continuation of those institutions depended on Christianity. According to Duncan, "No free government now exists in the modern world, unless where Christianity is acknowledged, and is the religion of the country." Unless people were restrained from "1. Denying the being and Providence of God. 2. Contumelious reproaches of Jesus Christ; profane and malevolent scoffing at the scriptures, or exposing any part of them to contempt and ridicule. 3. Certain immoralities tending to subvert all religion and morality," Duncan was convinced that "no free government could long exist." It was Christianity that provided "the purest system of morality, the firmest auxiliary, and only stable support of all human laws." With such unabashed clarity, Duncan declared the widespread conviction that religion—Christianity—was necessary to the existence and prosperity of the United States. Whereas previously this had been opinion, it was now interpreted as the law of the land.[27]

That Christianity was a part of the common law was accepted by the United States Supreme Court in 1844 through the ruling of Justice Joseph Story in the case of *Vidal* v. *Girard's Executors*. The evolution of law through judicial opinion was of extreme significance because it effectively introduced into American law the ancient, and contemporary, philosophy that religion was necessary to social stability. With only slightly different shading of meaning to reflect the "liberalism" of the times, the judicial process had established direct continuity with the legal tradition of the colonies and the laws of religious establishments.

In addition, however, state legislatures occasionally passed new legislation. In every case this legislation built on the foundation of existing laws and reflected concern for some immediate problem of the religious community rather than any fundamental change of philosophy. The development in Pennsylvania was representative. In 1798 the legislature passed a law allowing the churches to block the streets with chains or other devices during the time of worship in order to prevent traffic noise. The majority of the legislature believed it "would be nugatory" to allow rights of conscience "without securing the peaceable and quiet enjoyment of them."[28] In 1811 another act was passed to prevent the disturbance of worship services. This law was replaced by a similar one in 1822. Among other things, the act made illegal the blowing of horns, the shooting of guns, or the sale of liquor within three miles of a church during religious meetings.[29] Pennsylvania also passed laws against horse racing, drunkenness, and other things offensive to the religious community.[30]

Although the state legislators continued to enact laws supporting the religious community and the judges treated Christianity as part of the common law, the Reformed were not satisfied. A number thought more laws necessary, but the primary difficulty was perceived to be the enforcement of existing laws. From the Reformed point of view, the force of law steadily diminished from year to year. In 1827 when Gardiner Spring, pastor of the Brick Presbyterian Church in New York, was attempting to bring about Sabbath "reform," he could recall wistfully his early years in New York when the streets were chained off to prevent traffic during the time of worship.[31] Whatever the state of society, however, the Reformed thought greater law enforcement desirable. In 1780 the General Synod of the Reformed Dutch Church declared "that some defect is existing, either in the laws directed against vice and immorality, or the execution thereof" and asked the government of New York to "apply proper remedies."[32] That same body in 1782 wished "that the salutory laws of the land may be faithfully executed."[33]

These complaints were multiplied over the years.[34] In 1811 the Presbyterian Synod of New York and New Jersey appointed committees of five members each for the states represented in the synod. The committees were "to examine the laws of those States touching the observance of the Sabbath, and to enquire whether any, and if any, what alterations may be made, favourable to the interests of religion." Further, the committees were instructed to "apply to the Legislatures to make any alterations which may be thought advisable."[35]

Most references to law enforcement in sermons and other publications were of a general nature, but occasionally concrete circumstances were described that provided insight into Reformed thinking. An example of this was the appendix to John McDonald's July Fourth sermon preached in Albany in 1814. McDonald complained that "troops of negroes" nightly gathered in the "most public corners" and engaged in "obstreperous mirth, sham quarrels, obscene language, horrid and uncouth blasphemy." On Saturdays they were joined by whites "and the scene partakes of something infernal." McDonald called on the city further to "interpose" their authority and use "places of confinement and modes of correction" to eliminate this situation.[36] Nathaniel Prime of Cambridge, New York, called for a hundred men, "if necessary" to enforce the Sabbath laws in his community.[37] There is every indication that the Reformed would be satisfied with nothing short of conformity to their ideas of millennial society.

On a national level, there was no reason for the Reformed to comment before 1810. Following the constitutional settlement and the adoption of the First Amendment, the national Congress made no laws that affected the Reformed. This era of happy coincidence ended in 1810 when Congress enacted a law that required post offices to remain open "every day on which a mail or bag, or other packet or parcel of letters shall arrive."[38]

This law, which forced post offices to open on some Sundays, was violently opposed by the Reformed.

The sanctity of the Sabbath had been a Reformed doctrine of long standing and the concern did not fade in the new nation.[39] The proper observation of the Sabbath was considered by the Reformed to be the most essential element in the maintenance of morals and therefore the preservation of the nation. The centrality of the Sabbath to the total goal of the Reformed for the nation was well expressed by the Presbyterian General Assembly of 1814 in one of many petitions to Congress on the subject. The Assembly argued "that the Sabbath contributes to increase the amount of productive labour, to promote science, civilization, peace, social order, and correct morality." At the same time its observance "restrains mankind from those vices which destroy property, health, reputation, intellect, domestic peace, and national integrity and industry."[40]

When the national government violated this basic concept with the passage of the post office law in 1810, the Reformed launched an extensive and sustained campaign that illuminated their position on the desired relationship between civil and divine law. Meeting several months after adoption of the law, the Presbyterian Synod of Pittsburgh petitioned against it. The synod informed Congress that the new regulations were "very glaring violations of the laws of God, and therefore an infringement on the rules of conscience. . . ." The petition not only confirmed the Reformed position that the laws of the nation ought to be in accord with the "laws of God" and that anything short of that was a restriction on liberty of conscience, but also insisted that such action "may provoke God to inflict upon us, grievous judgments and calamities."[41]

The following year the postmaster general issued more definite orders regulating Sunday post office hours. The offices were to be kept open for one hour following the arrival and sorting of mail on Sunday, unless that time coincided with regularly scheduled hours of worship, in which case the offices would be opened for one hour "after the usual time of dissolving the meetings."[42] This concession did little more than to stir the Reformed to greater activity. Beginning in that year, the subject of Sabbath observance became a major item of deliberation in the various denominational bodies. In the state of religion message of 1811 the General Assembly of the Presbyterian Church decried "the prevalence of Sabbath-breaking" and warned that it would lead "directly to consequences of the most fatal and ruinous kind."[43] The message went on to point out that only a few "professing believers" were "directly chargeable" with this crime but they were "indirectly, by quietly suffering others to commit it, without endeavouring to prevent it, or to bring the offenders to punishment." The matter of Sabbath observance was not here considered a matter of individual choice, but a requirement for the whole nation.[44]

A fast day in 1812 gave the Reformed ministers an opportunity to plead their cause before their congregations. Joseph Clark labeled Sabbath breaking an "awful sin" and declared that "experience universally proves the fact, that in proportion as the religious observation of the Lord's Day declined, in any place, in the same proportion morals and religion decline." Clark's message was not a call for voluntary submission to Sabbath regulations but an insistence that "magistrates" and "private citizens" exert themselves "to enforce the laws."[45] Arthur Stansbury specifically pointed to the post office regulations in the list of national sins,[46] but John B. Romeyn preferred to list it as a national punishment for having made political rather than moral qualifications the "test of office."[47] John Latta felt that because this was "authorized, tolerated, and connived at by the civil authority, and practised by the magistrate and citizen," it was alone sufficient to bring on the providential judgment of war.[48] It was clear from the Reformed point of view that America's official and legal position on religious liberty did not free the American nation from the moral responsibility of obeying the commands of the God of providence.

The Reformed insistence that the national law be in accord with divine law, and the alleged relationship of this to the welfare of the nation, was well expressed in 1812 when the General Assembly petitioned Congress to repeal the regulation requiring post offices to remain open on Sunday. In the first paragraph of the petition, the Assembly pointed to the prior demand and authority of the natural law. "The institution of the Sabbath by the Creator and Ruler of the world . . . imposes upon [men] the reasonable obligation of devoting this day to his service." The petition declared that the post office practice violated this law, even to the extent of depriving the "brute creatures . . . of the rest to which they are entitled by the authority of God."[49]

This radical divergence of the civil law from the teaching of the church was difficult for the Reformed to comprehend. The occasion of the petition had been an appeal from the postmaster of Washington, Pennsylvania, who had been suspended from communion for opening the office on Sunday. While the Assembly refused to reverse the decision, a committee was immediately appointed "to consider the propriety of petitioning Congress relative to the repeal of so much of the post-office law as requires the opening of the post-offices and the delivery of letters on the Lord's day."[50] That the connection between these two events was no mere coincidence is confirmed in the petition. It declared, "Your petitioners, moreover, feel themselves constrained in their office as rulers in the Church, to exercise the discipline of that Church against those of their members who break the Sabbath in the carrying or opening of the mail on that day." If the commissioners were aware that their demand for legal enforcement of the Sabbath in any way could be construed as an infringement on liberty of conscience, they did not so indicate. While they were careful to answer the hypothetical objection based on an interpretation of Scripture, that the post office practice as a "work of necessity" was allowable on the Sabbath, they did not mention the more pressing legal and constitutional problems involved in the whole issue.[51] Such legal considerations seemed trivial when it was believed that the future of the nation hung in the balance. The commissioners sought to buttress their request by an appeal to providence. They feared "that the infractions of the Sabbath allowed by civil law, will draw down upon our nation the divine displeasure." They believed the prospect of war to be sufficient evidence of their concern.[52]

The failure of this petition in 1812 signaled a change in Presbyterian tactics. The 1812 petition had been sent in the name of the General Assembly. In 1814 the Assembly drew up another petition that began, "The subscribers, inhabitants of the town of .... in the state ....," printed 2,000 copies, appointed one minister in each presbytery as an agent to obtain subscribers, and appointed a committee to solicit the aid of other denominations.[53] The General Assembly had learned that the official voice of their denomination carried little weight in the nation's counsels, and it now sought to capitalize on the force that was the peculiar instrument of the "association between Religion and Patriotism"—public opinion.

That same Assembly addressed a letter to all Presbyterians that was designed to create support for the petition. This letter clearly voiced the Presbyterian conviction that the nation should adhere to Christian standards. According to the Assembly, "The Lord has instituted the Sabbath as a sign between him and his people—a visible test of their sincerity." If these people violated the duties of that day "or fold their hands in supineness and indifference when they are violated by others, he will regard their offerings as hypocritical and vain." The notion that the Sabbath was the foundation of religion and society was reiterated. "Without the Sabbath there will be no religion—without religion there will be no morality—and that where morality, sound and correct morality, ceases to form the basis of the public manners, the strongest bonds of society are dissolved." While the Assembly cautioned church members to avoid violation of this day themselves, they were also advised to guard the Sabbath against "encroachments made upon it by those who are unhappily ignorant of its blessings, and regardless of its authority and design."[54]

The General Synod of the Reformed Dutch Church did not take notice of the post office law until 1815. It had been their hope that the law would be altered at the close of the War of 1812. When this did not occur the general synod joined the Presbyterians in petitioning Congress. The petition, designed for general use, expressed the opinion that "the transportation and opening of the mail, on the Lord's day, is inconsistent with the proper observance of that sacred day, injurious to the morals of the nation, and provokes the judgments of the Ruler of Nations."[55]

The Reformed, as individuals and through denominational structures, continued to press for enforced Sabbath observation throughout the period.[56] After 1825, when the post office regulations were coordinated and a law was passed by Congress enforcing the delivery of mail on Sunday, opposition by the Reformed reached an even greater intensity than in previous years, but the earlier episode adequately reflected the Reformed demand that national laws conform to divine law as understood and interpreted by the Reformed.

The Reformed insistence that the laws of the nation conform to the natural law as interpreted by Christians, which was most characteristically presented in the debate over Sabbath mail, was in harmony with their interpretation of religious liberty and freedom of conscience. Religious liberty, as the right to worship God according to the dictates of Scripture and conscience, did not also free one from the laws of God. While the theological debates within Reformed denominations sometimes seemed acute, there was no instance of disagreement on that part of the Westminster Confession that read, "The moral law doth for ever bind all, as well justified as others, to the obedience thereof; and that not only in regard of the matter contained in it, but also in respect of the authority of God the creator who gave it."[57] This, for the Reformed, was that "unalienable right" with which man had been "endowed" by the Creator.

In addition to the insistence that the laws of the land accord with divine law, the Reformed believed that overt recognition of the deity and providence was necessary to secure national prosperity. Alexander M'Leod expressed this position by declaring that the Scriptures "required of the constituted authorities of a nation, that they officially recognize the Christian religion, and cherish the interests of the church of Jesus Christ."[58] Early in the period, this Reformed standard was applied to official documents, especially the state and national constitutions. Later, however, the emphasis shifted to the more frequent and less formal pronouncements of elected officials.

The Reformed standard requiring recognition of the providence of God was generally met in the state constitutions, and those documents received but slight comment. Some of the state constitutions even satisfied the more stringent demands of an explicit acceptance of the Bible as the revealed word of God. In some form or other, the constitutions of Delaware, Maryland, New York, North Carolina, Pennsylvania, South Carolina, and Virginia contained articles or clauses that could be construed as a recognition of the authority of God. This ranged from the Delaware requirement that its officials declare "a belief in the Christian religion" to the acknowledgment of "the duty we owe to our Creator" in the famous Virginia Bill of Rights.[59]

The federal Constitution, however, contained no explicit recognition of the authority of God, and because of this most of the Reformed thought it to be defective. The Reformed could rejoice in disestablishment, given the circumstances of the time, but they did not think that this justified the failure to acknowledge the existence of God and his providential government in the national Constitution. Samuel Stanhope Smith viewed this as "an unreasonable jealousy" of religion.[60] Archibald Alexander rejoiced in the constitutional settlement with this single exception, which he claimed "distorts the political features of our country." He hastily added that it was not his business to "meddle."[61] John B. Romeyn was less hesitant. He listed this "defect" in the Constitution as primary in the list of national sins. "Though it be thus the choice of a Christian people, in it are not recognized even the existence and government of God, much less the authority of his revealed Word." While Romeyn did not want to be understood as recognizing the right of government to interfere in matters of religion or as favoring "exclusive establishment of any particular denomination," he felt that "propriety, reason, and the Word of God" required "the recognition of the existence and providence of God" and "the acknowledgment of his revealed truth." Since the Constitution was "atheistic and unchristian," the whole American populace was "chargeable with irreligion."[62]

This "defect" in the Constitution was not so significant as to dampen the nationalism and patriotism of most of the Reformed. For the most part, the ministers stated their objections but placed their efforts in areas that had more promise of success. Some, like Eliphalet Nott could so completely forget the actual wording of the Constitution as to refer to it as "the vase of Protestant Christianity."[63]

Such was not the case for the members of the Reformed Presbyterian church, a small denomination that originated in Scotland and was transplanted to the United States. The largest single issue within the denomination for fifty years or even longer was whether their members should swear allegiance to the "atheistic" Constitution of the United States. Until 1812 the denomination refused to allow it, and after that many continued to deny the right of communion to those who did. In 1820 the synod responded to a query from Illinois respecting the legality of sitting on juries and performing other official duties with the ruling that "*no connection with the laws, the offices, or the order of the State, is prohibited by the church, except what truly involves immorality.*"[64] The problem was that the Reformed Presbyterians could not agree on what constituted "immorality" and in 1833 the denomination was split by factions favoring and rejecting the American Constitution.[65]

The Reformed Presbyterians who made their peace with the Constitution were led by John Knox, Jr., and Alexander M'Leod. In 1833 Knox supported his position with the publication of *An Essay on the Appreciation of Reformation Principles in the American Government.* He agreed in principle that Christians ought not to swear allegiance to an atheistic government because "experience has confirmed the truth of the fact, that Christian influence and political prosperity are inseparable." This principle could not be applied to the United States, because, according to Knox, "The Bible is virtually the supreme law of the land." The Christian duty was to cooperate with others in order to have the government administered according to divine law.[66] M'Leod argued in the *American Christian Expositor* that the clause, "on prohibiting the free exercise thereof," was a recognition of "the existence and utility of religion," and that the American Constitution was "worthy of our active support" even if not perfect.[67] This wing of the Reformed Presbyterian church realized rather perceptively that the only way to exert influence on the course of America was to accept the Constitution. As Gilbert McMaster, pastor of the Reformed Presbyterian Church in Duanesburgh, New York, noted, the "true members" of that church should "take vigorous hold of the machinery of government and employ it for the promotion of the interests of society, civil and religious."[68]

Apparently the majority of the Reformed would have been satisfied if the officials of government would have continually acknowledged the providence of God in more informal ways. Every official pronouncement, especially those of the presidents, was carefully scrutinized to discover if it contained recognition of the divine government. The most significant of these informal means of recognition were proclamations for days of fasting or thanksgiving. These were understood by the Reformed as an acceptable recognition of God. Jacob Brodhead labeled one such state proclamation in New York, "an official recognition of the almighty God, and a whole state thus acknowledges the Supreme Governor of heaven and earth." If all states would follow the same pattern, according to Brodhead, it "would constitute *a national confession of faith*, of the God of the Bible and salvation."[69]

The policy of each president was different and the Reformed made an appropriate response according to their ideology. George Washington, whom most Americans found it difficult to fault, was basically acceptable on this score. Washington responded to the resolution of Congress, presented by the staunch Presbyterian layman Elias Boudinot, with a proclamation of a day of thanksgiving.[70] This became a regular feature of Washington's administration. Washington himself wrote the proclamations and attempted to make them acceptable to all faiths. The Presbyterian General Assembly praised him for "on the most public and solemn occasions, devoutly acknowledg[ing] the government of Divine Providence."[71] Washington's failure to make an explicit commitment to Christianity, however, created some disappointment in Reformed circles.[72]

The administration of John Adams was more satisfactory from the

Reformed point of view. A fast day in May 1798 was first proposed by
the Synod of Philadelphia and then sanctioned by the federal government.[73] Unlike Washington, Adams had the chaplains of Congress,
Bishop William White and Ashbel Green, draft the proclamations. The
proclamation calling for a day of prayer in 1799 was written by Green.
Concerning this, Green recalled that he resolved to give the proclamation "an evangelical character" so as "to remove the complaint" of the
Christian community that previous proclamations "lacked a decidedly
Christian spirit." While Green feared Adams would reject or alter his
draft, he was pleased when it was published "with only the alteration of
two or three words not at all affecting the religious character of the
production."[74]

With this kind of cooperation the Reformed were pleased, but the
situation changed when Thomas Jefferson became president. Jefferson
refused to recommend days of fasting or thanksgiving because he believed such measures to be an indirect assumption of power that the
Constitution had directly forbidden. Jefferson's statement of this position came in response to a Presbyterian request in 1808.[75] During the
trying years between the Embargo and the War of 1812 the Reformed
had themselves proclaimed days of fasting and joined with others in
doing so on a local level, but they were convinced that nothing short of a
national humiliation could secure the favor of providence.[76]

When the United States became involved in the War of 1812, the
Presbyterians were convinced that the nation's sin was responsible, and
one manifestation of that sin was the neglect of national recognition of
God. Samuel Fisher did not hesitate to list as one of the most important
causes of the war the fact that the national government for a period of
ten years "did not, in a single instance, by any public act, make their ac-
knowledgments to God, either by an expression of gratitude or humility."[77]

The Reformed in their individual and denominational capacities
exerted as much pressure as possible, both at the state and national level,
to have the government officials proclaim a day of fasting and repentance for national sins. According to the General Synod of the Reformed
Dutch Church, Americans were "a guilty people, a sinful nation," and
the judgment of God could only be averted by national repentance.[78]
After James Madison gave in to pressure and, against his own better
judgment, issued a proclamation, the Reformed were partly placated
although dissatisfied by the general terms of the proclamation. Stephen
Rowan of New York interpreted this as the recognition on the part of the
administration that the church as the "only legitimate interpreter" of
providence had been just in seeing the conflict as God's "rod of . . . in-
dignation."[79]

The Reformed wanted more than the proclamation of days of
thanksgiving and fasting. They wanted every public statement, especially

of the president, to reflect dependence on the deity. Ashbel Green, while editor of the *Christian Advocate,* reviewed every presidential message. In January of 1823 he criticized President James Monroe for not acknowledging that American prosperity was due to "the smile and benediction of the God of nations." Green wished "to plead earnestly with our rulers to recognise, whenever a suitable occasion offers, a dependence on the God of providence, and never to shrink from the distinct assumption for this nation of a Christian character."[80] The following December Green went through Monroe's message to Congress and indicated appropriate places for the recognition of providence. With these additions, Green believed the message would have been acceptable to the religious community.[81] Whether it was the result of this kind of pressure or for other reasons, Monroe's fiscal message was not chargeable with the same "omission."[82]

A number of the Reformed objected generally to John Quincy Adams, whom they classified a Socinian,[83] but Green thought that he had made a good start because he "distinctly recognized his dependence on Divine aid" in his initial communication with Congress.[84] Throughout his term of office Adams continued to make such allusions to dependence on God.[85] However, even the attempts of Adams to placate the religious community brought criticism from the Reformed. Adams regularly attended the Unitarian services in Washington, but held seats in the Presbyterian and Episcopal churches and occasionally attended Catholic services. This practice only convinced many of his insincerity and negated his practice of constantly referring to the providence of God.[86]

The degree to which the Reformed desired even this kind of informal recognition of Christianity by the officials of American government made another requirement of the "association between Religion and Patriotism" even more pressing. With disestablishment having destroyed formal connections with Christianity, it seemed that the prior demand of national recognition could only be satisfied by the election of Christian officials.

Prior to 1800 the Presbyterians focused directly on the duties of rulers and tended to ignore the fact of election. This was based on the assumption that the officials would be Christian, compounded with the aristocratic point of view that envisioned the "ruling classes" as operating somewhat removed from the influence of the masses. As the molders of the morals and manners of the populace, the attitude of the elite formed the basis of the "national character," upon which depended the favor or condemnation of providence. On another level, it was believed that the workings of providence could depend entirely on the attitude of the government. John B. Romeyn, for example, rhetorically declared that "when the government of a nation is irreligious and immoral, God withdraws his protection, and they soon finish their career of folly."[87] As early as 1784 the Presbytery of New Castle complained of the presence of "debauchees and infidels" in places of public trust and wondered if "there is not a sufficient number of judicious sober professors, in good standing in their respective societies, or the respective denominations of Christians to which they belong, into whose hands we may put the reins of Government?" The concern at that time was that non-Christians in office would "by their pernicious example and opinions . . . corrupt the morals of the people, especially the young and rising generation,"[88] thereby altering the national character.

When Ashbel Green pointed out in 1798 the requirements of a nation to fulfill the laws of God, he emphasized primarily the duties of magistrates. They were to recommend Christianity by practice and example and enact laws for the "suppression of vice and immorality." They were to encourage "true piety" and recognize the providence of God in their public acts. Particularly, as those "whose station gives influence and fashion to their conduct," the magistrates were to regard the moral laws of God and thus render "in a sort the representation and expression of national sentiment on the subject of morals." As for the people, it was only necessary that the "great principles of piety and morality" should be "generally and effectually taught and inculcated on the public at large," which Green considered, again, to be the duty of the magistrates. If the officials did all of this it would "secure to a christian nation the benefits of the divine promise."[89]

After the election of Jefferson in 1800, the Reformed realized that this conception was inept. While the influence of rulers on the people was still held to be extremely significant,[90] in America it was the voter rather than the official who actually provided the better indication of the national character. As Eliphalet Nott put it in a Fourth of July address in 1801, "The government of our country is a government of opinion, rather than force." If rulers were corrupt they could be removed from office, "but if the people themselves become corrupt, it is an evil without a remedy."[91]

The election of non-Christian candidates was thus viewed by the Reformed as a national sin that could incur the wrath of providence and destroy America's liberties. The Presbytery of New Brunswick addressed a pastoral letter to the congregations under its care in 1801 informing the churches that "hitherto, in general, we have as a nation, together with our wise and pious rulers, revered God and his gospel." With recent political events in both France and the United States obviously in mind, the presbytery continued, "But, should the contrary take place, and we be carried away with the corruptions in principle and practice, so triumphant in the world, and join with the enemies of God, we must then also receive of their plagues." Without being more specific, the presbytery concluded, "You are then assuredly to expect, that a general rejection of

Christ and his gospel, corruption of morals, and reign of vices, will be followed, with as general, temporal and eternal ruin! Should the gospel leave us, earthly blessings will take soon after."[92]

The election of "infidels" also endangered America's peculiar liberties as the Reformed understood them. A few months earlier the Presbytery of New Brunswick had complained of the spread of deistic principles, "the manifest tendency of which is to relax or destroy the restraints of religion, and to set mankind loose, to walk after the way of their heart and the right of their eyes." Deists were declared to be enemies of good government who could "brook no restraints either from divine or human authority." The deists "preach up liberty while they themselves are servants of corruption." The election of such would open the "flood gates to licentiousness."[93]

The focus of Reformed thinking thus turned from the magistrate to the election of the magistrate. This change in outlook could be seen in the Reformed treatment of the traditional Christian duty of submission to lawful authority. Under the traditional two-authority structure, the inculcation of such submission was one of the prime functions of the church. This remained a decided element of Reformed thinking, and in the early days of the republic the Reformed were as adept in teaching submission to the new national government as they had been in undermining English rule. The American system, however, not only blurred the two-authority distinction but changed the locus of authority in the state from the magistrate to the people. When this began to become clear, the Reformed emphasis at this point was largely absorbed into the single issue of electing Christian magistrates.

This could be seen in the different response to the Whiskey Rebellion and the events from the Embargo of 1807 to the War of 1812. In 1794 the inhabitants of western Pennsylvania took up arms to resist what they considered to be an unfair excise tax on whiskey imposed by the Federalist government. The participants in this revolt were largely Presbyterian laymen, but a recent historian of Presbyterian involvement has concluded that "the Presbyterian clergy was unanimous in opposing the insurrection."[94] It is not surprising that the Federalist-oriented clergy of the coastal region opposed the rebellion, but it is highly significant that the local pastors whose sympathy might be presumed to rest with their congregations so completely concurred in the national Presbyterian judgment.[95]

However unjust they thought the law might be, the Presbyterian ministers firmly believed that rebellion against the "lawful authority" was worse. The magistrate and not the mob was the organ of justice. How unlike the Presbyterian clergy of only two decades earlier! The Presbytery of Redstone, most intimately connected with the affair, viewed the incident as a providential judgment and refused communion to all who had participated in the rebellion until they had given satisfactory evidence of repentance. In preaching from the text, "Let every soul be subject unto the higher powers. . . . They that resist shall receive to themselves damnation," Samuel Porter was giving credence to the Presbyterian contention that religion insured obedience to the law by adding the sanction of divine authority. Whether the religious teaching or the presence of federal troops contributed more to the suppression of the rebellion is an open question, but the Presbyterian ministers knew their role as interpreters of God's providential government and played it well in this national crisis.[96]

By the time of the Embargo of 1807 the Reformed had made an adjustment to the American situation. By focusing on the power and responsibility of the people to elect Christian magistrates, the Reformed were not faced with the alternative of commanding submission to an unpopular administration, as they had in 1794, or preaching sedition and rebellion, which was the characteristic response of the conservative New England clergy to these events.[97] The Reformed interpreted the ills of the nation as the judgment of providence for national sin. The free, responsible American electorate had embarked on a course unpleasing to providence, the only solution for which was a national reformation.

The Embargo was unpopular among leading Reformed divines, and in 1808 the Presbyterian General Assembly felt that its retraction called for a day of thanksgiving and prayer because it had "pleased Almighty God in his wise providence to avert in a great measure the temporal judgments which threatened us."[98] The General Synod of the Reformed Dutch church, in almost identical words, set aside a day of thanksgiving in 1809.[99] Although the Embargo was unpopular, the Reformed did not lay the blame solely on the administration of Jefferson. It was viewed, like the administration itself, as a product of national sin. James Muir, speaking before the Washington Society of Alexandria, set the tone of the Reformed response, which would be characteristic throughout the trying years ahead. While he counseled his highly partisan audience to submit to the government and not grow impatient under the judgments of providence, Muir emphasized that all was a result of national sin and that a national reformation was needed.[100] As John E. Latta of Delaware put it, "We shall admit, for sake of argument, that the conduct of our rulers is the proximate cause; but still it is evident that our guilt is the remote cause."[101]

In the same fashion, the Presbyterians viewed the War of 1812 as a divine judgment for national sin, part of which was electing non-Christian officials. In 1812 the General Assembly declared that "the indications of danger, no less than of guilt, are too visible to be mistaken." The "portentous and variegated visitations of Heaven's justice" called for a national humiliation in order "to preserve unimpaired, and perpetuate our happy constitution and republican form of government."[102] The Associate Reformed and the Dutch Reformed cooperated with the General Assembly in an attempt to have the public authorities proclaim a day of fasting and prayer "to be observed as such by all the citizens."[103] The next year the General Assembly affirmed that "we are all chargeable, both in our civil and ecclesiastical capacities, with many sins, of which it is our duty to repent before God," and called for a national day of fasting.[104]

On this fast day the Reformed ministers preached neither rebellion nor submission but national sin. In this approach the twin aspects of political behavior necessary to the "association between Religion and Patriotism" had merged into the single demand applicable to the American situation. Stephen Rowan emphasized providence. If America continued in sin it would only be "laying up in store, some more awful judgments, and preparing the way for the execution of divine vengeance."[105] Nathan Perkins brought providence and liberty together and indicated the connection of America's sin with the election of national officers. The growth of "infidel and immoral principles" was to be greatly feared "in a free elective government . . . as it has an inauspicious influence on the choice of men, who shall be elevated to places of honour and trust." Perkins believed it to be an undeniable dictum that good people will choose good rulers; bad people, bad leaders; and he believed immoral leaders to be the greatest curse for a republic.[106]

The insistence that the elected officials be Christian created some conflict with the national constitutional settlement that had clearly prohibited a religious test for government officials. The Presbyterians had by this time become accustomed to making the distinction between the formal or voluntary character of certain national policies. By making this kind of distinction, inherent in the "association between Religion and Patriotism," the Presbyterians could declare absolute and unqualified support for the prohibition of a religious test and at the same time insist that if the nation were to prosper its leaders would have to be Christian.

Samuel Fisher made this explicit in two sermons preached on a fast day in 1814. He defended the thesis that "a wicked man, at the head of a nation has it in his power to destroy much good." But a wicked man could only rule in America if elected by the people. He did not wish, Fisher insisted, to have a law requiring "that a man should be a professor of religion in order to be eligible to a civil office." Rather he wished the people to scrutinize the candidates and vote only for those "who manifest by their upright conduct, that they are men who fear God."[107] This subtle distinction, which demanded on an informal basis what could have been law under an establishment, did not always satisfy members of the congregation. Fisher thought it necessary to publish his sermon because he had been accused of being an enemy to his country on the basis of these remarks.

Nor were the ministers always consistent. John B. Romeyn, for example, listed as a national sin the "election of men, avowedly immoral and irreligious, to office." In the printed edition of this sermon, Romeyn appended a note exempting Connecticut from the charge because "morality and religion, in the opinion of her sons, are essential qualifications for office." While Connecticut had a religious test for office, Romeyn had declared in the body of the sermon, "Think not that I desire the establishment of any particular denomination of Christians, by law, or the introduction of a religious test. No; by no means."[108] The question of the sincerity of the denials of desire for law to enforce election of Christian rulers is decidedly secondary to an understanding of the Reformed purpose, which was to achieve the relationship between religion and civil government that formerly would have existed in a society with an established religion. In the American context this cooperation would have to be informal rather than legal.

By concentrating on national sin and the election of Christian officials, the Reformed were able to sustain a more varied response to partisan politics during the War of 1812 than their New England counterparts. The Reformed of the middle and southern states could be for or against the Madison administration, for or against the war, without violating their basic agreement about the desired nature of American society. A number of the Reformed were definitely antiadministration, and it was to be expected that they would emphasize the factor of the election of non-Christian officials.[109] However, others who were vigorous supporters of the war argued that it was indeed a divine judgment for national sin, but that the United States was slated to be victorious because England's sins were more offensive to God. The most significant contribution to this train of thought was Alexander M'Leod's work, *A Scriptural View of the Character, Causes, and Ends of the Present War*. M'Leod, of Scottish descent and strongly anti-British, did not differ substantially from those who opposed the war. He went so far as to declare that the Bible described proper election proceedings and should "direct our political conduct."[110] Thus while the Reformed of the middle and southern states took a variety of positions on the War of 1812,[111] they were agreed on basic philosophy. James M'Chord was following the most consistent Reformed position when he argued that the issue was neither the immorality of England nor of the American rulers, but the sins of the American people who had disregarded God and failed to acknowledge his providence.[112]

The mildly partisan Reformed response to the events surrounding the War of 1812 was merely reflective of a broader position. In their contention for the necessity of Christian rulers, the Reformed rather consistently disavowed partisan politics, and the War of 1812 encouraged the most bitter expression of that phenomenon. In the midst of the war Daniel Clark expressed the opinion that "the existence of two *hostile* political parties" was proof of the sinfulness of the American people.[113] The Reformed would have preferred that adherence to Protestant Christianity be the only criterion for election. Party allegiance often meant alignment with persons whose religion was suspect. Paschal N. Strong was vehemently opposed to electing any person just because he was "regularly nominated" by a certain party. According to Strong, "when we find in our city, men, and Christian men too, men of high consideration and influence, maintaining, and publicly abetting the election of an infidel in preference to a christian . . . what, I ask, has become of the *authority of God* as the consciences of men, in the discharge of their political duties?"[114]

Condemnations against "party spirit," similar but distinct from those in Federalist literature, were frequent in Reformed publications throughout the period. Reformed ministers generally refused to comment on party issues but did so as the most effective means of securing the religious domination of political affairs. The ministers maintained a rather clear distinction, which was often not discerned by their congregations, between party politics and the general direction of national affairs. Seth Williston, Presbyterian pastor in Durham, New York, noted that "it does not fall within the province of the Christian minister, when there are two merely political interests in the state, to make it any part of his religious instruction, to direct his people which side to espouse." But he was equally convinced that "it came within his sphere, even as a *religious* teacher, to tell his people, it is their duty and their interest, to choose into office men as will be pleasing to Him who presides over the destinies of nations."[115]

Thus, characteristically the Reformed surrendered their legal rights to work for partisan issues in order to more vigorously defend their demands that the nation operate on Christian principles.[116] Ashbel Green, the "Christian Advocate," refused to comment on the tariff and "concerns which will not long appear to be of the highest moment," but he consistently called for the election of men who would "rule in the fear of God."[117] As he noted in 1828, this could be accomplished "only by the diffusion of knowledge and piety among our citizens at large." This was the case, according to Green, because "an ignorant, immoral, irreligious people never did, and never will, long maintain a free government."[118]

The best remembered of the Reformed publications on this subject was Ezra Stiles Ely's proposal in 1827 for a "Christian party in politics." The idea of a Christian "party" was new, but actually represented a weakening of the long-established principle by suggesting that Christianity become partisan rather than dominating the whole.[119] Ely appears to have been moving in this direction as early as 1822 when he published "A Proposal to Christians of All Denominations," in the *Presbyterian Magazine*. In this essay Ely stated the accepted position that "every man's religion ought to regulate his politics," a principle he assumed would "not be controverted by any Christian in argument, even though his whole conduct in civil society should be in opposition to the maximum." His proposal at this time was that "Christians of every denomination abandon party politics" and vote only for Christians. Since Christians formed the majority, this would "secure the lasting happiness of America."[120] This general sentiment was so frequently expressed in 1822 that it was the occasion for little comment or notice. By 1827, however, the public was already aroused by other factors that heightened interest in Ely's sermon.

From a twentieth-century perspective it appears that American civil governments were essentially compatible with Reformed ideology. If these governments failed to conform in certain respects, such as the overt recognition of divine authority, they more than compensated in such areas as the development of law. By the 1820s all aspects of the Reformed national ideology had resolved themselves into a single issue. Recognition of divine authority, legal enforcement of Reformed morality, and the election of Christian officials all depended on the control of public opinion. In America constitutions and laws have tended to vary in relationship to public opinion. The informal relationships between government and various pressure groups has been as significant as the more formal arrangements. At this point the Reformed were very perceptive. The single largest problem that the Reformed faced was how best to control public opinion.

Chapter 6

Voluntary Societies: Locus of the "Association of Religion and Patriotism"

At the same time the Reformed were constructing a viable ideology linking American prosperity with a national commitment to Protestant Christianity they were also attempting to foster institutions that would accomplish the major goals of that ideology by molding American public opinion. The existing institution, the denomination, had come into being in the context of Erastianism and was designed primarily to regulate the religious life and to promote the uniformity of doctrine and morals of ministers and members. Although some attempts were made to make the denomination a more aggressive instrument for implementing the national goals of the Reformed, the institution could be changed only slowly. The more significant factors, however, were that the denomination failed to meet the ideological requirements of Christian unity and could not claim the disinterestedness required for "the association between Religion and Patriotism." The Reformed turned to the voluntary association as the most appropriate institution to implement their goals in the American context.

When the Reformed were organized in the wake of the American Revolution,[1] they conceived of the denomination almost solely as a means for the internal government of the church. Each denomination was based on a presbyterial form of government with varying numbers of local or regional bodies between the local church and the highest body in the denomination. Each denomination's constitution specified in great detail the duties and responsibilities at every level of church government. Only the Presbyterians provided for expansion, and that in a single page in an otherwise lengthy document. Even at this point, however, the Presbyterians were primarily concerned with supplying vacancies in already existing churches. The only provision for expansion was that "the general assembly may, on their own knowledge, send missions to any part to plant churches, or to supply vacancies."[2] In fact, the American Reformed church organizations differed little from that of the established Church of Scotland. Differences were of detail rather than basic design, function, or structure.[3] As Sidney E. Mead has observed of the 1780s, "There was as yet little indication and less awareness that the church patterns of America would be markedly different from those of Europe."[4]

There were several factors at work during the 1780s that produced such a narrowly defined concept of the denomination. The first of these was the belief that the United States was a Christian nation whose policy and laws would conform to the standards of Christianity taught by the existing denominations. The presupposition was accepted as fact and found explicit statement in the Presbyterian constitution, which declared, "And if at any time the civil power should think it proper to appoint a fast or thanksgiving, it is the duty of the ministers and people of our communion, as we live under a christian government, to pay respect to the same."[5] The Reformed Dutch standards contained a similar provision.[6]

Implicit in this thinking was the idea that in some way Protestant Christianity, as distinguished from any single denominational expression of that religion, was to be the established religion of America. By continued use of the expression "nursing fathers," the Presbyterian revision of the Westminster Confession concerning civil magistrates expressed the idea of an informal establishment. Having affirmed that civil magistrates had no religious jurisdiction, the revision continued, "Yet as nursing fathers, it is the duty of civil magistrates to protect the church of our common Lord, without giving the preference to any denomination of Christians. . . ."[7] The Dutch Reformed assumed in 1790 that the United States Congress was the most logical body to secure copies of the Bible for Americans.[8]

Since the rapidly developing historical situation soon belied these presuppositions, there was never a theoretical or practical demonstration of how the system was to function. A letter from the first Presbyterian General Assembly to the recently elected Washington, however, breathed this spirit. After reciting the providential formula, "Public virtue is the most certain means of public felicity; and religion is the surest basis of virtue," the Presbyterians praised Washington as an "avowed friend of the Christian religion; who has commenced his administration in rational and exalted sentiments of piety; . . . and on the most public and solemn occasions, devoutly acknowledges the government of Divine Providence." While entertaining the hope that such an example would have the "most happy consequences," the Presbyterians promised "to add the wholesome instructions of religion . . . to render men sober, honest, and industrious citizens." But this important function was not to be the work of Presbyterians alone. "In these pious labours, we hope to imitate the most worthy of our brethren of other Christian denominations, and to be imitated by them; assured that if we can, by mutual and generous emulation, promote truth and virtue, we shall render a great and important service to the republic; shall receive encouragement from every wise and good citizen, and, above all, meet the approbation of our Divine Master."[9] Thus, at the time of the reorganization, the Presbyterians envisioned themselves and "the most worthy of our brethren," meaning primarily those of the Reformed tradition, as serving collectively in the capacity of a state church.

The Presbyterians of 1788 were of the opinion that they could do most to influence the nation by maintaining the doctrinal and moral integrity of their own denomination. This belief is reflected in a letter from the first General Assembly to the four newly created synods. According to the commissioners, "The dignity of our church, its weight and influence in the United States . . . will depend much on the unity of our counsels; and on the order and efficiency of our government." While they did not want to promote sectarianism at the expense of "the interest of religion," they felt that it was "necessary, for that great purpose, to preserve our character as a body, and our consequence in the republic, in comparison with other denominations of Christians.[10]

A second factor that produced an intense concern with internal church government was the fact of religious liberty in America. As has been demonstrated, the significance of this for the Reformed was that religion—the church—was now free from the control of civil government and free to conform as nearly as possible to the Scriptural ideal. In the Presbyterian revision of the Westminster Confession the sentence following the one designating magistrates as "nursing fathers" of the church stated that "as Jesus Christ hath appointed a regular government and discipline in his church, no law of any commonwealth, should interfere with, let, or hinder, the due exercise thereof."[11] The Presbyterians were at complete liberty to organize their denomination in line with what they believed to be the will of God.

That the Presbyterians recognized the uniqueness of the situation and determined to use it to best advantage was illustrated in the introduction to "The Form of Government and Discipline," which was written to "make the several parts of the system plain." After declaring in the first paragraph that "they consider the rights of private judgment, in all matters that respect religion, as universal and unalienable," the founding fathers of modern Presbyterianism indicated the implications of this for their task of reorganization. Every denomination was thereby "entitled to declare the terms of admission into its *communion*, and the qualifications of its ministers and members." If, in exercising this right, the denomination erred, it was not an infringement "upon the liberty, or the rights of others," but an "improper use of their own."[12]

The Reformed Dutch reflected the same attitude in the preface to their constitution of 1792, which began, "In consequence of that liberty wherewith Christ hath made his people free, it becomes their duty as well as privilege, openly to confess and worship him according to the dictates of their own consciences." Since membership in the denomination was "wholly voluntary, and unattended with civil emoluments or penalties," they could "bear a proper testimony" without "infringements upon the equal liberties of others."[13]

Since the concept of the denomination was limited primarily to the internal government of the church, the national endeavors of the Reformed were promoted primarily through a number of voluntary associations that were established in America with a frequency that heralded a new era in the history of this type of organization, which had actually originated in the era of the Reformation. The creation of these societies grew at an accelerated pace in the first quarter of the nineteenth century so that by 1826 the local societies numbered in the thousands and seven societies claimed "national" status. Although any initial definition of these societies as institutions would require subsequent qualification, they were usually nonecclesiastical organizations of individuals sufficiently concerned with some given issue to unite, pay annual dues, and promote the designs of the society with their time and energy. The names of the national societies suggest in broad outline the nature of all the societies. They were, in order of founding, the American Board of Commissioners for Foreign Missions (1810), the American Bible Society (1816), the American Education Society (1816), the American Colonization Society (1816), the American Sunday School Union (1824), the American Home Missionary Society (1826), and the American Temperance Society (1826).

The trend toward the preference of voluntary societies in areas of national concern was evident as early as 1800 when the trustees of the Presbyterian General Assembly presented to that body a comprehensive statement of the Reformed national goals. The trustees presented four areas for consideration. The first was the "gospelizing" of the Indians and a plan for their civilization, "the want of which it is believed has been a great cause of the failure of former attempts to spread Christianity among them." The second goal was the "instruction of the negroes, the poor, and those who are destitute of the means of grace." The third suggestion was for "the purchasing and disposing of Bibles, and also books and short essays on the great principles of religion and morality." The fourth called for "the provision of a fund for the more complete instruction of candidates for the gospel ministry, previously to their licensure."[14]

The General Assembly agreed with the report and added to the second recommendation, suggesting the possibility of instituting an "order of catechists" to instruct the poor and others "destitute of the means of grace." These men, who would not have the education necessary for the ministry, could offer private religious instruction and lead devotional exercises "with a view to prepare the way for a few regular and ordained ministers to follow them, to organize churches and administer ordinances." While not ministers, these functionaries would be examined and recommended by the presbyteries and work under their direction. This program was not to be viewed as replacing missionary work but "to be considered as additional to it."[15]

There was in this report the essence of the entire program that was launched to make the American nation conform to the requirements of the doctrine of providence and the vision of the millennium. But this program was not to be implemented through the Presbyterian denomination or any of the other Reformed denominations. In ordering these statements published so that "the judicatories and people at large . . . may be acquainted with the views and wishes of their highest judicature," the Assembly noted that it could not "attempt to carry into immediate effect all that is here suggested." It would implement some items and "the judicatures and people will judge for themselves what other objects it may be proper for them voluntarily to regard."[16] What the Assembly meant by "voluntarily to regard" was not clear. What was clear, however, was what the program suggested was attempted primarily through the system of voluntary societies formed specifically to carry out a single phase of the program. In this report were clearly the germs of the missionary, Bible, tract, and education societies, with the Sunday school unions reflecting a revised version of the "order of catechists" and "instruction of the negroes" giving way to a scheme for their removal.

In addition to the positive advantages of the voluntary societies there were several considerations that made the denomination a secondary institution for action designed to affect the nation. The task of internal government for which the structures had been created occupied a large portion of the time and energy of the various judicatories, produced disharmony, and thereby made the denomination less efficient than the voluntary societies. The denominations attempted only missions and the education of ministers and in these two areas they were constantly frustrated by inadequate accomplishment and inability to stimulate greater exertion. There was a tendency for the denominations to mold their own organizations on the pattern of the voluntary societies. These maneuvers worked to destroy the coherence of the original hierarchical structures so that the judicatories functioned more like autonomous societies than links in the chain of a larger integrated organization. By the 1820s the strictly denominational efforts had become nearly indistinguishable from those of the voluntary associations.

This tendency toward the society principle was most pronounced in the area of missions. Formation of standing committees of missions was the first step in that direction by the Presbyterians in 1802, the Reformed Dutch in 1806, the German Reformed in 1813, and the Associate Synod in 1822.[17] With slight variations these committees had the power to solicit and distribute funds, appoint missionaries, and carry on all of the missionary business of the denomination. They were required to make annual reports to the denomination.

The standing committees proved to be largely ineffective and the denominations went through a series of reorganizations that moved them further in the direction of the voluntary societies. Between 1802 and 1816 the Presbyterian committee was able to supply only the equivalent of four full-time missionaries per year.[18] The Reformed Dutch committee was never able to raise more than $400 in any given year during the first decade of operations.[19] The standing committee of missions of the Associate Synod of North America employed only one missionary in 1822 and was attempting to get missionaries from Scotland or Ireland by offering $100 to any who would come and accept the principles of the Associate Synod.[20] In 1816 the Presbyterians organized a board of missions, which they believed would "be able to carry on the missionary business with all the vigour and unity of design that would be found in a society originated for that purpose."[21] This movement toward the society principle within the denomination in order to gain efficiency was followed by the Reformed Dutch in 1822, the Associate Reformed in 1824, and the German Reformed in 1827.[22]

The pattern developed in missions was transferred to the denominational efforts to educate ministers. After preliminary experimentation with "Cent societies," the Presbyterians in 1819 and the Reformed Dutch in 1828 formed boards of education on the society principle.[23] This "new and more efficient measure" was fraught with difficulty that became significant in the development of a new concept of the denomination. These problems were illustrated by developments in the Presbyterian board of education. In the early years of its existence the board of education was completely overshadowed by its two largest auxiliaries, the Presbyterian Education Society, located in New York, and the Philadelphia Education Societies. The New York branch functioned as an autonomous society with no denominational connection, while the Philadelphia society worked in close harmony with the board of education. The New York group believed that the denominational judicatories should do nothing other than manage the internal concerns of the denomination and that voluntary societies should attend to those things designed to convert the nation. From the Philadelphia group, which believed that all such concerns should come under the control of the denomination, emerged the new concept of the denomination as a "missionary society" that was ultimately to dominate in America. The fact remains that during the period before 1826, when the great national voluntary societies were being established, the Reformed denominational organizations did not appear to offer a viable alternative.[24]

From a point of view of a study of early nineteenth-century Reformed tradition, the voluntary societies represented the best means to promote the "association between Religion and Patriotism." In the wake of the fragmentation of Protestantism and the retreat of civil government from jurisdiction in matters of religion, the societies seemed to be the most efficient way to encourage religion and therefore promote the national welfare in light of a theory of the denomination that had relied on civil government to provide religious cohesion to the society. In the societies the Reformed could appear to be unsectarian and therefore cooperate with the nation's patriots in a way that was impossible within the framework of the denomination. For the Reformed, the societies rather than the denomination seemed best suited to promote the "association between Religion and Patriotism," and the societies seemed to foreshadow the unified millennial church that would reign in theocratic splendor.[25]

Through the societies the Reformed could act in a way that was not possible in the denominations. In the societies the Reformed could associate in "patriotic" activities that might otherwise appear to be selfishly motivated or engaged in for sectarian advancement. In addition, they could work with "patriots" who formerly would have supported religious affairs through the civil government but who would tend to shy away from denominational activities for political or other reasons. The societies not only provided a method for this kind of association but also performed tasks either considered too large or inappropriate for the denomination. The societies could promote those activities necessary to the "association between Religion and Patriotism" that were believed to be of national concern but which found no appropriate place in the denomination as it was then conceived. Initially it was hoped that the societies could serve as intermediate institutions between the denominations and civil government that would not suffer the stigma of disestablishment. When this failed to materialize, the societies turned almost solely to the task of shaping public opinion by "the knowledge of the Lord." The societies could instruct those groups in America that were beyond the influence of organized religion but who seemed to endanger the national character and threaten the nation with providential ruin.

After 1826 participation in the societies became a matter of dispute among the Reformed, but the early societies had elicited their united support. One indication of this was the numerous, constant, and unqualified statements of praise in the minutes of the Reformed denominations, especially the Presbyterian General Assembly. The Assembly first took cognizance of voluntary societies in 1798 in response to a letter from the General Association of Connecticut, which had formed itself into a missionary society. The Assembly answered that while it had had "no convenient opportunity" to engage in this work, it was the "fixed resolution to undertake the same whenever the means shall be in our power." The Assembly noted "with great pleasure," however, that "in-

stitutions" for missionary purposes had been formed in New York and
Albany and that one was planned in Philadelphia. This same year the
Assembly gave its blessing to a society formed in Philadelphia "to aid the
civil authority in the suppression of vice and immorality."[26]

Several years passed before the General Assembly again took notice of
the voluntary societies. During that time a number of societies had been
formed and the Assembly demonstrated the unity of purpose in these
societies by giving a blanket approval rather than pointing to specific
associations. In 1804 the summary of the state of religion message noted
briefly that "the Assembly have likewise heard with uncommon satisfaction, of the increasing number of societies for the purposes of prayer,
and for the promotion of piety and good morals."[27] On the same occasion in 1808 the Assembly declared that "among the visible fruits of an
increased attention to the gospel, we recognize the establishment of benevolent institutions, as peculiarly characteristic of the religion of
Jesus."[28] In the following year, after listing the work of various societies,
the Assembly praised them as "nurseries of the Church" that were producing "almost incredible effects upon the moral and religious state of
the community."[29] This recognition of the value of the societies to influence the community beyond the organized life of the denominations was
an important consideration in the pattern reflected for the next several
years in the Assembly's commenting "with peculiar pleasure" on the
activity of the societies.[30]

Prior to 1812 the General Assembly confined its activities largely to this
policy of recommendation. Presbyterian ministers often formed the core
of the local societies and in 1812 the Assembly recognized the possibility
of cooperating organically with societies. In 1812 the Assembly *"Resolved,* That the Committee of Missions be authorized to expend in support of a mission to the Cherokees, annually, $500; and that they be
authorized to revive that mission, in conjunction with the New Jersey
Missionary Society."[31] Thus began, on a denominational level, a pattern
of cooperation between ecclesiastical and extra-ecclesiastical institutions
that was to continue for a number of years.[32]

The usefulness of the societies led the General Assembly not only to
recommend societies already established but also to recommend that
new ones be created. As early as 1809 the Assembly's committee of
overtures recommended the establishment of a "general religious tract
society." The national society approach had not as yet received general
acceptance and the Assembly called for the formation of more local tract
societies.[33] Again in 1814 some of the commissioners to the General
Assembly wished to use the influence of that body in the formation of a
"general Bible Society." While there was by that time considerable support for such a society, most of the commissioners desired to relieve the
prospective society of the charge of "sectarianism" and the subject was
"indefinitely postponed." It was thought that the better approach to the

formation of a national society would be for some state society to bring the measure forward. Elias Boudinot, president of the New Jersey Bible Society, was present at the meeting and, having been convinced of the utility of a national society, used his influence toward that end.[34]

By 1815 the General Assembly was convinced that the societies could be powerful agents in the promotion of the "association between Religion and Patriotism." In reviewing the state of religion in America, the Assembly spoke of the "judgments of pestilence and war.... [that] the alien from the commonwealth of Israel, the man of earth, the unbelieving servant of the corruption which is in the world through lust has regarded ... with indifference," and wished for "a more general amelioration of manners and habits, that improvement of the dispensations of Almighty God, which he expects, and mankind are obligated to exhibit." Turning to the work of the societies, the Assembly reflected, "The social principle is mighty in its operations." Although the society principle was not new, "the practice of uniting the talents, influence, and resources of individuals, by these hallowed bonds" had never before "been pursued with such vigour, extension, and success."[35]

The General Synod of the Reformed Dutch Church was less prone to statements on the societies in the early years of the century, but their support for the movement was not less enthusiastic. In 1823 the General Synod gave a favorable account of the societies and in 1826 gave a considerable portion of the address on the state of religion to a discussion of the progress of the societies. The General Synod felt that the societies reflected the glorious situation "which has been promised in the latter day glory of the Church."[36]

One of the most attractive things about the societies for the Reformed was that they served as agencies of Christian unity that enforced the millennial vision and signified its imminence. The connection between the millennium and missionary societies in America was recognized long ago by Oliver Wendel Elsbree.[37] More recently, Lefferts A. Loetscher has confirmed the importance of the millennium to Christian unity in early nineteenth-century America.[38] The millennium became a favorite subject for sermons preached before the various societies. William Linn, collegiate minister of the Reformed Dutch Church in New York City, delivered his influential sermon on the millennium before the New York Missionary Society in 1800. The published version, which had extensive notes, was one of the period's most thorough studies of the millennium.[39] John B. Romeyn, in addressing the same society in 1812, presented his fullest exposition of the millennium and affirmed that "no subject ... can be more suitable to our present meeting." In considering the "future state of the Church," Romeyn dwelt at length on unity and declared "missionary Institutions" to be "founded upon the prospects of the Church according to Prophecy."[40]

John Holt Rice believed that the founding of the various societies was an omen "of no doubtful interpretation, of the approach of the day of millennial glory, when the earth shall be filled with the knowledge of the living and true God."[41] The societies also claimed to have a significant role in bringing in the millennium. The American Tract Society declared that as a result of its activity "the day of millennial glory in our world will be hastened in its time."[42] The front cover of the American Sunday School Union's report carried an impression of the peaceful cohabitation of the lion and the lamb with the motto, "Knowledge of the Lord."[43]

While there was a difference in the rhetoric used about the exact relationship of the societies to millennial unity, it was universally affirmed that the relationship did exist. The Northern Missionary Society in upstate New York declared in 1797 that such "extraordinary union" foretold the coming millennium.[44] John Mason, who delivered the first sermon before that body, believed the unity represented by the society conformed to the millennial vision. He rejoiced that "while the spirit of discord rages in the world, the spirit of love descends upon the Church," and declared that "the spell of party is broken."[45] The New York Missionary Society, formed a year earlier, was more cautious. It viewed the societies as a way to transcend denominational differences and work toward unity while maintaining denominational distinctions. In its initial address to the public, the society disclaimed any "conspiracy against the outward distinctions that prevail among us," while affirming that "the hearty concurrence of Christians of different denominations . . . will be a token for good, that the Lord is about to build up Zion, and to appear in his glory."[46]

The weight of conviction seems to have been that the societies would lead to unity, although occasionally in moments of exuberance unity could be pronounced as complete. Declamations such as that of Gardiner Spring before the initial meeting of the United Domestic Missionary Society that "every suspicion and animosity" had been buried and that "we are now ONE" were in the minority.[47] The more consistent view was that expressed by the Bible Society of Philadelphia in 1809 when it declared that the unity of Christians would be a "by-product" of the society. The distribution of Bibles would open the way for "the fulfillment of the prediction of the prophet 'the earth shall be full of the knowledge of the Lord as the waters that cover the sea.' "[48]

For the Reformed the Bible was the supreme source of the "knowledge of the Lord," hence the Bible societies offered the most promising avenue to unity. This is not to say that the Reformed believed that the distribution of the Bible "without note or comment" was sufficient to produce the millennium. The emphasis on a trained ministry as a vital source of instruction also demanded missionary and education societies.[49] While these societies could produce disagreement, however, there was a consensus on the Bible as the source of that truth that would eventually lead all men to see "eye to eye." For this reason Bible societies were the most significant in terms of Christian unity.[50] Matthew LaRue Perrine reflected this opinion before the Presbytery of New York in 1816. He believed that "the rough edges of bigotry and superstition are wearing off, and Christians are coming gradually nearer and nearer together." The most important aspect of the growing unity, which would be complete in the millennium, was that Christians "agree in having confidence in the Scriptures, as being a plain, and sufficiently sure, guide in all matters of faith and practice." Since Perrine believed that "religious truth is one and the same; and all Christians have one and the same source of information," the distribution of Bibles by Bible societies would be the most significant step in bringing about ultimate unity.[51]

In his description of the "signs of the times," James Blythe recognized all the societies but gave preeminence to Bible societies. Significantly, Blythe too was addressing a denominational judicatory. He hailed the *"spirit of association,"* which he saw pervading Christendom, as "the great restorative of love, concord, and peace to Christ's church." A feature of great moment was that in fifty years every man would have a Bible. "It seems as tho' it were designed by God, that Bible societies should accompany those other momentous events we have noticed above—that they should all break upon the world together . . . to light up that glorious day."[52]

These were not the exuberant declarations of a few optimistic individuals. It was the expression of the consensus of Reformed opinion. The General Synod of the Reformed Dutch Church hailed the formation of the American Bible Society as the approach of that period "when God's people 'shall see eye to eye,'" and when the confession *"One Lord—One Faith—One Baptism*—will become the jury of all the earth."[53]

The Reformed ejaculations on unity were more ideological and propagandistic than reflections of reality. Most of the societies were in fact of a sectarian nature in the sense that they operated on broad Reformed principles and worked to the benefit of the denominations adhering to the Westminster Confession. In spite of rhetoric to the contrary, most of the societies gave evidence of some sectarian bias in their organization and, as has been demonstrated by Frederick Kuhns and Whitney R. Cross, most of the societies were sectarian in activity as well.[54]

The societies reflected this basic sectarianism in a number of different ways. The Northern Missionary Society and the New York Missionary Society adopted Calvinist confessions of faith.[55] The Pennsylvania Missionary Society would hire only Presbyterian or Dutch Reformed ministers. By 1816 the sectarian spirit so prevailed in the New York Missionary Society that a resolution to appoint any minister in good standing in the Dutch Reformed, Associate Reformed, or Presbyterian denominations failed by a vote of 182 to 91. The majority did not want "Hopkin-sian" ministers even if in good standing in one of these strongly Calvinis-tic denominations. This affair led to the formation of the New York Evangelical Missionary Society of Young Men, which was supportive of Hopkinsianism.[56] The Young Men's Missionary Society of Richmond was wholly Presbyterian, but auxiliary to the Young Men's Missionary Society of New York.[57] The New York Religious Tract Society reflected its Reformed bias by printing 5,000 copies of the Larger Catechism and labeling it "one of the best systems of Divinity which has ever been collected from Holy Scriptures."[58]

Some of the larger societies demonstrated sectarianism only by weight of numbers. This was the case, for example, with the American Bible Society, which was so scrupulously nonsectarian that it refused to open its meetings with prayer or to have sermons. The managers went so far as to invite a Catholic, William Gaston of North Carolina, to be one of the first vice-presidents. The society was so dominated by members of the Reformed denominations, however, that early critics labeled it as a Presbyterian organization and a number of Episcopalians and Baptists were alienated at a very early date.[59]

Not only were the societies sectarian in a theological sense but in a regional sense. Before the late 1820s the "national" societies were very largely regional and therefore dominated by either the New England Congregationalists or the Reformed of the middle and southern states. The American Board of Commissioners for Foreign Missions was a New England society with token representation from the rest of the nation. The American Education Society was likewise primarily Congregational-ist, while the Presbyterian Education Society of New York and societies auxiliary to the General Assembly's board of education were supported by Presbyterians. The American Tract Society was located in Boston and the New York Religious Tract Society, which was larger, served the mid-dle and southern states. On the other hand, the American Bible Society, the American Colonization Society, and the American Sunday School Union were largely controlled by the Reformed of the middle and south-ern states. Perhaps of even greater significance was the fact that the United Domestic Missionary Society was the creation of the Presbyterian, Dutch Reformed, and Associate Reformed.

After around 1826 this pattern of regional sectarianism began to break down, but the basic sectarianism was so great that this created problems in the society movement. In 1825 the American Tract Society and the New York Religious Tract Society joined to form a new Ameri-can Tract Society. In that same year the Presbyterian Education Society of New York united with the American Education Society. In 1826 the United Foreign Missionary Society, organized by the Presbyterian, Dutch Reformed, and the Associate Reformed denominations in 1817, united with the New England-based American Board of Commissioners for Foreign Missions. The American Home Missionary Society, organized in 1826, was a unification of the United Domestic Missionary Society with various New England societies. In 1829 the powerful Connecticut Bible Society became auxiliary to the American Bible Society. It was only after this series of mergers that the hegemony of the Reformed in the middle and southern states in the societies in which they participated was in doubt. It was also only after this development that various factions among the Reformed began to criticize the societies and propose that all activity carried on through the societies ought to be conducted under the responsible eye of the denominational judicatories.

However sectarian or regional the societies were in fact, it was essential to Reformed ideology and purposes that the emphasis on nonsectarianism be sustained. In the associated activities, as in the Reformed ideology, unity was understood as necessary to the ultimate domination of society. Consistent with the millennial vision, the societies unified Christians to extend the "Kingdom," or to promote the universal domination of Christianity. The Philadelphia Sunday and Adult School Union, which declared as its first purpose "to cultivate unity and christian charity among those of different names," made explicit the relationship of this unity to universal domination. "Every union formed in the spirit" accelerated the hour when Jesus "shall deliver up to the Father the mediatorial kingdom, tranquilized, *united,* and holy." The minority status of genuine Christians made this necessary. If "*Divide* and *Conquer*" was the maxim of their enemies, Christians should adopt for their motto "*Unite* and triumph."[60]

In the millenial context the societies offered the most fruitful source of unity for a divided Protestantism both in terms of its internal life and in terms of its theocratic vision. In case of the latter, however, the vagueness of the millennial symbol, while remaining the long-range goal, gave way to the more specific formulation of the American Corollary as a directive for action in the present. If Christian unity would not be consummated until the millennium, there were still the more immediate concerns with America that demanded unified action. The societies provided Christians with a way to cooperate without surrendering their peculiarities, but also made available institutions that would promote and allow the "association between Religion and Patriotism" in a way that was not possible in the denomination. It was the societies that would promote "that sort of union which makes every patriot a Christian, and every Christian a patriot."[61]

That the societies' primary focus was national was verified in their literature from the establishment of the earliest local societies to the founding of the national societies. To an amazing degree these statements of national purpose reflected the symbol system of the Reformed.

The necessity of Christianity to civil and religious liberty, and the maintenance of republican government formed the basic concept of the societies. Lyman Beecher established a society "for the suppression of vice and immorality" on Long Island as early as 1803. Pastor of a Presbyterian church at the time, Beecher pointed to a resolution of the General Assembly of 1798 in support of such action. His own opinion was that such societies were a "probable, and perhaps the only method, to preserve the liberties of our nation," because "in a republic, the virtue of the citizen is the life of the government." While Beecher recognized that his society was only for a single small town, he hoped that the society system would spread.[62]

When the Bible Society of Philadelphia gave its first report in 1809 the national concern was apparent. As a local society, the Philadelphia group hoped that other such societies would be formed. "However, the managers believe, that if no similar societies should be formed in any part of this country, then it will be the duty of the Society, to extend its arms from Maine to Georgia, and from the Atlantic to the Mississippi."[63]

In 1815 Nathaniel S. Prime, pastor of the Cambridge, New York, Presbyterian Church, informed the Cambridge Moral Society that he appeared before them "as the advocate of the common cause of God and of my country." Reiterating the Reformed position that no country, especially a republic, "can long exist" without the influence of virtue and religion, Prime declared that the societies were the solution. "Success in this undertaking will give more stability to our government, and security to its citizens, than all the constitutions and treaties that human wisdom can devise."[64] Jabez Chadwick managed a more dynamic assertion when he informed the Genesee Missionary Society in 1816 that "every nation which does not submit to Christ must be dashed to pieces." The way for America to escape was to have more missionary, Bible, and tract societies and more educated ministers.[65]

The American Bible Society, one of the first of the national societies, expressed similar concerns in its first communication with the public. The society noted that "the political world has undergone changes stupendous, unexpected, and calculated to inspire thoughtful men with the most boding anticipation." The fear was that the population of the United States would revert to a "species of heathenism which shall have all the address and profligacy of civilized society, without any religious control."[66]

As the societies became larger and more numerous the national aspirations continued to dominate. In addressing the United Domestic Missionary Society, John Holt Rice pictured America as a great nation consisting of two hundred million people of a "homogeneous race." The big question in his mind was, "Can this degree of liberty be enjoyed, and the order of society be preserved, and the interest of religion be promoted?"

His decided opinion was that America could only fulfill that destiny if his generation were successful in extending the influence of Christianity throughout the nation. The only hope for accomplishing that task was the united effort of the societies.[67]

The American Tract Society, in its initial communication with the American public in 1825, affirmed its national purpose. Their primary concern was with "securing and augmenting our civil and political liberties." In America, "so long as public opinion maintains its existing supremacy," this could only be done by molding public opinion "by a moral and religious influence." America's political existence, they believed, "depends on the intelligence, and more especially on the integrity of the people."[68] The American Sunday School Union, in its report in 1826, claimed that it was "laying the foundation of our nation's prosperity."[69]

Perhaps the most concise statement of the national concern was that of the United Domestic Missionary Society as that body was in the process of joining with other missionary societies to form the American Home Missionary Society in 1826. The society explained the uniqueness of the American situation when compared with England and the European nations. America was "practically a government of opinion," and progressively the representation of the people in both the national and state governments was becoming "more literal and perfect." In order to preserve "our political institutions from ruin," it was necessary to "purify the twelve million sources of political power and public influence." This could only be accomplished by "the permanent establishment of Christian ordinances."[70]

Such open statements of national purpose would have been considered altogether inappropriate for a denomination. Charges of sectarianism and an attempted amalgamation of church and state would have been immediately forthcoming. Even though the societies were basically sectarian, however, the Reformed did not hesitate to make their claims on the nation through them. The pretense was steadfastly maintained, and perhaps believed, that a society, unlike a denomination, was such that "local feelings, party prejudice, sectariansim are excluded by its very nature."[71] This identification was so consistently a part of the society movement that a society made up of members from only one denomination could still "disclaim all sectarian, and party principles and prejudices."[72]

As in the case of the Reformed belief about the ultimate triumph of their perceptions of truth, however, many viewed the associated activity as a step in the ascendency of their own denomination. Most of the Reformed would have been in basic agreement with the sentiments of John Holt Rice. When Rice surveyed the religious world in 1819 he concluded that Presbyterianism would, "should no unforeseen disaster occur, be the prevalent religion of the land." In the meantime, however, Rice was willing to cooperate with other denominations because "religion is the glory and safety of our land."[73]

The societies not only satisfied the Reformed ideological requirements of Christian unity and provided a means for making demands on the American nation, but also offered the possibility of a different kind of unity that would have been impossible in a denomination. Politicians, businessmen, and others among the American upper classes could participate in the work of the societies and there serve as "nursing fathers," a role for which there was no place in America's civil governments. Such men would participate in the societies who otherwise would have been only loosely associated with organized religion. By uniting in one group of religious and secular leaders, the societies became preeminently the locus of an "association between Religion and Patriotism."

The drive toward a closer association of religious and political figures was apparent in 1816 when Nathaniel S. Prime published *A Plan for the More Successful Management of Domestic Missions.* Prime was a Presbyterian minister who graduated from the College of New Jersey in 1804 and served churches in various parts of New York. His plan anticipated in several particulars the later development of the societies in America. Prime called for a greater centralization, replacement of itinerant missionaries by resident pastors, curtailment of expensive Indian missions for a greater concentration on the white citizenry of the United States, and an increase in efforts to educate the ministry. Within this broad framework, however, Prime wished to enlist greater participation from the nation's lawmakers. He proposed that each state form a central society to meet annually at the "seat of government." According to Prime, "On the proposed plan we may calculate on securing the influence of the members of the Legislature in favor of the institution." The American public, he believed, was well disposed toward religion and the members of the various legislative bodies would "cheerfully enrol [*sic*] their names as of the institution; and contribute their exertions as well as their money to promote its success." The "high standing and extensive influence" of these men would lead to the founding of auxiliary societies and the whole cause of missions would flourish.[74]

Many of the nation's political leaders actively joined in the labor of the societies. Some simply allowed the organizations to use their influence to sanction the enterprise in a subtle form of advertising. From an early date it became the custom to elect as vice-presidents of the societies a number of men who were well known in the community and whose support was deemed valuable. There were no duties connected with this office and those elected were sometimes informed only after the election had taken place. By merely accepting the position, the person sanctioned the purposes of the society. John Holt Rice, always anxious to portray the best of motives, said of this practice, "When men, who have the confidence of the country on account of their intelligence and patriotism" support the societies, it assures the public "that these associations have no object in view but that which is avowed."[75]

The cooperation of religious and secular leaders, which had been present to some degree in all the early religious societies, became pronounced with the formation of the "national" societies. At the convention for the formation of the American Bible Society, which was composed primarily of Reformed delegates from the middle and southern states, twenty-two prominent secular figures were elected as vice-presidents. The men were apparently selected with concern for regional distribution as well as status. In this case, lack of careful planning led to some embarrassment. Ten of these men, including three governors or former governors, one lieutenant governor, and one attorney general, refused to serve and their names were conspicuously absent in the next public announcement of the society.[76]

The American Bible Society, however, commanded active support from a number of political figures. At the request of the board of managers, a public meeting of the citizens of New York was convened at the city hall on May 13, 1816. The meeting was chaired by Smith Thompson, chief justice of the state of New York, with the mayor of New York and two United States Supreme Court justices participating. After several speeches laudatory of the society, John B. Romeyn, secretary of domestic correspondence for the organization, read its constitution. At the conclusion of the meeting the group of citizens "Resolved, That this meeting will cheerfully support this great National Institution." While it is apparent that this assembly had no legal power, it was nevertheless an example of the "association between Religion and Patriotism."[77] This kind of meeting became an established pattern for support of the religious voluntary associations.[78]

The American Colonization Society, founded less than a year after the American Bible Society, also reflected the "association between Religion and Patriotism." The fact that it was supported strongly by many of the nation's most powerful political figures often eclipses its religious, if not totally Presbyterian, origin. The prime mover behind the society was Robert Finley, pastor of the Presbyterian congregation at Baskingridge, New Jersey, who was trained at Princeton by Witherspoon, Smith, and Green. Reflecting his heritage, Finley was convinced that "should the time ever come when slavery shall not exist in these states, yet if the people of colour remain among us, the effect of their presence will be unfavourable to our industry and morals."[79] Having determined to establish a colonization society, Finley easily secured the support of neighboring Presbyterian ministers. In 1816 he brought up the idea before the Synod of New York and New Jersey, which had but recently established the African Education Society to train Negro preachers and teachers for the blacks of America. At this meeting, even before the colonization society was formed, the synod agreed to train missionaries and magistrates for the proposed African colony.[80]

With the support and encouragement of his friends in New York and New Jersey, Finley went to the "seat of government," Washington, D.C., to enlist the aid of the nation's political leaders. This he succeeded in doing in a very short period of time. When the constitution for the society was adopted on December 28, 1816, the meeting was held in the hall of the House of Representatives, chaired by no less a figure than Henry Clay and attended by "a score of men of rank and renown." The thirteen vice-presidents "were highly placed politicians or men of national reputation," including Secretary of the Treasury William Crawford, Speaker of the House Henry Clay, and General Andrew Jackson.[81]

All of the other major societies were established on the principle of an "association between Religion and Patriotism." There was, however, at least one unsuccessful attempt to obtain an even closer connection between religious figures and the national government, as opposed to eminent political figures. In 1822 the American Society for Promoting the Civilization and General Improvement of the Indian Tribes in the United States was formed. The object of the association was "to facilitate the operations of the Government, and of all of those wise associations, which have been formed by different denominations of Christians" for the purpose of providing the Indian with "the blessings derived from our common Christianity, and the various improvements peculiar to civilized man." The organization of the society was based on the structure of the federal government with ministers controlling the board of directors. The surviving presidents of the United States were listed as "patrons." The vice-president of the United States was the ex-officio president of the society. Members of the Supreme Court were ex-officio vice-presidents. Any government officials associated with the Indian in any capacity were members of the society. The board of directors, who would control the operations of the society, numbered thirteen, seven of whom were ministers.[82]

Although this society claimed to be formed "under the eye and auspices, of the general Government of our country; with its knowledge and sanctions of its principle officers," the grand design ultimately failed. James Madison, John C. Calhoun, and John Jay supported the society but a number of the most powerful persons declined their offices. Among these were John Adams, Thomas Jefferson, John Marshall, and the members of the Supreme Court. Some of those declining expressed support of the society but others rejected the concept. Thomas Jefferson was foremost among the latter, claiming that "the clergy will constitute nineteen twentieths of all the high authorities of the United States."

Jefferson believed that such "uncontrollable power" could not "be viewed without dismay."[83]

In spite of the failure of this grand design, a great number of significant political figures participated in the religious societies. Indeed, it would be difficult to determine the precise degree or percentage of involvement, but it would be staggering by twentieth-century standards. Among prominent national figures, James Madison, James Monroe, John Quincy Adams, Andrew Jackson, Henry Clay, John C. Calhoun, William Wirt, John Jay, Charles C. Pinckney, John Marshall, and Daniel Webster all supported some facet of the society movement. While some gave but scant aid, others were active leaders. John Jay was president of the American Bible Society from 1821 to 1827. Late in his life John Marshall began to lend his extensive support and was a vice-president in both the American Sunday School Union and the American Colonization Society.[84]

A host of lesser political figures supported the societies. Elias Boudinot, president of the Congress in 1783, was the first president of the American Bible Society and supported all of the societies. DeWitt Clinton, governor of New York, was active in most of the religious movements. Stephen Van Rensselaer, America's only nobleman and an active politician, was perhaps the most influential man in the societies. Joseph Hornblower, Supreme Court justice of New Jersey, Henry Rutger of New Jersey, and Bushrod Washington of Virginia, to name a few, were also active supporters of the religious societies.[85]

An analysis of the political figures involved in the societies indicates that men of very different political ideology and alignment came together in support of the religious societies. Although no complete quantitative and statistical data exist, it is apparent that at no time before the 1830s did the religious societies reflect any strong orientation toward one political party. Often political opponents appeared on the same platform in support of one society or another.

That political parties had no decisive influence was illustrated by the alignments of the first group of vice-presidents of the American Bible Society. Of the original twenty-two, ten declined to serve. Seven of these were political figures. Although 1816 is a bit late to assert clear distinctions between Federalists and Republicans, three of these would be classified as Federalists and four as Republicans, one of whom later supported the society.[86] Of the eleven identifiable political figures who accepted the position, six were Federalists and five were Republicans.

The same generalization applied in the later realignment of political parties. The bipartisan support for the movement was well illustrated by a meeting in Washington in 1831 for the purpose of supporting the American Sunday School Union's attempt to establish schools in every area of the Mississippi Valley. The meeting was chaired by Felix Grundy, the Democratic senator from Tennessee. Letters were read offering support for the endeavor and apologies for their absence from Andrew Jackson and William Wirt, attorney general under Monroe and Adams who backed Clay in 1828. Resolutions and seconds were made by both Democrats and Whigs. Elisha Whittlesey, a representative from Ohio who was one of the founders of the Whig party, moved a resolution of general support. He believed that the American Sunday School Union was "calculated to give strength to our political union." His Whig colleague from Ohio, Joseph H. Crane, seconded the resolution. The Democratic representative from Kentucky, Nicholas D. Coleman, then expressed concern for the "poorer classes" and moved that the meeting approve all measures of education, "especially such as contemplate the moral cultivation of man." This was seconded by his Democratic colleague from Georgia, Charles E. Haynes. The third resolution was truly bipartisan. The motion offered by Theodore Frelinghuysen, Whig senator from New Jersey, was seconded by the Democratic representative from Kentucky, Charles Wickliffe.[87] This bipartisan support of the religious societies indicated that a number of the nation's political figures shared the world view of the Reformed and that they too were interested in the "association between Religion and Patriotism."

In addition to this informal kind of support from the nation's "patriots," there was some hope that the societies could achieve a more direct form of government aid that had been denied to the denominations. The most fortunate society in this respect was the American Colonization Society, the success of which was thought to be a necessary step toward accomplishing the national goals of the Presbyterians and their associates in the societies. P. J. Staudenraus has portrayed the connection of this society to the religious life of the nation and pointed to its specific function in relation to the other societies. Operating on a belief "that a ruling Providence guided nations to ruin or salvation," the supporters of colonization believed "the American nation could root out its social and political deficiencies, atone for past misdeeds, and shape the course of unborn generations." This particular society sought to remove "a socially inferior and repressed nation," thereby hastening "the coming of the American nation's millennium."[88]

Robert Finley had determined from the beginning that such a scheme would require the support of the federal government, and within two weeks after its organization the American Colonization Society petitioned Congress to create an African colony. As recorded in the first report of the society, "The first step of the board of managers was to present a memorial to Congress."[89] Congress did not immediately comply and efforts were made by Finley and Samuel J. Mills to form auxiliary societies. The auxiliary system in this case was "merely supplemental to the larger goal of federal assistance," and the money raised in this fashion was used primarily to gather information and assimilate arguments that would convince Congress of the necessity and feasibility of the plan.[90] In the meantime the society was endorsed by several state legislatures as well as several Presbyterian judicatories. The General Assembly recommended the colonization society "to the patronage and attention of the churches under their care, and to benevolent individuals throughout the union."[91]

By 1819 a committee of the society was convinced that all arguments had been settled except "the simple question, whether the undertaking shall be adopted and patronized by the Government, so as to become essentially national in its means and its objects; or whether its ultimate success is to depend upon the responsibility and exertions of individuals."[92] The society finally secured the support of President James Monroe in 1819, and the first American ship sailed for Africa in 1820. But, as Staudenraus concluded, "tacit aid fell short of total acceptance of the principle of government-sponsored colonization." The colonization society remained "a private agency, a mendicant no different from the many benevolent societies of the time."[93] While the society continued through the years to solicit government aid, the whole scheme of colonization became an object of political contention, "and in a short time the unsuccessful contest for federal aid grew small in importance compared with the bitter contest for public opinion stirred by an angry Boston editor in gray steel spectacles—William Lloyd Garrison."[94]

A second area in which the societies obtained some cooperation and financial support from the federal and state governments was Indian missions. As in the case of free Negroes, it was believed that the presence of "ignorant, uncivilized and savage" Indians on the fringes of American society threatened both national and social security.[95] The proposed remedy was to civilize and Christianize the Indians. The early efforts at Indian missions in this period were based on a philosophy coinciding with the Presbyterian concept of "civilization." It was generally held that Christianity was necessary to the civilization of the Indians, but in practice the missionary societies did not distinguish between the two. Even the General Assembly reversed the generally accepted formula when it considered a plan for Indian missions in 1800. The Assembly proposed that the "gospelizing" of the Indians be "connected with a plan for their civilization, the want of which it is believed has been a great cause of the failure of former attempts to spread Christianity among them."[96]

R. Pierce Beaver has delineated the cooperation between the government and the societies in his recent monograph, *Church, State, and the American Indians: Two and a Half Centuries of Partnership in Missions between Protestant Churches and Government.*[97] According to Beaver, Henry Knox, the first secretary of war and the man responsible for shaping the government's Indian policy, "shared many of the opinions of the directors of the missionary societies, and he envisaged a program of civilization carried out through Christian missions as the key to a successful policy." In a report to President Washington in 1789 Knox outlined his policy. "Missionaries, of excellent moral character," he advised, "should be appointed to reside in their nations, who should be well supplied with all the implements of husbandry, and the necessary stock for a farm." Knox did not feel that this would "fully effect the civilization of the Indians," but he thought it would at least attach them to "the interest of the United States."[98]

This coincidence of purpose and method led to cooperation. The missionary societies furnished men and the government supplied land, financial assistance, and a certain amount of prestige—or coercion. State governments also joined the effort. The missionaries in return often served as semiofficial agents for the government. This relationship in action comes to light in the diary of Joseph Bullen, first missionary of the New York Missionary Society. He reported having "a good long talk with Wolfe's friend, head man of this nation." After explaining the gospel, Bullen informed the chief "of the great love the council at New-York have for the Chickasaws, and of the good-will of his great father the President." Later in a large meeting with the tribe, Bullen began by announcing the arrival of presents from the United States government, explained the Christian religion, and concluded by teaching the alphabet.[99]

In 1818 the level of cooperation was intensified through the efforts of President Monroe, and in 1819 the government set up a permanent fund to be made available to missionary societies for use in Indian missions.[100] At an earlier date the Presbyterian General Assembly had received some support from the federal government in its own efforts in Indian missions. While this aid had more recently been denied, the Assembly noted their approval of the new arrangement in a resolution praising "the general government" in its exertions "to promote the civilization of the Indian tribes." They hoped this would result in the reclamation of "the aborigines of our continent from the darkness and ferocity of their savage state, to the privileges and enjoyments of Christian civilization."[101]

If the societies were able to attain the aid of the government in their attempts to purify American society by removing the blacks and civilizing the Indians, they were not successful in those areas designed for the white citizenry of America. The civil governments were more respectful of the rights of white Americans. This was highlighted, for example, when the Pennsylvania legislature granted a charter to the Western Missionary Society that prohibited the society "from expending their funds in preaching the gospel to any other objects but the Indians." The society had sought incorporation as a missionary institution for both Indians and "destitute" American citizens.[102]

The hopes of those who supported the societies and the reluctance of the government emerged most clearly in the discussion surrounding a petition to Congress by the managers of the American Bible Society requesting free postage and exemption from duty on paper used in the printing of Bibles. The petition, dated December 4, 1817, was pigeon-holed by Congress and in 1819 the managers published the document along with their arguments in support of such legislation. While the author remains anonymous, the probability of his being a Presbyterian is substantial. John B. Romeyn, secretary of domestic correspondence, and John M. Mason, secretary for foreign correspondence who became a Presbyterian in 1821, are the most likely candidates.[103]

The American Bible Society based its case for special government aid on the twofold argument that its operation would be beneficial to the nation and that such aid would conform with intentions of the constitutional provisions against an establishment of religion. Both of these arguments were consistent with the Reformed position. In support of the first contention, Congress was reminded that the governments of Russia, Prussia, Saxony, Wertemberg, and the Netherlands had felt Bible distribution to be of such national importance as to warrant government support. Noting that Congress had exempted postage on letters of a "Vaccine Institution" in Baltimore, the pamphlet declared, "While it is readily conceded that the public health is an object of sufficient importance to justify the granting of this privilege, can it be denied, that the promotion of religion and morals, and the consequent improvement of society, is no less important in a national view." In fact, the American Bible Society felt it had a more valid claim for public support than any other "benevolent agencies" because it was "a *National Institution,* founded for, and directing all its efforts to *national objects.*" The society was "not for the accommodation of any prescribed district, or religious persuasion, but for the *public good,*" since its efforts "tend to the improvement of society in knowledge and virtue." Since Congress had granted exemption "in cases of *inferior* national importance," it should not fail to grant the society's request.[104]

In arguing that such aid would be consistent with the Constitution, the managers claimed that the relevant articles were not intended to work "against the *principles of Christianity.*" According to the society, "The *real* evils . . . intended to be averted, were the dominant influence of any one religious sect, the union of *ecclesiastical* with *civil* power, the tyranny of *one* favoured and usurping religious denomination, and the consequent degradation and persecution of every other *dissenting* persuasion." Such laws could not apply to Bible societies, which were "composed of persons of *various* religious sentiments" and which aimed at "demolishing the barriers that separate christians from each other." Congress was again reminded, from the society's address to the American public, "that local feeling, party prejudices, and sectarian jealousies" were excluded "by the very nature of the Society." In fact, the society claimed, by absorbing funds that were intended for religious purposes through taxes and postal fees, the government was violating the spirit of the Constitution "by '*prohibiting,*' to a certain extent, '*the free exercise of religion.*' "[105]

Had the American Bible Society been successful, the way would have been opened for government aid to the societies generally. While the petition did not press this point, as it may have tended to make their own appeal less acceptable, it did note that circulation of "printed Reports of Bible Societies, and other religious publications" could not be called "an establishment of religion."[106] The millennium had not yet arrived, however, when all would see "eye to eye" and the magistrates would be "nursing fathers," and the government resisted these attempts, forcing the societies to rely on the support of individual public figures to promote the "association between Religion and Patriotism."

Another attempt to establish a more direct cooperation of churchmen and magistrates through the society method also failed to become an established pattern in American life. This was the creation of "moral societies," which generally listed as their purpose "to aid the magistrates in the suppression of vice and immorality." The extent of these societies is difficult to determine. Unlike Bible, missionary, and other societies, the reports of the moral societies were seldom published and, since this particular aspect of the society movement produced no permanent or national society, many of the records have disappeared. There were probably more than has generally been recognized. Charles I. Foster listed only three, all of which were located in New England. There were several others in the middle and southern states founded between 1798 and 1817 in which Reformed participation was conspicuous.[107]

These societies were in accord with the Reformed tactic of attempting to have enforced those existing laws of which they approved, Sabbath laws being a prime example. The Presbyterian General Assembly of 1815 specifically recommended the formation of this kind of society. Such recommendation was adequate to produce greater activity at the local level. The minutes of the Presbytery of Erie, meeting a month after the General Assembly, indicate the effect. Upon being informed by their commissioner "that moral associations have been formed . . . and have been successful in checking immorality," the preachers of the presbytery agreed "that they will cheerfully give their united aid in endeavoring to suppress Sabbath-breaking, drunkenness, profane gambling, and all immoralities within their bounds."[108]

Again in 1817 the General Assembly praised the moral societies. Speaking of the prevalence of various vices, the Assembly noted that "in many instances, however, a check has been given to these degrading and sinful practices, by the salutary operation of moral societies." The Assembly believed that these societies, "if instituted on proper principles, and conducted with suitable prudence, promise to be very useful in laying, at least, an outward restraint upon the disturbers of the peace and order of society."[109]

The largest of these moral societies, the New Jersey Society for the Suppression of Vice and Immorality, was founded in 1816 and affords some insight into the nature of these societies. Fifteen ministers were listed among its managers, eight of whom were Presbyterian. Of the fifteen, six were also managers of the New Jersey Bible Society.[110] The constitution of the society listed as its principle object, "to carry into full effect the laws of the state against vice and immorality, by aiding the civil authorities." The society would seek to prevent rather than punish crime and resort to legal coercion only when "persuasion, admonition, and other mild measures, are found ineffectual."[111]

In 1818 in an address to the public, it was noted that the society had been formed because efforts to enforce the existing laws were insufficient. While the society did not intend to invade the province of the civil magistrates, it would prod those who failed to do their job and support those faithful servants who would appreciate the help of the "most worthy part of the community." The society assured the public that they had no intention of trespassing on the rights of conscience, but declared that freedom of conscience did not mean "liberty to perpetuate vice and practice immoralities." It was the society's conviction that, "in opposing what all admit to be vicious or injurious to society, no man's conscience can be violated." The exact nature of the society's concerns became clear when the address called upon all Sabbath breakers, "profane swearers, men of intemperance, and those who openly violate the laws of our country and corrupt public morals, by horse-racing and gambling . . . to turn from such evil ways." The society designated such crimes as "weapons of rebellion against civil government, social order, domestic enjoyment, and true piety."[112]

These societies emphasized the work of persuasion in their publicly announced intentions, but there is some evidence that at least some of the individuals involved wanted to use immediately the full force of the law to attain these ends. The Cambridge Moral Society in New York announced in its constitution that its methods would be "example, affectionate persuasion, admonition, and in the extreme, legal coercion." In a sermon before the society in 1815, however, Nathaniel Prime called for a hundred men, "if necessary," to arrest Sabbath breakers in that town.

Prime felt that it was simply a matter of legal force. If the law were enforced "vigorously" for two or three weeks, Sabbath breakers would soon learn "that there is not the smallest hope of escaping, and that all who *obstinately* transgress will be punished with rigour." For Prime the question was not "whether men shall be permitted to break the Sabbath or not, but which is the most eligible and effectual way to prevent them?"[113]

It was the hope of the New Jersey moral society that their venture would succeed and "lead to associations of a like kind, in every part of the Union," as had been the case with the Philadelphia Bible Society.[114] Such overt activity, however, simply was not a viable approach, as it produced immediate hostility from large segments of the American population. The response to Gardiner Spring's attempt to promote Sabbath "reform" in New York was illustrative. Spring preached a series of sermons relative to the observation of the Sabbath, in the course of which he obtained the cooperation and help of the mayor and other local officials. A public meeting to carry out the reform was arranged, over which Spring was to preside. Upon arriving at the city hall, Spring and a companion came face to face with an angry mob. In recalling the incident, Spring wrote, "We forced our way through the crowd, and found ourselves in the midst of an indignant assemblage, passing resolutions *requesting the ministers to mind their own business.*" Spring was forced to flee for his life.[115] This somewhat minor incident was reflective of the mood of many Americans in the late 1820s that made socially unacceptable the use of political power to support a religious culture.

A series of events between 1827 and 1829 brought into the open and stimulated widespread opposition to the overt political designs of the Reformed. The first of these, Ezra Stiles Ely's sermon, *The Duty of Christian Freemen to Elect Christian Rulers,* was significant only in that it elicited publicity about and debate on the broader Reformed program. The refusal of the Pennsylvania legislature to charter the American Sunday School Union and the failure of the General Union for Promoting the Observance of the Christian Sabbath marked a decisive defeat of the Reformed desires for closer formal cooperation with American governments. In retrospect, these events were an extension of the attempts by the Reformed to secure support for the American Bible Society. The major difference, however, was that by 1829 American public opinion was decisive, and the Reformed were forced to retreat.

Ely's proposal for a "Christian party in politics" may not have been so explosive had it not been obvious that he considered Andrew Jackson as the only "Christian" candidate. While the basic content of the sermon merely reflected established patterns of thought, the apparent involvement in party strife was a significant deviation. In this case, the divergence from the long-range theocratic vision to the immediate political situation unavoidably embroiled the Reformed ideology in party politics. Each of the contending political parties attempted to use Ely's sermon in the most advantageous fashion and as a result the Reformed suffered a loss of prestige in the community.[116]

The political antagonisms were vented most forcefully when the American Sunday School Union applied to the Pennsylvania legislature for a charter in 1828. What ordinarily would have been looked upon as a harmless request by a benevolent association became an object of political debate. Those wishing to discredit the Sunday school movement, with which Ely was closely associated, had no difficulty finding damaging evidence in the printed records of the society. The Reformed designs on the American nation, apparent in all the literature, were blatantly stated in the Sunday school material. Laid on the desk of each legislator was a document exposing the American Sunday School Union's intentions of becoming "dictators to the consciences of thousands" and of monopolizing publication in America. What in the abstract would have been recognized by few Americans as a threat to individual liberty became a burning issue because it was politically expedient. The managers of the American Sunday School Union were accused of determining "to subject the consciences, and persons of the *free citizens of these United States*, to the tyranny of an ecclesiastical domination," and the legislature refused the charter by a vote of 21 to 9. This incident served further to publicize the national ambitions of the Reformed and to arouse unfavorable public opinion.[117]

In the same year a number of the Reformed constituted the General Union for Promoting the Observance of the Christian Sabbath. This society was very similar in design and purpose to the moral societies, except that it was "national." The work of the society was widely acclaimed by the Reformed in individual and denominational expressions. The Presbyterian General Assembly believed that the loss of the Christian Sabbath "would be the inevitable doom of all that is splendid in our national prospects."[118] The Reformed Dutch General Synod rejoiced that efforts were being made "in behalf of the due public observance of the Lord's day."[119]

The society immediately focused its energies on the one federal law, the post office law, which had been a source of concern to the Reformed since 1810. The primary tactic used by the society was essentially the same approach that the denominations had used earlier, except now the voluntary association was the locus of action.[120] Theodore Frelinghuysen, an ardent supporter of the Reformed cause, presented the case to the Senate. The whole effort failed when the Senate postal committee chaired by Senator Richard M. Johnson issued an unfavorable report in January 1829. Senate acceptance of the report ended the Reformed hopes for political implementation of their ideology.[121]

The failure of the Reformed to secure direct governmental aid for their societies or to implement their desires for American society through the police powers of the state did not mean a failure for their program. Although unable to circumvent the legal disestablishment of religion, the societies did provide an effective union between religious and secular leaders who desired an "association between Religion and Patriotism." This advantage alone was sufficient to make the societies a more attractive alternative than the denominations as institutions for promoting the national ambitions of the Reformed.

Chapter 7

Voluntary Societies: Focus on Poverty, Population Explosion, and Popular Suffrage

The attempts of the Reformed to establish a more formal relationship between religion and American government through the societies reflected only one part of the Reformed ambition for the nation. After the failure to obtain a charter for the American Sunday School Union and to secure repeal of the post office law, the Reformed turned almost entirely to the other tactic, the control of public opinion, which had been implicit in the ideology from the beginning and had been instrumental in the development of the societies. However much the Reformed would have appreciated the use of law to place an "outward restraint upon the disturber of the peace and order of society,"[1] their contention that ultimately even the proper functioning of law depended on the religious character of the population was more basic. It was the "knowledge of the Lord" revealed in the Bible that taught "the magistrate how to rule and the citizen how to be governed."[2] The major task of the Reformed was to shape and mold American character through voluntary means, and the societies seemed to be of greater utility than the denominations.

The enormity of the power of public opinion in America was a subject of considerable discussion in the early nineteenth century. Alexis de Tocqueville noted that "public opinion pressed with enormous weight upon the mind of each individual; it surrounds, directs and oppresses him; and this arises from the very constitution of society, much more than from its political laws."[3] The Reformed gave a similar analysis. DeWitt Clinton, addressing the Presbyterian Education Society, declared that since the American Revolution the power of public opinion had "risen up to direct the energies of mankind." According to Clinton, "Its authority is unlimited, its progress irresistible, and its force irrepressible."[4] Theodore Frelinghuysen, addressing the American Sunday School Union, agreed that "opinion is, under heaven, become the *Arbiter of Nations.*"[5]

Although the Reformed literature conveys the strong impression of the undesirability of this situation, it was nonetheless a reality they could not escape. The power of public opinion alone, however, was not

considered necessarily evil. It was a neutral force that could be used to
further Reformed goals if it could be properly directed. It was a common sentiment that "as we believe our form of government to be *best,* so
it might be worst."[6] The determining factor was the control of public
opinion. After discussing the power of public opinion, Clinton was quick
to add, "This power, in order to be beneficial, ought to be predicated on
just and proper grounds. It ought to be directed by piety and knowledge."[7] The Reformed found themselves in a situation that has appeared to many a contradiction, an anomaly, but for them the logic was
clear. If America, with her republican form of government and free
institutions, was to survive and prosper, then public opinion must be
carefully controlled. Jacob Brodhead, the highly influential pastor of the
Reformed Dutch Church in Broome Street, New York, was convinced of
the truth of his words when he said, "Let the salutary restraints of religion and morality be put upon the possession of men, to regulate their
opinions, and keep *them* in a correct and uniform course; and more will
be done to save this republic, than can be effected by all appeals made to
patriotism."[8]

Consistent with the Reformed ideology, it was believed that only religion was powerful enough to control public opinion. Philip Milledoler
responded to the rhetorical question, "What power or craft can resist the
force of public opinion?" with the declaration that "it can be controlled
by no voice but the voice of God."[9] The Reformed understood their
pronouncements as the "Voice of God" and believed themselves capable
of, and even responsible for, exercising that control. Eliphalet Nott
managed a forthright statement of the position. Recognizing that public
opinion in America commanded authority even above the law, Nott
noted that "public opinion is itself directed, and settled among the many,
by the few who, either by merit or by management, have acquired an ascen-
dancy, and become the acknowledged arbiters of faith and of practice."[10]

In former times and places this task would have been the responsibility
of the established religion, but in America it fell to the societies. In
commenting on the power of public opinion, Frelinghuysen noted that
"the spell of long-established systems . . . is broken," and he hastened to
add, "what a public mercy was it, that the Sunday-School should come up
just as the elements began to quicken, and shed its healthful, purifying,
forming influences over whole masses of minds. . . ."[11] The specific mention of the Sunday school came only as the result of his addressing the
American Sunday School Union. All the societies were engaged in the
same concern. As DeWitt Clinton noted, "Monitorial education, Sunday
Schools, and Bible societies are the great levers which must voice public
opinion." Combined with "the ministrations of a virtuous and enlightened clergy," these would firmly establish "the cause of liberty, order, and good government."[12]

The Reformed ambition for the American nation could have been achieved only with great difficulty if American society had remained stable after the Revolution except for the process of political reorganization. The decades following the acquisition of political sovereignty, however, were characterized by rapid change. The rapid growth of population, always a dynamic feature in social change, was a significant aspect of that change. In America that factor was complicated by the scattering of the population over an increasingly larger land area and, simultaneously, by the concentration of people in growing industrial cities. Both of these quantitative changes tended to accelerate changes in the quality of American life already effected by industrialization. Poverty, which the Reformed equated with viciousness, increased at a time when other developments isolated the poor from the religious community. The extension of the suffrage to large numbers of people not controlled by Christian influence greatly complicated the Reformed task of building a Christian civilization by controlling public opinion. The Reformed had to concern themselves with the entire population of the United States— "Men and women, and children, and strangers within the gates; within a field of labor, extending from Florida to Michigan, and from ocean to ocean."[13]

The population of the United States grew from 3,929,625 in 1790 to 17,069,453 in 1840. The absolute growth was not as significant as the rapidity of growth. By decades the percent of increase was 35.1, 36.4, 33.1, 33.5, and 32.7. This is to be compared with a growth rate of 13.3 percent between 1960 and 1970, supposedly a decade of "population explosion." The social problems stemming from the growth of population, however, were different in the early national period from those of the present. There was no shortage of space in the early nineteenth century, although the number of residents per square mile increased from 4.5 to 9.8.[14] The problem from the Reformed point of view at that time was that the population was "outgrowing its institutions."[15]

For the Reformed, the most significant problem related to the inability of religious institutions to multiply as fast as the population. The American Sunday School Union calculated in 1835 that it would require a "daily increase of eleven new Sunday-schools of thirty pupils each, on an average, and of thirty-three teachers" to keep pace with "the natural increase of the white native population" of the United States.[16] Societies to educate ministers were needed, according to Ashbel Green, because "our population was increasing a great deal faster" than the number of religious teachers.[17] Even the energy and effectiveness of associated activity produced little more than enough ministers to replace the dying, according to the American Education Society, in a population that was growing by 1,000 per day.[18] In 1826 the American Home Missionary Society complained that those "most destitute" of religion were in places

that were "most rapidly increasing in population." Since these were destined "to control the moral influence of the nation," it was necessary to
unite and "possess the land."[19]

It is significant that the primary emphasis was on the growth of population rather than the westward movement. The intense concern of the
Reformed that the frontier would relapse into "barbarism" and shift the
social and political balance of power actually developed late in the
1820s.[20] The initial concern was with the concentration of the population in the cities. The nation's major cities, except for Boston, were all in
the middle and southern states, and Boston did not grow as rapidly as
the other cities during the period. Compared to the growth of population in the nation generally, the rate was much faster in the cities. From
1790 to 1830 the total population of the United States increased by
227.4 percent while the population of its four largest cities increased by
397.4 percent.[21] The most rapid increase came between 1790 and 1800
when New York and Baltimore nearly doubled in size, while Philadelphia grew by almost 50 percent. As Constance McLaughlin Green has
argued, "The swift rise of its cities is a feature of American heritage no
less significant and drastic than the swift march of the frontier."[22]

The Reformed orientation was decidedly futuristic. They were as
much concerned about 1925 as they were about 1825. Those who projected into the future predicted a population of at least 200,000,000
within a century.[23] While constantly aware of their inability to multiply
religious institutions as fast as the population, the Reformed measured
their task in terms of the millennium. It was a common conviction that
"the men of this generation will be the patriarchs of the millennial age"
and that "the impressions which we will leave will endure forever."[24]

With such an awesome sense of responsibility, the Reformed became
acutely aware of their failure at the close of the War of 1812. Religious
institutions, especially churches and pastors, had so emphatically lagged
behind the population growth, Ward Stafford reported in 1817, that the
"most populous places, it will be found from examination, are more
destitute than the surrounding country." Using the desirable optimum
of one church and minister to every 1,000 people, Stafford pointed out
that eight major cities in the middle and southern states were 210
churches short, leaving a population of 210,000 destitute of the gospel.
If the different growth rates remained constant, however, New York and
Philadelphia alone would be short of the desired figure by 280 churches
in 1820.[25]

The problems of growth, from the Reformed point of view, were
greatly intensified by the chracteristics of the added numbers. The cities
in particular were increasingly populated by the poor. Until recently
American historians have stoutly resisted the notion of a permanent
proletariat, especially during the formative years of the American repub-

lic.[26] American historians and Americans generally, have preferred to view America as a dynamic and fluid society where wealth could not survive the industry of its possessors, and where the energetic poor could climb to the pinnacle of wealth by honesty, industry, and frugality. This conception has received sustained attacks but continues to be accepted by many as valid.[27] One reason that it has been possible to escape a consciousness of the awesomeness of poverty in the early national period is that poverty, especially pauperism, was considered to be primarily a religious problem. As such, most of the surviving source material is confined in religious publications that have been largely ignored. The Reformed of the early national period considered poverty to be one of the most pressing social, political, and religious problems of their era. Whatever judgment one would make on their response to that problem, they were certainly not excessively concerned with a nonexistent phenomenon.

The growing numbers of persons receiving aid from public institutions in the large cities during the early decades of the nineteenth century certainly indicated a growth of poverty but represented only a portion of the overall picture. In New York in 1811 there were 2,600 poor residing in all the city's public institutions. Ten years later the number had grown to 3,428. While these comprised about 2 percent of the population, the figures do not represent adequately the total number of the poor institutionalized in a given year. The poor were in and out of the public institutions, and these figures were based on the number of residents on a given day. A much larger percentage of the population would have experienced the horrors of institutionalized poverty.[28] The figures for Philadelphia were kept differently. In the three years between 1824 and 1827, 10,730 were admitted to the Philadelphia almshouse alone. Allowing for the fact that a number of these were admitted several times, it probably still represented 5 percent of the population.[29] By 1830 nearly 5,000 were admitted in a single year. Baltimore, which generally reflected more traditional patterns of living and caring for the poor, in addition to its larger percentage of slaves, was admitting over 1,000 persons per year to its almshouses by 1830.[30]

All of the poor receiving public assistance, however, were not confined to the public institutions. Outdoor relief, while deemed an undesirable form of aid, was nonetheless common. In New York, 3,516 families, consisting of 16,417 persons, or approximately 10 percent of the population, received some assistance between April 1, 1814, and April 1, 1815.[31] In the 1820s the New York Dispensary was aiding six to ten thousand of the poor per year, and the society's strongest claim for public support was that they kept many of the poor from the almshouse.[32]

In Philadelphia there were 1,036 pensioners receiving outdoor relief in August 1826, not counting those being supported by the "Committee on Bastardy." While these figures indicate extensive poverty, they still do not adequately reflect the reality of the situation. There was considerable discrimination against certain classes of the poor, the blacks in particular. Of the 1,036 receiving outdoor relief in Philadelphia, only 41 were blacks, whom the committee on pauperism confessed to be "the class most notoriously improvident among us." While the free blacks of Philadelphia, making up about 10 percent of the total population, were by definition the poorest, they also constituted a small percentage of the institutionalized poor of Philadelphia.[33]

In addition to public agencies for the relief of poverty, there were incalculable numbers of private associations of varying sorts designed to aid the poor. In his detailed study of poverty in New York City, for example, Raymond A. Mohl discovered more than a hundred voluntary associations concerning themselves with poverty. Lamentably, Mohl made no attempt to determine the exact extent of poverty, although his evidence clearly supported his contention that poverty was increasing during the period before 1825. One committee estimated that one out of every seven New Yorkers received some kind of public or private assistance in 1817.[34]

In the absence of hard statistical data, it would not be inappropriate to determine the extent of poverty in the major cities by available religious data. In the early nineteenth century, unlike any other period in American history, attendance at religious services was a relatively precise indication of social status and wealth. The change in Reformed thinking about poverty, which evolved from a conception of divinely ordained social classes to one viewing poverty as the result of irreligion, was based largely on an analysis of social classes in America. However much the Reformed analysis ignored such basic phenomena as unemployment and lack of opportunity, it was correct in one aspect. Clearly the upper and middle classes in the cities attended church. The poor did not.

This situation was created in part by sociological conditions peculiar to the new industrialized urban environment. In colonial society the entire social atmosphere had been based largely on an extended family unit. Although this pattern was breaking down in the cities by the time of the American Revolution, early laws required that every unattached individual be connected with a family. The head of the household was responsible for the oversight of his extended family, which included servants or slaves and other individuals employed by the family, as well as immediate members of the family and other relatives. In this manner, nearly all classes of society were represented in the family unit.[35] Even when unfortunate members of society became wards of the state, they were normally placed in families who received compensation for their service.[36] These arrangements diffused the poor throughout the community and placed them under the constant surveillance of the substantial members of the community.

As a result of this social pattern, the poor, as well as the immediate family, were the responsibility of the head of the household. One of the most important of his social duties was to insure the attendance of his entire household upon divine worship. Throughout most of the colonial period, therefore, rich and poor, slave and free attended church together. All classes were subject to the religious instruction and discipline of the community.[37] The poor participated in and were affected by religious movements along with the rich.[38]

In the process of rapid growth and industrialization that followed the American Revolution, this pattern of housing began to disappear. As the number of employees per business establishment grew, the older household arrangements disappeared and the first working-class ghettos emerged. The churches were supported by the wealthier members of society and they were confined almost exclusively to their residential areas. This pattern of segregation and consequent lack of churches for the poor was well developed before it was noticed. By that time, in many instances, a whole generation of the poor had grown to maturity without religious instruction—without that "wholesome discipline" that the Reformed believed essential to social order.

It has been a powerful temptation for American historians to ascribe most of the nation's poverty to blacks or immigrants.[39] To be sure, immigrants increased the problem, but most of the poor before 1825 were American-born whites. Ward Stafford noted in 1817 that "many foreigners are lamentably ignorant, and the people of color have been sadly neglected; but no small proportion of the ignorant and destitute are white people, who were born in the city, and have lived there all their days."[40] Some reports greatly exaggerated the number of foreign paupers. The Philadelphia Committee on Pauperism, for example, emphasized that 385 of the 837 people in the almshouse in August 1826 were "foreigners." The committee, however, used place of birth rather than citizenship as the determining factor. It noted simply that of the 385, "many of these . . . have recently arrived in the country."[41]

Archibald Alexander's assessment of the situation late in the period accurately reflected prevailing Reformed opinion. According to Alexander, the poor needed religious instruction more than others because "their time is commonly completely occupied and their education defective." One could not hope to change this situation through political or social change; "the true remedy can only be found in raising their character, by instilling in to their minds sound religious instruction." Alexander believed poverty to be particularly appalling in America, since it was his firm conviction that "no evil is more threatening in free countries than the increase of pauperism." Fully convinced that religion was the only remedy, Alexander could only lament that "in most protestant churches in our large cities, you see very few of the poorest people."[42]

John Holt Rice reflected the same problem but in his own fashion. He explained that persons taught and disciplined as Christians "were industrious, frugal, and economical." For that reason there were no Christian paupers. The church people, Rice claimed, were the "most thriving people in the country."[43] Without considering the merits of his argument, he seems to have been correct in the final assertion.

When Stafford enumerated the lack of churches in the major cities, he made it clear that those without access to houses of worship were the poor. Stafford's description of the situation in New York in 1817 vividly portrayed the concentration of the poor in the nation's first ghettos. "While almost all the churches are in the lower, the great mass of the people are in the upper part of the city. When we find that in the upper part of the houses, which are comparatively small, contain from 4 to 12 families each, and that with these houses, the ground is almost completely covered, we cannot doubt that there are in that part of the city five times as many people on an area not one half as large, as there are on an area of equal size in the lower part." In the wealthiest section of town there was a concentration of sixteen churches in an area not one-half the size of the poverty-ridden seventh ward, which had a population of 12,000, an estimated 2,000 prostitutes, and one church. In three other wards with a population of 41,000 there were only eleven churches.[44] The situation was about the same in Philadelphia. Most of the churches were located in the residential area of the wealthy, while the poorer sections, Southwark and Northern Liberties, were practically destitute. Various estimates in Philadelphia between 1823 and 1826 were that there were between 55,000 and 80,000 unchurched poor.[45] By 1831, 130,000 of the 200,000 Philadelphians could not have found room in the churches had they desired to attend.[46]

This concentration of the upper classes in the Reformed churches in the cities was assisted by the deliberate action of the Reformed clergy. Rice himself gloried that many of the Virginia aristocracy who "formerly never went to church at all," had become Presbyterians. When Rice went to Richmond in 1812 as pastor of a newly formed church, one of his first activities was to persuade the congregation to sell the partially completed church and build "more centrally" so they could attract a larger and wealthier clientele.[47] John Blair Smith succeeded in transforming the Pine Street Presbyterian Church in Philadelphia from a lower middle class church to an upper class congregation in a new location with a chandelier from London and a wigged sexton, "the crucial rung on the ladder of social prestige."[48] The Brick Presbyterian Church in New York, which paid Gardiner Spring a salary twelve times the size of the annual missionary wages of the General Assembly, moved locations twice in the first quarter of the nineteenth century in order to keep near its wealthy members.[49]

Other social and economic factors militated against the poor attending church. Throughout most of the period, Reformed churches continued to charge pew rents that the poor could not afford to pay. Beyond this there is substantial evidence that the poor were not welcome in the churches. Stafford believed that "should the poor . . . so far overcome their natural diffidence, or, as some would say, be so impudent, as to enter these churches," they would not be given seats.[50] The social bigotry stemming from the segregation of the poor and rich reached the point in 1828 that "few masters are willing to have their apprentices with their families in church."[51] Indeed, the colonial system of social control by means of religion and the family structure had disintegrated in the large cities. Well over half the population—the poor—were beyond the reach of organized religion.

The society movement in its initial phases was the major Reformed response to this urban dilemma. If the churches were providing religious instruction for the substantial citizen, the societies would serve as agencies of social control for the poor. This dichotomy was pronounced in the period before 1825. Apparent in much of the society literature, it was bluntly phrased by an exuberant and youthful writer for the Bible Society of Union College. "Callous, indeed, must be that heart, which is unmoved by the degradation and impiety which abound among the destitute and the uncivilized." He had personally witnessed "scenes, which shock the ear of modesty, and benumb the sensibility of the virtuous and refined." While vice was not confined to the poor, the "middle and the higher walks of life" were served by the churches. The Bible Society of Union College would turn its attention "to the profligate and the vicious among the children of poverty.[52]

From an early date the Reformed recognized that some extraordinary measures were required for the religious instruction of the poor in the cities. The Presbyterian Society for the Promotion of Religion in the Benevolent Institutions of the City of Philadelphia was founded in 1802 to provide a chaplain for prisons and almshouses. The society acknowledged that its motives were "partly of the political kind," since without religious instruction the occupants of these institutions "may become the pests of society."[53] A similar effort was made by all the Reformed denominations in New York to provide religious instruction for the poor in that city's institutions. Ezra Stiles Ely initiated the action of 1810 with *A Sermon for the Rich to Buy, that They May Benefit Themselves and the Poor*. This called the attention of the religious public to the problem and a "subscription was drafted, and subscribed by a number of individuals who were principally of the Presbyterian and Dutch communion," to hire Ely as the "stated chaplain" of the city's institutions. Again the need for religious instruction of the poor was recognized in terms of "future pests of society." Ely's published diary, called *Visits of Mercy*, contains vivid descriptions of life in New York's public institutions.[54]

This kind of effort was only partial, as it ignored the vast numbers of the poor who were never confined to public institutions. In the first decade of the nineteenth century the Reformed made other limited efforts. In 1797 women from the large Presbyterian and Reformed Dutch churches in New York City founded the Society for Relief of Widowers and Orphans. Incorporated in 1802, this society was more concerned with the religious instruction of the children than with financial aid. The society declined to give aid in a "lavish or indiscriminate manner" but established four schools for the children, who were "placed, at a suitable age, in respectable families," where they could become "blessings to themselves and to their country."[55] A similar society was founded in Newark in 1803. This society gave some material relief, "never in money," and refused to aid any widow who refused "to put out at service or trades, such of her children as are fit, and to place the young ones of a proper age at school."[56]

Other early efforts emphasized solely religious instruction. Archibald Alexander organized an "Evangelical Society" in 1806 for the poor of Philadelphia who could not afford to pay pew rent. Alexander secured the services of about twenty "gentlemen" of various Philadelphia congregations to teach Bible classes in the poor districts. Divie Bethune, the active New York layman, was the moving force behind early efforts to provide religious instruction for the poor in New York.[57]

The efforts of Alexander and Bethune were early expressions of the Sunday school movement, which has long been acknowledged as designed for the poor. The first large-scale associated religious activity to reclaim America's poor, however, came in the form of Bible societies. The first of these, the Bible Society of Philadelphia, announced that "the poor, generally will thus claim the peculiar notice of the society."[58] Bible societies proliferated rapidly in the cities, and invariably the primary concern was with the poor. Founded in 1810, the New York Bible Society believed that the absence of Bibles in most homes could be "attributed to poverty."[59] The Bible societies of Charleston, Washington, Norfolk, and Somerset also declared poverty and the poor to be their primary concern. The new Jersey Bible Society in 1810 determined to put Bibles "into the hands of every poor family throughout the state."[60]

The Bible societies were joined by tract societies. Tracts were initially designed for the poor. They were small, could be printed and distributed easily and inexpensively, and were more apt to be read than books. According to the initial public communication of the American Tract Society, "This method of instruction is peculiarly calculated for the poor, and is especially demanded by the poor of an extended population. It is a method by which the blessings of a religious education may, to no inconsiderable degree, be extended to the lower ranks of society with peculiar facility."[61]

From 1809 to 1816 the Bible societies dominated the Reformed movement to provide religious instruction for the poor. After 1816 the Sunday school unions came to occupy a place of central importance. This was caused in part by the formation of the American Bible Society in 1816. Prior to this, Bible societies performed the various tasks of visiting the poor and some provided schools. To secure as widespread support as possible, however, the American Bible Society limited its activity to the distribution of the Bible "without note or comment" and would only recognize as auxiliaries those societies with this sole function.[62] It is not then surprising that Sunday school unions were founded with rapidity after that date.

Bibles and tracts were useless unless they could be read, and the American poor did not read. According to Samuel Blatchford, addressing the Female Union Society for the Promotion of Sabbath School in 1818, the multitudes in America could not afford the "time" necessary for an education because their "daily labour was requisite to procure their daily bread." As a result, "while the Bible was put into their hands, they were unable to read it." Using the Bible as the basic text, Sunday schools were to eliminate this problem.[63] Through the Sunday schools the poor were provided "such an education as might be attained in pious and well regulated families." In this fashion the New York Sunday School Union Society promised to curtail the "innumerable evils which spring from ignorance and want; that idleness, larceny, mendicancy, and the various forms of wickedness perpetrated by the lower classes."[64]

The Reformed efforts to reach the poor through the society method were climaxed by the formation of numerous local domestic missionary societies. These associations hired missionaries, who were more often than not Presbyterian, who worked in the poor districts and coordinated the activities of the other societies. The missionaries preached, organized Sunday schools, distributed tracts and Bibles, and kept the churches informed of conditions in the poor neighborhoods, where no "decent character" would go.[65] Some of the primary societies of this type were the Charleston Female Domestic Missionary Society, the Young Men's Domestic Missionary Society of Philadelphia, the Philadelphia City Mission, the Female Domestic Missionary Society of Philadelphia, and the Young Men's Missionary Society of Richmond. The Reformed Dutch Missionary Society also provided missionaries for New York City.[66]

If the societies were varied in regard to specific duties, their function was one. They were designed to perpetuate America's "free institutions" and bring in the millennium. An analysis of their statements and actions indicates that in many instances this meant nothing more or less than the maintenance of the existing social and political order. With religious instruction, or "the knowledge of the Lord," as the central agency of social control, the societies hoped to prevent pauperism and crime without necessarily eliminating poverty, to protect the rich, and to preserve republican government by forming the character of the voters. Believing that religion was the only force powerful enough to do this, the Reformed supporters of the societies rejected all other solutions and considered but few.

The Reformed believed that the work of the societies could prevent, and possibly eliminate, pauperism by making the poor industrious and frugal through religious instruction. According to the managers of the Bible Society of the District of Columbia, virtue spread proportionate to the distribution of the Bible. "Idleness had been supplanted by industry, intemperance by sobriety, and general improvidence by prudent management." Thus the Bible became "a powerful antidote . . . to pauperism and all its direful train of miseries."[67] The New York Bible Society claimed that as a result of its work many were "fast yielding to a settled character for sobriety, frugality, and industry."[68] J. P. K. Henshaw of Baltimore, addressing the American Sunday School Union, declared the Sunday school system the best ever devised to do away with the problem of poverty.[69] Jonas King, Presbyterian missionary for the Charleston Female Domestic Missionary Society, asked the rhetorical question, "What renders some parts of our own society, better men than others?" and quickly answered, "Because they have received more *religious* instruction." Only religion could cure "the prodigality . . . , idleness . . . , and indigence" that produced the poor.[70]

The Reformed community's beliefs about the connection between poverty and religion were perhaps never more elaborately stated than by Jacob C. Spears, of the Reformed Dutch Church of Spring-Garden Street in Philadelphia, in an address before the American Home Missionary Society in 1826. He saw poverty as the direct result of sin. The poor then were often "excluded from common social advantages" and "over-awed by the stern aspect of poverty." Under these circumstances "every ambition is suppressed, every incentive to exertion is lost." Only religion could supply the force necessary to overcome such poverty. Let the missionary enter the "forlorn habitations" of the poor and "indolence, discord, and ignorance are chased from their dwellings." Then the poor would "rise in the scale of being" and become "useful members of society," promoting both the "happiness of the community" as well as the Kingdom of God.[71]

This view of religion as the cure for poverty was not only the belief of the specifically religious organizations but was at the core of most early nineteenth-century plans to cope with poverty. Raymond A. Mohl, in his study of poverty in New York City, isolated four "cures" for poverty offered during the period, which he categorized as work, education, religion, and temperance.[72] David J. Rothman, in his study of the asylum, pointed to the same categories but stressed that the contemporary emphasis was on the total environment.[73] Actually, religion stood at

the core of all of these "cures." Religion, as already noted, was believed
to produce industry and sobriety. Education was almost synonymous
with religious instruction. Any environment without religion would have
been considered defective.

The Female Hospitable Society of Philadelphia illustrated perfectly
the connection between religion and work as a cure for poverty. The
society was best known for its "manufactory," which employed the poor
mostly in sewing. According to the second article of its constitution,
however, the society was designed "to administer spiritual as well as
temporal relief." One of the society's functions was the distribution of
Bibles and tracts.[74] Other societies operated on the same conceptions.
Shortly after the Charleston Bible Society was organized, "a small society . . . for the promotion of Honesty and Industry" dissolved and transferred its funds to the Bible society.[75] The Provident Society of Philadelphia also furnished work for the poor and provided religious instruction.[76]
The missionary for the Philadelphia City Mission was also the agent
for the Society for Bettering the Conditions of the Poor.[77] The American Society for the Encouragement of Domestic Manufactures argued
that manufacturing establishments prevented pauperism, not only
because they provided work but also because in most places the morals of the workers were directly supervised. It is not surprising that
the leadership in this society was also connected with the distinctly religious society movement. The president was the governor of New York,
Daniel D. Tomkins, who supported many religious societies, and the first
vice-president was Stephen Van Rensselaer.[78]

In the community generally, and among the Reformed specifically,
industry was considered to be the product of religious training. This
aspect of the so-called "Protestant ethic" had not yet developed into the
vicious justification for extreme wealth that emerged later in the century, but it did serve the function of making a moral distinction between
the haves and the have-nots. In spite of abundant evidence in the society
literature that poverty and extreme suffering occurred in the face of
unremitting toil, the Reformed continued to insist that work would overcome poverty.[79] The Female Domestic Missionary Society of Philadelphia suggested to those not willing to give to any society "not designed to
give immediate employment to the poor" that "many of the poor are not
willing to be employed." The Bible, tract, and missionary societies could
overcome that by teaching "that industry brings its own reward; that
idleness is the root from which great evils spring; and that it is a crime,
for which they will have to give account, at that great day."[80]

The emphasis on temperance was a more obviously religious phenomenon that enjoyed a rather remarkable evolution during the early
nineteenth century. In the early part of the period temperance was
merely one of the many desirable traits inculcated by religious instruc-

tion. The Bible Society of Philadelphia noted in 1809 that the Bible teaches "the drunkard to be sober."[81] It was assumed that the religious instruction fostered by the societies would produce temperance. The American Sunday School Union, for example, contended that its efforts had "produced habits of sobriety, [and] temperance."[82]

During the 1820s, however, intemperance came to be classified as the largest single cause of pauperism. Persons responsible for the public institutions began giving statistical data on those committed to their care, and from those figures intemperance appeared to be the primary cause of poverty, disease, and crime.[83] The label of intemperance, like that of "foreigner," was easy to apply. Once this pattern was established in the public mind, any evidence of alcoholic consumption was deemed sufficient to establish cause. Nevertheless, the Reformed were motivated to action by their own easy answers to complex problems and engaged fully in associated activity to eliminate poverty by banning the demon.

The initial emphasis on temperance quickly developed into a widespread conviction that even temperate usage of intoxicating beverages was harmful. This analysis of the problem of poverty, however, called for a rather drastic change in the religious community itself. The Reformed clergy and laity had traditionally sanctioned the use of alcohol in moderation. In promoting temperance, and later "entire abstinence," as a means to prevent poverty, the Reformed themselves had to abandon a long-established social tradition among the upper classes. As a result, the Reformed entered the temperance crusade somewhat belatedly. The American Temperance Society was organized in 1826 with only partial support from the Reformed denominations of the middle and southern states. A representative from the American Temperance Society asked the General Synod of the Reformed Dutch church for support in 1827. The synod approved a resolution "to discourage the *indiscriminate* use of ardent spirit in family and social orders." By the next year, however, the movement was too strong to be resisted, and the General Synod unanimously adopted a resolution recommending "total abstinence" and encouraging the formation of auxiliary societies.[84] Thus, while the Reformed always emphasized "temperance" as a characteristic promoted by religious instruction, in the 1830s "total abstinence" became almost synonymous with communicating membership in the churches.[85] Temperance as a solution to poverty can not be divorced from religion.

The same was true with other solutions to the poverty problem. Religion was basic to both educational and institutional solutions to poverty. Almost all schools, elementary through collegiate, in the early nineteenth century featured Bible study. What was true in general was especially the case in schools designed for the poor. The Philadelphia Society for the Establishment and Support of Charity Schools had as its first regulation that the Bible should be studied daily. The charity schools in New York were dominated by the Reformed and had the same features.[86] While the Reformed insisted that the Bible form the basic text in all schools, they considered Sunday schools, which were more distinctively religious, the best form of education for the poor—and the one most likely to prevent poverty.[87]

Religion also formed a vital part of the institutions designed to eliminate poverty by creating controlled environments. The efforts of the Reformed to provide chaplains for the almshouses and other public institutions in New York and Philadelphia have already been noted. Actually, the New York group found it necessary to support the chaplain only for two years, as the city took over the responsibility. The general principle was nowhere better illustrated than in the houses of refuge in Philadelphia and New York. These asylums for juvenile delinquents were initiated by associated activity, featuring largely Reformed membership, but received extensive financial aid from local governments. The inmates, assigned by the courts, were educated and taught trades in the context of a "frequent exercise in religious duty." The twenty-eight hours of work each week were designed more for "moral benefits" than for "profits." The daily routine, similar in both places, featured daily worship at 5:30 A.M. and evening prayers at 8:00 P.M. Sundays featured preaching by different ministers in addition to Sunday schools.[88]

The extent to which religion was deemed to be *the* solution to the problem of poverty was best illustrated by the work of the New York Society for the Prevention of Pauperism, perhaps the best-known antipoverty organization of the early nineteenth century. The society did not hope to eliminate poverty but felt compelled to "lay the powerful hand of moral and legal restriction upon everything that contributes . . . to diminish, in any class of the community, a reliance upon its own powers of body and mind for an independent and virtuous support." With this in view the society attempted to list the causes and cures of poverty. They believed the causes to be: (1) "Ignorance," (2) "Idleness," (3) "Intemperance in Drinking" (the "cause of causes"), (4) "Want of Economy," (5) "Improvident and Hasty Marriages," (6) "Lotteries," (7) "Pawnbrokers," (8) "Houses of Ill Fame," (9) "The Numerous Charitable Institutions of the City" (the committee noted that indigence and helplessness multiply nearly in the ratio of those measures that are ostensibly taken to prevent them "by encouraging idleness"), and (10) "War." The committee's suggested "cures" were in line with its analysis of the causes of poverty. They suggested that the poor be visited and advised; that savings banks be promoted; that nonresident paupers be deported; that street begging be prevented; that employment be furnished; that most liquor shops be abolished; and that all charities be placed in one "well-regulated system." All of these "cures," however, were secondary to the necessity of religion. The committee noted, "If, as

we believe, nine tenths of the poverty and wretchedness which the city
exhibits, proceeds directly or indirectly from the want of correct moral
principle, and if religion is the basis of morality . . ." then the formation
of societies and "the opening of places of worship in the outer wards of
the city" were essential.[89] This society was, in fact, nothing more than
another association fostered by the Reformed. Three of its most prominent officers were Matthew Clarkson, Divie Bethune, and Zachariah
Lewis, who also participated in nearly all of the specifically religious
societies both locally and nationally.[90]

If religion was believed necessary for the prevention of poverty, its
social significance was enhanced in that poverty was believed to be the
most immediate and powerful threat to social order. In early nineteenth-
century America, as in other societies in other eras, no motivation was
more powerful than self-interest. As the Union Benevolent Association
of Philadelphia noted in 1831, "the comfort and well-being of every
individual are liable to disruption by the disorderly conduct and crimes
which too often accompany poverty."[91] The Reformed efforts to prevent
poverty through the religious societies was stimulated more by fear than
by any altruistic concern for the poor. The committee of the New York
Society for the Prevention of Pauperism voiced the common conviction
when it expressed the opinion that without a "radical change . . . the
numerical difference between those who are able to bestow charity and
those who sue for it, would gradually diminish, until the present system
must fall under its own irresistible pressure, prostrating perhaps, in its
ruin, some of the pillars of social order."[92] James Patterson, Presbyterian
missionary for a Philadelphia missionary society, warned the society that,
unless "religious instruction" was provided for the 80,000 poor of
Philadelphia, they would see "the very foundations of society sapped
before your eyes." The Christian religion, Patterson contended, "alone
contains in it the seeds of social order and stability."[93]

That the Reformed religious attack on poverty was preventive reform
cannot be seriously questioned. The elite and middle classes clearly
viewed religion as the most powerful means of sustaining the social
order—the status quo. While this point is verifiable by historical analysis
of the society movement, it was also confirmed by the frank statement of
leaders in the movement. Jacob Brodhead in 1831 called for "a uniform
system of national education" modeled on the Sunday school movement. This was particularly demanded for the poor who formed the
"majority . . . either absolutely or comparatively." Such religious education was necessary because "whenever industry, frugality and obedience
to the laws, form the decided character of the poor, *there* the rich will
have their rights respected, and at the same time, the poor will be contented and happy."[94]

The form of social control that characterized all the societies was dem-

onstrated in microcosm by those societies designed specifically for seamen. On the whole, this group of men, who spent a large portion of
their time at sea, were beyond the reach of organized religion and had a
reputation for boisterous behavior while in port. They were, however, a
very significant factor in the nation's economy. From an early date many
of the religious societies gave particular attention to them.[95] Since they
were regarded as a separate and special social class, societies specifically
designed for them soon emerged. The activity of the Marine Bible Society of New York, formed in 1817, clearly indicates how the Reformed
hoped to provide security for the rich by giving religious instruction to
the seamen. The society was supported by the same persons generally
involved in the religious societies of the city, with the addition of a
number of ship captains.[96] The society noted that "most of our Seamen
are unenlightened, and addicted to vices, which are peculiarly injurious
to themselves, to their employers, and to all with whom they are connected." The emphasis was clearly on "the ships which have been
wrecked" and "the property which has been wasted," by the "superstition, the intemperance, the insubordination, and other misconduct of
Seamen." The society proposed to remedy this situation through the
agency of "this blessed Book."[97] In 1821 the society produced the testimony of forty shipmasters that the distribution of Bibles made "better
men" of the seamen, and in 1822 the society noted that money donated
"would in all probability put ten times the sum into the hands of the
giver, by putting a trusty, careful and honest heart into the men to whom
his property is intrusted."[98]

The society hoped to aid the influence of the Bible by making employment of seamen contingent on moral character. This was to be accomplished by using a "record book" to "ascertain the moral character of
Seamen." Only those coming up to the standards of the society would be
recommended for employment. Seamen joining the society would be
given an identification card, which would certify their good character to
prospective employers and "recommend them to the benevolent and
pious in times of distress." These seamen, the society believed, "cannot
fail to exhibit a powerful influence over their brethren and induce them
to abstain from those vices, which disqualify them from the discharge of
their duties as Seamen, and as members of civil society."[99]

In 1826 a national society, the American Seamen's Friend Society, was
formed that retained most of the characteristics of the Marine Bible Society of New York but with expanded goals. This society supported
preaching and religious instruction for the seamen, and continued the
use of the "register's office." In addition, the society promoted
"boarding-houses of good character," to protect the sailors from temptation, and "savings-banks" to promote frugality and keep seamen from
becoming public charges.[100]

The self-interest of the Reformed attack on poverty was evident in the literature of other societies. The managers of the American Sunday School Union confirmed this sentiment in their *Eleventh Annual Report* in 1835.

> It has been well said, substantially, that the question of a system of moral education is, as it regards the great mass of citizens, a question of RE-DUCTION OF TAXATION—as it regards the few who constitute the wealthier class, it is a question of SECURITY. In the former case, it is a question what shall be the weight of public burdens; and in the latter, what proportion of wealth, or influence, or power, property-holders may retain; but cannot, if the multitude who represent the physical force of the country be not so enlightened as to become also a righteous moral force.[101]

The matter of taxation for the support of "idleness" was a significant social concern, and the Reformed promised that the religious instruction afforded by the societies would eliminate the necessity of poor taxes. The citizens of New York, Philadelphia, Baltimore, and Charleston were spending approximately $300,000 each year during the 1820s for the support of the poor.[102] This expenditure of funds was a necessity, but it received support from almost no one. The Reformed in particular viewed the bestowal of "pecuniary aid" as encouraging idleness and re-moving the incentive to labor.[103] James Patterson, missionary for the Philadelphia Missionary Society, warned that the poor tax would "in-crease unless some measures be taken to prevent the increase of vice and immorality."[104] Jonas King argued that the poor tax of Charleston would be better spent "for the support of missionaries." If, as he believed, "the greater part are rendered poor by *prodigality*, by *idleness*, and by *intemperance*—vices, which nothing but religion can remove," then a few thousand dollars yearly "from the public treasury" for missionaries could "save hundreds of thousands to this city."[105] Ward Stafford, who estimated that the actual cost of poverty in New York in 1816 was $750,000, argued that this could be saved by providing churches and Sunday schools for the poor.[106]

On the whole, however, the general religious society movement tended to define the threat of poverty more in political terms. One of the most prominent reasons for the Reformed concern about poverty was simply that in America the poor, potentially at least, had political power—they could vote. Historians have debated extensively the conse-quences of the extension of popular suffrage in the early decades of the nineteenth century. While it now seems most likely that it had very little real effect on the political process,[107] it did provide a significant motiva-tion for a parallel extension of social control. This was the primary focus of the societal activity of the Reformed.

The societies acted on the Reformed ideas that Protestant Christianity was necessary to the existence of civil liberty and republican government. In many ways the rationale that demanded religious instruction for the poor was the same used by the Reformed through most of the period to justify the continuation of slavery. Slaves could not be freed, they argued, because they were not prepared by religious education to exercise the responsibilities of citizenship. The poor, however, already possessed citizenship and were considered a much more immediate threat to social order.

The free blacks obstensibly occupied a similar position to the poor whites except for the operation of racial prejudice. The Reformed attitude toward the free blacks, in fact, demonstrated some inconsistencies in their attitude toward slavery and emancipation. Although the societies, and the Sunday schools in particular, devoted some attention to the religious education of free blacks in the cities,[108] the primary emphasis was on deporting free blacks through the American Colonization Society. It was a widespread conviction that "as American Citizens these men could never be free. And as American freemen, they could never be valuable."[109] For this reason, the other societies concentrated on "the white native population."[110]

A related factor was the gradual disfranchisement of the free blacks during the period. Having no effective political power, the blacks were less of a threat from the Reformed point of view. The largest number of free blacks were in New York, New Jersey, and Pennsylvania. New York disfranchised the Negro in 1821 by constitutional "reform," and New Jersey accomplished the same through legislative action. Pennsylvania did not formally exclude blacks until 1837, but the force of public opinion effectively prevented the blacks from voting much earlier.[111] The presence of a given number of free blacks, who increased from 59,481 in 1790 to 233,530 in 1820, was a cause of considerable concern, but the solutions offered by the Reformed were different than for the poor whites. In part, the supremacy of the debate over slavery in the social consciousness of Americans, from the 1830s to the present, has served to deemphasize, and in some cases suppress, the equally significant relationship of white social classes.[112]

During the period after the War of 1812 the suffrage was considerably extended. Ten states revised their old constitutions or wrote new ones, in each case extending the franchise. The New York constitution increased the number of eligible to vote by about 30 percent. Perhaps of equal or greater significance in the urban areas, however, was the diminishing of deferential voting that accompanied the breakdown of the household system.

The religious voluntary societies were concerned that the voters be controlled by religion. A speaker at a July Fourth Sunday school gathering in Utica, New York, came straight to the point with the rhetorical question, "Does not the vote of a poor man at your polls count as much as the vote of a rich man?" Without religious instruction "this interesting and important class of citizens" would "corrupt the whole body politic," and the government would be controlled by "an unprincipled mob, who care neither for law nor religion."[113] J. P. K. Henshaw, rector of Saint Peter's Church in Baltimore, advised the audience at the annual convention of the American Sunday School Union in 1833 that the franchise could not be given to the ignorant and irreligious without some restrictions. According to Henshaw, "where the government is dependent on the popular will, and, without preference of birth or fortune, all are entitled to the rights of citizenship . . . our only security . . . is the intelligence and virtue of the people."[114]

The desire to in some way control the votes of the poor, the distinctly political expression of public opinion, was not necessarily motivated by party considerations. While some politicians may well have hoped to enhance their political prospects through the operation of the societies, the total movement was more basic and fundamental. Through contending political parties America's elites vied with each other for power. Through the religious societies, many of these same elites came together to make this possible. The society movement represented the most sustained and concerted attempt of the minority—the rich—to control the majority—the poor. William Wirt explained the situation while arguing for the necessity of Sunday schools. In this concern "the narrow spirit of political party, or of temporal domination of the church" had no place, for "the great objects in view are of universal concern." In monarchies, he pointed out, the great and powerful were influential. In America the situation was different. "The people in truth hold the upper place among us." They were in fact "the natural fountain of all powers." The only "power" that could control them was "the Gospel of the Redeemer carried home to the heart by his spirit."[115]

The related concerns of poverty and political stability, a feature of the society movement from the beginning, became more pronounced with the formation of the "national" societies. The American Bible Society noted in 1816 that "the political world has undergone changes stupendous, unexpected, and calculated to inspire thoughtful men with the most boding anticipation." The society feared that the population of the United States would revert to a "species of heathenism which shall have all the address and profligacy of civilized society, without any religious control."[116] In 1817 the New York Sunday School Union Society saw its activities as related to "the continuance of civil and religious liberty, which, from a form of government adopted to secure that blessing to the country, is so dependent on the intelligence, the morality, and the happiness of the lower classes of Society."[117] The parent of the national Sunday school society, the Philadelphia Sunday and Adult School

Union, warned in 1823 of the futility of electing men "renowned for wisdom, to enact laws . . . if the body of the people remained uninstructed in the great leading truths of divine revelation."[118] The American Tract Society in its initial communication with the public in 1825 expressed its purpose as "securing and augmenting our civil and political liberties." In America, "so long as public opinion maintains its existing supremacy," this could be done only by molding public opinion "by a moral and religious influence." America's "political existence," they believed, "depends on the intelligence, and, more especially, on the integrity of the people."[119]

If the society movement was fostered by the concentration of the population in urban areas, it was easily adapted to a population expanding to the frontier. The Reformed concern for the frontier developed parallel to that of the cities and was expressed in similar terms. The pressures of urban poverty, however, were closer at hand and tended to absorb most of the associated resources. By the time of the formation of the national societies in the late 1820s, the already awesome political power of the West led them to concentrate on that region. The city mission movement continued unabated, but was supervised by local societies that were auxiliary to a national society. Since the concern for the frontier is well known,[120] it need not be extensively reviewed, except to point out the similarities to the urban religious movement. The constants were expanding population, poverty, political power, and the Reformed ideology. The only significant variable was space.[121]

From the Reformed point of view, religion and wealth were related on the frontier as well as in the cities. The Presbyterian Education Society noted in 1824 that there was a flaw in the plan to trust "the extension of our religious institutions to the voluntary and unasserted efforts of the people." The primary problem in the "new settlements" was that "the first settlers are men of little or no property."[122] John F. Bliss, the Presbyterian missionary for the New York Evangelical Missionary Society, reported in 1821 that the major problem in western New York was that "the inhabitants are so poor . . . it is impossible to find permanent materials for constituting churches."[123] The editor of the *Panoplist,* in reviewing a report of the American Education Society, noted that the "emigrants have usually been destitute of property, and not strongly attached to their religious privileges." The best way to establish religion on the frontier would be for "men of considerable property" to form "well organized little colonies." It was his belief that "there are no circumstances, in which wealth does so much good, as in the settlement of new countries."[124] It would be a long time before the West would have enough wealth to support religion. In the meantime, the eastern upper classes would have to furnish it for the frontier as they did for the urban poor.

The rapid growth of the population and the acquisition of political power were synonymous. The American Tract Society calculated in 1828 that the West would contain 12,000,000 inhabitants within twenty years, making "the majority of our whole population." The society was sure that those who cared about America's "free institutions and civil privileges . . . will not fail to pray and labor, that a knowledge of the Gospel may be diffused throughout our destitute population." Without such immediate effort, the managers could envision "civil revolutions and dissensions, the tumult of arms, the confiscations of property. . . ." Only Christianity could maintain America's "free institutions."[125]

The methods that the Reformed presented to regulate and control the American population, in order to perpetuate "civil and religious liberty" and "free institutions," were as significant as the attempt itself. The poor in America were not easily controlled. One writer for the *American Sunday School Magazine,* identifying himself as "S," argued that the very "spirit of our republican institutions" made the poor of the United States harder to control than the poor of Europe. American institutions imparted "the earliest bias of independency to the minds of the poorest and most ignorant class." To this writer the poor presented a "moral anomaly, being at once abject, yet high minded and independent." According to "S," the character of the American poor and previous unsuccessful attempts demanded that any steps taken for their reform "should be in the most engaging disguise and in direct conjunction with a plan that proposes some secular promotion, profit, or advancement." He suggested that Sunday schools, free schools, savings plans, and houses of industry were the most appropriate tools.[126]

The principal method of the Reformed was "the knowledge of the Lord," or religious instruction—indoctrination. The Reformed merely transferred their ideas about the way to train their own children to the dependent classes in America. Ashbel Green frankly compared the Indians, blacks, and the poor with children and emphasized the need to "instill into the minds of the rising generation, the principles of sound morals and of Christian piety."[127] Religious instruction in this case had nothing to do with salvation; in Reformed thought, it would prepare the mind for the later reception of the Holy Spirit. While the Reformed believed that salvation was solely the work of God, they believed as firmly that everyone should be controlled by Christian teaching. As Charles Hodge noted, there were actually very few active Christians, but many were under the influence of the Bible. The principle aim was "to bring the word of God to bear effectually on the formation of human character."[128] Therefore the work of the societies was to control the development of character by control of the mind. In this work the Sunday school and tract societies were most significant. If the education and missionary societies provided and supported the ministers, and the national Bible society furnished the basic textbook, the tract societies and Sunday school unions established the proper emphasis and dealt with the poor directly. The American Sunday School Union, because it furnished both reading material and teachers, was the most important.

The Reformed intended to educate the poor in such a way that every action, every response, would be predictable, controlled by their instructions. In the language of the twentieth century, they hoped to "program" the entire American population. Heman Humphrey, addressing the American Sunday School Union, characterized it as "*simplification.*" No child was educated properly, he argued, until his mind was formed by a pious education "commencing with the dawn of intellect, and continued till his character is formed and settled" so that he has "virtuous habits of thought, of feeling, and of action." Humphrey was convinced that "there is something in the power of habit . . . which is extremely difficult to overcome."[129] At the same occasion a year earlier, Francis Wayland, the Rhode Island Baptist, emphasized that "education consists in so cultivating the mind, as to render it more powerful, and a more exact instrument for the acquisition, the propagation, and the discovery of truth, and a more certain guide for the regulation of conduct."[130] The supporters of Sunday schools believed that the only way to regulate conduct this precisely was to control the mind from the earliest age. In 1831 the managers of the American Sunday School Union asserted that "every thing a child sees or hears, or reads, should be in strict conformity to truth." This was the case not only with religious and moral instruction, but with history or the study of nature. Impressions on the mind were "so deep, vivid and permanent," that "the utmost care should be taken to have them rigidly exact." Any reading material not coming up to these standards should be excluded with "scrupulous fidelity."[131]

As a result of their convictions, both the American Sunday School Union and the American Tract Society exercised close censorship of the materials they published. At a later date, when this practice created considerable antagonism among the contending factions in the Reformed denominations, it was questioned, but as applied to the poor there was no disagreement among the Reformed.[132] The committee on publication of the American Sunday School Union, consisting of five members from different denominations, admitted to "the immense responsibility which they assume, in becoming dictators to the consciences of thousands," while vowing that they were "not backward to become the responsible arbiters in these high points." The committee found it necessary not only to modify "the language and even the ideas" of some material, but in some cases of "directly opposing the opinions of the original writers."[133] The American Sunday School Union approached a claim of infallibility when it declared that "nothing contrary to sound doctrine or morals has been, or will be tolerated, except from the short-sightedness, which is incident to humanity."[134]

But the societies could not accomplish the desired goal without doing something about literature generally. The managers of the American Sunday School Union complained that many books were "abounding with foolishness, vulgarity and falsehood, or otherwise deficient in relation to their moral influence." Among the books specifically criticized were *Robinson Crusoe, Mother Goose,* and the Waverly novels.[135] The managers of the American Sunday School Union believed that the only solution was to make their own books "so abundant as to force out of circulation those which tend to mislead the mind."[136] When the American Sunday School Union was criticized for the statement of these intentions, the action was justified as being as open and public as it was "necessary."[137]

In devising a total body of literature for the American poor, however, the American Sunday School Union found it necessary to conceal the religious instruction in an "engaging disguise." Some students rejected "truth, broadly exhibited, though with apostolic eloquence and zeal." In this case, according to the American Sunday School Union, "that which offends must be so mingled with that which is agreeable, as scarcely to be discerned." Operating on these convictions, the American Sunday School Union attempted to print enough books to supply entire libraries. Many of the books were "edited," and others were written expressly for the American Sunday School Union.[138] One of the American Sunday School Union's favorite books was a biography of George Washington designed "to present to the mind of the youthful reader something of novelty, and entertainment, and instruction in almost every paragraph." In commenting on Washington at Valley Forge, for example, the author noted, "But though he was 'walking in the midst of troubles,' he was not forsaken by God." It was also said that had Washington lived, "he would have rejoiced" over the existence of Sunday schools.[139]

The policy of total indoctrination followed by the American Sunday School Union was also reflected in the evolution of teaching methods. At first the scholars were encouraged to memorize verses of Scripture and the catechism. While some students performed prodigious feats, it was discovered that they often did not understand, or understand properly, that which they had committed to memory. It was argued that such mental activity produced hydrocephalous. In 1825 the American Sunday School Union introduced a uniform lesson system. In addition to its uniformity, this system allowed the teachers to explain the lesson, thereby insuring that the right sentiments were communicated.[140] The more significant change, however, was concerned with the intellectual tools taught in the Sunday schools. At first the students were taught reading, spelling, and writing. By the later 1820s, however, the teaching of writing was discontinued.[141] One-way communication was more conducive to total indoctrination.

One other adjustment was made in the late 1820s to make indoctrination more effective. The Sunday schools did not work with very young children. Yet many of the Reformed were convinced that it was impossible to mold a child to the desired characteristics without religious instruction from a very early age. Again the initial drive came from the large cities. In 1827 infant school societies were formed both in New York and Philadelphia, designed to teach children from eighteen months to six years of age. The New York group, encouraged by DeWitt Clinton and meeting in the Brick Presbyterian Church, complained of the "neglect of indigent or uneducated parents" that produced toddlers "addicted to the vices of stealing, lying and swearing." The societies' first school featured a little room with barred windows, "styled the Bridewell," used for punishing the children.[142] But the primary emphasis was still on mental indoctrination. According to one argument for infant schools in the *American Sunday School Magazine*, "the mind must be laid hold of, the dawn of thought must be directed, a bias must be given and then the difficulty in forming the character is removed."[143] The American Sunday School Union immediately began to promote infant schools. By 1832 it was printing a substantial quantity of material for use in such schools, and in 1833 and 1834 the American Sunday School Union determined to place greater emphasis on infants.[144]

If the societies offered secular advancement as an inducement to the poor, the burden of their teaching was to promote contentment with poverty. The religious instruction featured an emphasis on industry, frugality, sobriety, contentment, and submission in the context of piety. The whole thrust of the movement was to eliminate the social and political problems imposed by poverty by changing the character of the poor rather than their circumstances. It was a common conviction that "it will rarely be found to happen, that poor persons ... who had also the advantage of suitable instruction have become mendicants."[145] According to John M. Krebs, "The influence of the Gospel on its subjects is to make them sober, chaste, contented, humble, industrious, gentle, benevolent, and just." Therefore religious instruction was "preventive of crime; of pauperism."[146] Such submissiveness also made the poorer classes easy to rule. There was, in fact, a direct parallel between the Reformed argument for religious instruction of the poor and of the slaves. Slaves, it was alleged, needed religious instruction because it made them better workers and more content.[147]

The emphasis was the same whether taught directly or veiled. For example, the New York Female Union Society for the Promotion of Sabbath Schools had its scholars recite Scriptural proof to the following questions.

51. Of the sin and consequence of lying.
52. That we ought to be content, and not wish for anything that belongs to another.
53. That we ought to esteem the ministers of the Gospel very highly.

54. That we ought to honour the King and obey Rulers and Magistrates.
55. What are duties of Masters and Servants?[148]

Samuel Byard's catechism, widely used in Sunday schools, instructed that the "duty of the poor" was "to be humble, patient, laborious, and resigned to the will of God, without envying, nor taking from others by any unlawful means their property; but after they have by all lawful means sought to supply their needs, remain content with that portion which God permits them to possess."[149] The catechism further taught submission to magistrates and masters, even if wicked.

The extent to which the poor were expected to be content and submissive, however, emerged more clearly in the tracts published by both the American Sunday School Union and the American Tract Society. Some of the more popular ones are illustrative. "The Poor Man's Friend" was the narration of a conversation between a poor man and his wife, as overheard by a man who had sought shelter from the rain in a nearby shed. To his wife, who expressed dissatisfaction with her position in the world, the man replied, "Riches would never make us happier, so long as the Lord sees it good that we should be poor." His wife reminded him that a neighbor had "risen" in the world. "Wife," he responded, "having food and raiment, let us therewith be content." Even if God should withhold food and clothes, the man admonished, they should still be satisfied because "he gives us more than we deserve." His wife then said that she objected to preaching and Bible quoting, to which the man replied, "Why, that book has taught me, that it is an honor and a comfort to be a poor man."[150]

Through a story called the "Remarkable Benevolence," the poor were encouraged to be content even in the face of wrongdoing by their superiors. A poor man who worked "long hours" for a "Christian man" but was never paid remained patient and prayed. One day a passing stranger gave the poor man a piece of silver. The tale ended, "If the poor Christian is led to further perseverance in his confidence in God ... this memorable instance of God's paternal care will not have been recorded in vain."[151]

The American Tract Society's publication, "Blind Ellen," emphasized contentment under the severest of circumstances. Ellen was described as a poor, lame, and blind old woman "whose habits of frugality and industry afford a useful example to persons in humble life; and whose cheerfulness, thankfulness, and submission to the providence of God, may be considered with advantage, by persons in every station." Blinded at a young age, Ellen worked "from Monday until Saturday, excepting the few moments which her meals required." In order to conserve time, she prepared enough bread to last for three or four weeks. By tireless labor she managed a normal diet of bread, "blue milk," and potatoes. When she could not secure that, she fixed a broth made of onion, salt, and pepper. Ellen never complained. Her best dress was fifty years old, but clean. She never begged, being convinced that "God knows better what I want than I do myself, and he always sends what is needful for me."[152]

The favorite story of many of the Reformed was "The Dairyman's Daughter." The daughter was "hired out to service" at an early age, but spent all of her money on clothes. After she became religious, however, she saved her money to help her aging and indigent parents. "My dress," she was made to say, "like that of too many gay, vain, and silly servant girls, was much above my station." Although her clothes were not fancy, they were clean and neat, "those sure marks of pious and decent poverty." Although dying of tuberculosis and overwork, she was content. She died in peace.[153] The managers of the American Sunday School Union said of this tale, "who that understands the immortal relations of his being, would not rather be the author of "The Dairyman's Daughter," than of the Waverly novels?"[154]

In the large cities the policy of indoctrination was supplemented by an attempt to bring the poor under the surveillance of the religious community. This was in effect an effort to recreate in the city a form of social control believed to be effective in smaller places or with the colonial household arrangements. Again Ward Stafford's analysis was perceptive. He noted, "It cannot be in the city, in every respect as it is in the country, where the character and circumstances of every family is almost necessarily known." In villages the factor operated "as a strong motive to restrain those who are not under the influence of the gospel." Stafford pointed out that many people who attended church in their native place of residence did not do so when they came to the city. "Let every man's character and conduct be known," he contended, "and a change in the state of society will be effected."[155]

Many of the early societies pursued this line of control. In 1811 the Philadelphia Bible Society appointed men to visit the poor and make "the most particular inquiries into the character of those who should apply for bibles."[156] The New York Society for the Prevention of Pauperism recommended in 1818 that the city be divided into small districts and that the poor be visited on a regular basis.[157] The Female Domestic Missionary Society of Philadelphia appointed committees to visit the poor.[158]

Later this technique of social control was greatly expanded. The efforts in Philadelphia illustrate the point. In 1831 the Philadelphia City Mission, which was primarily a religious organization supported by the Presbyterians, Associate Reformed, Baptists, and Episcopalians, divided the city into thirty-four districts and each district into sections of about twenty families. The society proposed to hire an agent for each district to visit the poor personally and to supervise a core of visitors. It was the intention of the society that each family "shall be visited once in two weeks by a male or female member of the society."[159] That same year the Union Benevolent Association was formed to devise "permanent measures for ameliorating the condition of the poor, and preventing pauperism." This society, pledged to work with all religious sects, also proposed to divide the city into districts to provide "direct supervision" and keep the poor "constantly under the eye of the visitors."[160]

It would be impossible to assess with any precision the extent of influence the religious societies had on the American nation. However, if there was any relationship between the quantity of material published for and extensiveness of contact with the American people, the influence of the societies must have been great. By 1836 the American Tract Society alone had published 43,647,590 items, almost three for every person in the nation, consisting of 711,853,750 pages. By 1829 the American Bible Society had managed to print over a million Bibles. The quantity of publication by the American Sunday School Union was equally impressive. By June 1828 the society had published over five million books in addition to other Sunday school materials. At the same time the American Home Missionary Society was aiding about one thousand churches a year and the American Education Society was supporting an equal number of youth studying for the ministry. In 1833 the American Sunday School Union claimed 760,000 scholars and 109,000 teachers in 14,550 schools. In 1830 the combined income of the twenty-nine leading societies, eleven located in New England and eighteen in the middle and southern states, was $600,000. When compared to other American institutions, even the federal government, the religious societies were by far the most intimately involved in the daily lives of American citizens. Such widespread and sustained activity could not fail to make a significant impact on the character of American society.[161]

Chapter 8

Revivalism:
Salvation and the
Social Order

The religious society movement prospered in the decade after 1826 in spite of deep-seated and growing divisions among the ranks of the Reformed in the middle and southern states. By 1837 these contentions had destroyed the possibility of reaching the societies' goals of controlling the United States by religious instruction. The divisiveness affected all the Reformed denominations but was most severe among the Presbyterians. The schism between the Old School and New School Presbyterians in 1837 symbolized the end of an era. The period from 1826 to 1837 was as eventful in religious developments as it was in political, social, and economic areas. Because of the significance of this decade, many historians have turned their attention to its outstanding features—schism, abolitionism, temperance, and revivalism. In national terms, however, the most significant development was an evolution in the religious mode of social control from indoctrination to salvation. The national goals of the Reformed of all parties remained relatively unchanged. All continued to argue the necessity of religious control for the preservation of republican government and civil and religious liberty. All parties still believed that America would lead the world into an imminent millennium. The argument was over how these goals could be achieved. During this period the Old School method of social control through religious indoctrination gave way to the New School method of social control through individual conversion. In this evolution the influence of New England was pronounced, but the major change occurred among the Reformed of the middle and southern states.

This analysis may indeed give some insight into the larger questions arising from Jacksonian America. The temptation has been great to argue that the broader diffusion of religious salvation was an expression of Jacksonian Democracy. William G. McLoughlin, for example, noted that revivalism represented "the essence of the quarrel between the Whigs and the Jacksonians: the fight against aristocracy and privilege had a clear parallel in religion."[1] The extension of salvation, however, was clearly believed to be a more effective way of controlling the masses. At the same time, there seems to have been some shift in the constituency of the ruling elite. If indeed there was some "clear parallel" between religious and political developments, Jacksonian "democracy" would represent the methods of a new elite to secure and augment their power. Whether exercising the suffrage or claiming salvation, the common men, the poor, were functioning in behalf of others. Whatever personal satisfaction the common man gained came from a sacrifice of power.

It is often asserted that the "benevolent societies . . . had come about as the fruit of what were called 'revivals of religion.'"[2] Whatever may have been the case in New England, an analysis of the Reformed tradition in the middle and southern states indicates that there was no connection between revivalism and the society movement before 1826. In fact, in terms of social function the two phenomena were polar opposites. While the societies were designed expressly for the poor, revivals were occasions for the upper classes to claim salvation and the right of church membership. In the 1820s this type of revivalism, associated with the Old School Presbyterians and most of the other Reformed denominations, was threatened and ultimately surpassed by the type of revivalism supported by such New School men as Charles Grandison Finney and Albert Barnes. The new revivalism was applied to all classes of society and was therefore compatible with the society movement. The amalgamation of revivalism with the societies was one of the most divisive issues among the Reformed from 1826 to 1837.

The older form of revivalism was a time of "refreshing" within the church. It was characterized by increased attention to religion among church members and by the addition to the church of those persons properly instructed in orthodox theology. These were usually the children of established church members. It was believed that these were converted by the action of the Holy Spirit, but it was assumed that only those having an intellectual and rational grasp of orthodox theology could be subjects of conversion. Church sessions carefully examined all those professing salvation to see if they could give "reason of the hope." Such examinations called for rational and orthodox explanations of the Christian religion. The emphasis on such detailed knowledge of theology required extensive religious instruction and indicated that revivals occurred primarily among the elite. Thus the old type of revivals were usually confined to those already influenced by the churches and were more properly a part of internal development than an instrument to implement the national goals of the Reformed.

The best single exposition of this form of revivalism appeared after the new revivalism was firmly established. In 1832 William B. Sprague published *Lectures on Revivals of Religion* in order to counteract the influence of the new revivalism. Sprague declared that it was his intention to "vindicate and advance the cause of *genuine* revivals." To do this he would point out the distinction between a "genuine revival and a spurious excitement," because it was necessary to "guard against the abuses to which revivals are liable."[3] Sprague's efforts were supported by the most influential ministers from both the moderate and militant Old School. The work contained an appendix with twenty letters of recommendation by such well-known figures as Archibald Alexander, Samuel Miller, William Neill, Ashbel Green, and Edward D. Griffin.

Sprague wrote with a perceptive awareness of the increased social significance of revivals. He noted that the church in America was "more deeply and practically interested" in this subject than any other. Already most conversions occurred "during revivals of religion," and "as the millenial day draws near, these effusions of the Holy Spirit will be yet more frequent and powerful." Sprague also discerned that in the future revivalism and the society movement would be united. Declaring that achievements in the "moral renovation" in America were attributable to the operation of the "benevolent institutions," Sprague noted, "Now, this moral machinery, so far as our country at least is concerned, is evidently to be sustained and increased through the influence of revivals." These two great forces were "hereafter to go hand in hand—the one being sustained and cherished in a great degree by the other, until the earth shall be filled with the Redeemer's glory." Because of their extreme significance then, revivals needed to be properly understood and directed.[4]

In defining a "genuine" revival, Sprague stressed the primacy of a rational understanding of Christianity. A revival was "a revival of scriptural knowledge; of vital piety; of practical obedience." The first stage of a revival occurred when there was "an *increase of zeal and devotedness on the part of God's people.*" Only then did the unconverted become concerned about their salvation. Of these perhaps only a few would be "indulging a hope" that they had been "born of the Spirit." It was no mark of a genuine revival that there was a "*great excitement*" or when "*great numbers profess to be converted.*" Orthodox, doctrinal preaching rather than the exercise of "animal passions" characterized a genuine revival. According to Sprague, "the Holy Spirit employs the truth . . . in the work of conversion; and the truth can never find its way to the heart, except through the understanding."[5]

When applied to revivalism this emphasis on "knowledge," which permeated all Reformed thought for the first quarter of the nineteenth century, necessarily limited salvation to the middle and upper classes. During the early part of this period Reformed revivalism consistently reflected three primary characteristics. It was associated with educational activities, confined primarily to youth, and was therefore essentially elitist. This was particularly the case in the urban areas and the established regions generally. In developing areas before 1825 Reformed revivalism often served what Donald G. Mathews has characterized as an organizational function.[6] In these places, the revivals brought the local elite, who may not have been so defined in more established locales, together in churches and helped organize these communities along the same patterns already existing in the more settled regions. While this phenomenon largely occurred in the West, including the Southwest, it also occurred in new communities in urban areas. This stage helped break down the prevailing social functions of revivalism and prepare the way for the new revivalism, which featured salvation by a single human decision rather than knowledge and was extended to all classes of society.

The Reformed firmly believed that most people were saved in their youth and only as the result of a proper education. John M. Mason pointed out that it was the "ordinary method of providence to call sinners into the fellowship of Jesus Christ in the *days of their youth.*" For those receiving "the benefit of religious instruction," the "instances of conversion after middle life" were "extremely rare."[7] An anonymous contributor to the *Christian Advocate* affirmed that "a majority—probably a large majority—of all that are ever pious, have become so between the ages of fifteen and thirty."[8] Thomas DeWitt explained that this was the case because youth were "more manageable" and their consciences were "more readily impressed."[9] Because of this emphasis on salvation during youth, the Reformed either denied the possibility or doubted the probability of conversion in old age, and particularly death-bed repentance. Many connected this wholly with the declining rational powers accompanying old age. According to Samuel Stanhope Smith, "the powers of reformation and repentance are lost with the powers of reason and reflection."[10] This conception of the ordinary process of conversion reflected the existing pattern. The hope of salvation usually came to church members' children in their youth as the result of their religious instruction.

This normal and highly desired pattern was sufficiently interrupted in the decades around the turn of the century to cause extensive concern among the Reformed. In many ways the situation was comparable to that of prerevival colonial New England, which produced the Half-Way Covenant and communion as a means of conversion. The "infidelity" abounding in the nation's colleges in the 1790s has been elaborated upon frequently. It was estimated that in the decade following 1800 only one out of six college students was "hopefully pious."[11] Almost by definition, these college students were the male children of the Reformed elite who had been baptized in infancy.

One of the most persisting problems faced by the Reformed during the period was the discipline of baptized children. Baptism itself was carefully guarded. The Reformed Dutch refused baptism to children of parents with "such a want of knowledge in the first principles of our holy religion, as to render them unfit to make a public profession of their faith."[12] The Presbyterians attempted to uphold the same standards.[13] As one man said to Gardiner Spring, after Spring had refused to baptize the man's child, "I perceive, sir, that you baptize only the children of the aristocracy."[14] In spite of these precautions, the children of the Reformed came to maturity without experiencing conversion. The Presbyterian General Assembly addressed this problem repeatedly from 1799 to 1818.[15] The situation was so bleak that the editor of the *Christian's Magazine* complained that "old Christians are dying off, and a proportionable number of young ones does not step forward to occupy their stations."[16]

These developments prepared the way for a number of revivals that occurred from 1815 to 1818. These seasons of religious arousal uniformly reflected the prevailing notions concerning revivals of religion. Perhaps the best example was the revival at the College of New Jersey in 1815, which epitomized both the elitist aspect of salvational thought and the connection with education and rational processes. Occurring under the leadership of Ashbel Green, one of the staunchest opponents of the new revivalism, the students became "unusually serious" and attentive to religious instruction. Many were convicted of sin and, in the acceptable Reformed style, agonized for weeks. A number of the students "expressed a hope" and others remained "serious."[17]

At the same time there were a number of revivals in various congregations that reflected the same pattern. A revival in the Presbyterian Church in Fairfield, New Jersey, began with the conversion of "twenty lads from twelve to sixteen." It was noted that "most of them belong to the Academy." The revival then spread to "the girls of the Academy," who "became gradually more thoughtful." This revival affected "almost all the first families in the town" and "a great majority of the awakened" were members of those families.[18] Early in 1815 there was a revival in the Reformed Dutch Church at Poughkeepsie. The pastor, Cornelius C. Cuyler, reported that the revival was "deep and solemn" and noted that "the work has been chiefly among the young, and a considerable part of them have been my catechumens." In this case, the young converts were primarily from "among the middling class of life."[19] This revival was fairly widespread, affecting most established areas of New York and New Jersey, and was favorably mentioned by the Presbyterian synod of that region.[20]

In late 1816 and early 1817 the Presbyterian Church at Newark experienced a revival. This also began among the young people "not perhaps older than 13 or 14 years of age." These first converts were assembled often and gave a "most rational" account of their conversion. From this the revival extended to other elements of the congregation, including some "heads of families," but the "greater number" were "in the morning of life."[21] During this same month a revival at Hartwick, New York, "made its first appearance in the Academy for young Gentlemen and Ladies." This revival also "soon spread to society" and resulted in the conversion of several "heads of families," but "the greater part" were "youth, and from pious families." Henry Chapman, the pastor, noted, "God has indeed blessed the attempts to give youth and children a pious education."[22]

These revivals, confined to the middle and upper class church members and their households and occurring in the context of religious instruction, were characteristic of all Reformed revivals. John McDowell, for many years the pastor of the Presbyterian Church in Elizabethtown, New Jersey, witnessed a number of these in his church. In 1810 he informed his church's young people's Bible and church history class that "knowledge is of very great importance in religion; and I doubt whether persons grow in grace any faster than they grow in knowledge of the truths of God's word." Almost all of these children were converted in a revival. In 1812 during another revival in the church there appeared signs of "bodily agitation," and McDowell dismissed the congregation in order to restore the desired calm. Of a revival in 1817 McDowell noted, "Almost all of the youth who have attended my catechetical and biblical instructions give evidence of having experienced the saving change."[23] In his autobiography McDowell noted that these revivals came as a result of "the ordinary means of grace," and that no new convert was admitted to the church "in less than six months."[24]

In some instances similar events were not characterized as revivals. When William Neill became pastor of the Presbyterian Church in Albany in 1809, he immediately initiated a Bible class for the young people. He noted that the youth "generally became hopefully subjects of renewing grace." These periods he preferred to call "seasons of refreshing" rather than "strongly marked revivals of religion." The pattern was repeated when he moved to Philadelphia. According to Neill, "We had peace and concord, and a gradual ingathering of souls, though we never had any special revival of religion."[25]

Before 1820 any tendency toward revivalism of a different sort usually meant separation from the main stream of the Reformed tradition. This was most notably the case with the Cumberland Presbyterians whose revivalism went beyond the bounds of accepted Reformed practice. The revivalists were accused of heresy and for making "their spirits the rule, by which to judge the word of God." But the heresy was social as well as doctrinal. Robert Stuart, a member of the "orthodox" party, initially approved of camp meetings as a means of gathering the religious families to observe the "ordinances." The problem, as he perceived it, was that "they soon became popular, and spread all over the whole state. . . . All classes of society flocked to these meetings. . . . There were the hunter, the black-leg, the robber, the prostitute, etc., as well as the devout worshipper."[26]

The educational requirements for salvation were also a prominent feature in Alexander Campbell's separation from the Presbyterians. The well-known *Declaration and Address* of the Christian Association of Washington denied the necessity for people to know "all divinely revealed truth" before they could become members.[27] John Wenebrenner, founder of the Church of God, was locked out of his German Reformed Church in Harrisburg and finally expelled from the denomination because of his revival techniques.[28]

That such schisms did not occur in other places only indicated that the revivals were more compatible with accepted practice. This was the case with the revival that swept through North Carolina in 1802. It started from a single congregation that traveled to a spot for a meeting. The congregation had been engaged in Bible study and prayer meetings for eighteen months before this outing. The first convert was a man of thirty who had been "pious from an early period of youth." After that nearly all the young people of the congregation "were deeply impressed." James Hall, the pastor, noted, "I have seen an answer given to the prayers of those pious parents who sent, or conducted, their children on that happy tour."[29]

From this altogether acceptable beginning the revival spread rapidly and in the process produced some contrary tendencies. The Associate Reformed disapproved of this work, but the Presbyterians, led by Samuel M'Corkle, attempted to control it within accepted guidelines. M'Corkle observed that those "persons who had obtained a religious education . . . had greatly the advantage in the regularity of their exercises, and in the facility and perspicuity with which they communicated them." He was convinced that "though very young people have gone as far as education or genius could go; yet I have never seen them go beyond." All candidates were thoroughly examined and many were rejected because they could give no rational account of their conversion. M'Corkle secured agreement on a "rule" for the meetings that no prayer of thanksgiving be given "in such terms as if conversion and salvation were entirely certain; but only in the judgments of charity hopefully begun, and to be manifested by a future humble active course of obedience. . . ."[30] This revival was not without its "excesses" and schismatic tendencies, as M'Corkle's own congregation split into revivalistic and nonrevivalistic sides in 1805, but the Presbyterian clergy attempted to maintain approved standards in the face of difficulty.[31]

The North Carolina revivals brought criticism from more-established localities, particularly from neighboring Virginia. The Reformed tradition of revivalism was firmly established in Virginia, where in 1787 a revival had started in Hampden-Sydney College and extended to

Washington College. The revival of 1802 also spread to Virginia, but there it was characterized by greater solemnity. In the midst of the Virginia revival, Moses Hoge criticized the "worthy brethren both in the South and the West" for allowing exercises that "would not be tolerated in any civilized society."[32]

On the basis of outward appearance, the revivals in western Pennsylvania from 1800 to 1803 were an even greater exception to this general rule. Under predominantly orthodox Presbyterian leadership, these revivals were characterized by extreme emotional outbursts and physical exertions. The Presbyterian ministers, however, taught publicly and privately that there was no "religion" in these exercises and a number of them were accused of "coldness" toward the revival. According to James Carnahan, an eyewitness of these events, "People were exhorted to restrain their feelings and listen to the truths of God's Word."[33] Elisha Macurdy and John McMillan, the most active preachers during the revivals, spent more of their time in promoting religious education than in preaching. Macurdy carefully catechized his entire congregation. McMillan continued to write and memorize his sermons and personally taught theology to over one hundred ministers. McMillan's church at Cartiers only admitted 450 members on examination during his thirty-three-year pastorate. The revivals of western Pennsylvania appear to have been the product of a popular expression of religion that the Presbyterian ministers sought to tame rather than oppose.[34] The ministers continued to argue that a rational understanding of the Christian religion was a prerequisite to conversion. In this the ministers of western Pennsylvania were in agreement with national Reformed sentiment and for that reason did not run into the same difficulties as the Cumberland Presbyterians in Kentucky. The fact is that even when there were emotional expressions in Reformed revivals before 1826, the priority of the catechism and the intellectual apprehension of the "knowledge of the Lord" was unquestioned and thus the revivals were confined to those "classes" already under the influence of the church.

The tendencies in the revivals at the turn of the century reappeared in the late 1810s. At this date, however, the pressures of a growing and expanding population were more severe and revivalism went through a permanent evolution. In recently settled parts of the nation, the old form of revivalism was a sociological impossibility. There were no firmly established churches and no prepared class of youth ripe for conversion. The vast majority of those moving west were not among that 10 percent of the population possessing wealth and church membership, nor were they necessarily the poor. As communities developed, however, the same need for social control existed as in the well-established communities. In this context, revivalism became the agency whereby the emerging elite organized themselves into churches as part of the total process of bringing order to the community.

Whitney Cross has convincingly demonstrated part of this development in western New York. According to Cross, the revivals of Charles
Grandison Finney did not occur in the sparsely populated or "frontier"
areas, but in already-formed communities.[35] The revival as an agency of
social organization, however, predated Finney. The revival at DeKalb, in
Saint Lawrence County, New York, in 1817 and 1818 illustrated this
development. With a population of less than a thousand, DeKalb was a
thriving village with thirty "professors" of religion of different denominations but no church. In August 1817 a minister named James Johnson
came into the town. Eighty-six days later he reported that a revival had
occurred. According to Johnson, "There is now a regular church of
fifty-six members, embracing almost every influential man in the town."
Noteworthy among the converts was an unnamed general in the War of
1812 who was "a man of liberal education, and brilliant talents" and who
had "amassed a large fortune" and "enjoyed all the honors the town
could bestow upon him."[36]

By 1825 many towns in western New York were ripe for this kind of
organization, and revivals probably would have occurred with or without
the aid of Finney. Finney's major revivals in the towns of Western,
Rome, Utica, Auburn, and Troy all represented this process of social
organization. At Rome, many "who had regularly attended public worship for twenty years" were subjects of the revival. Apparently the revival
made a clean sweep of the local elite. "Four lawyers, four physicians, all
the merchants who were not professors before, and men of the first
respectability in the place, are hopeful converts." At Western, the prime
convert was the 80-year-old widow of General William Floyd, officer of
the Revolution and signer of the Declaration of Independence.[37] A similar phenomenon occurred at other places not visited by Finney. At
Whitesborough, "Some of the most intelligent and respectable people in
the place were convicted of sin." Of special interest, the superintendents
of the cotton factories in the area were converted. These men, it was
reported, "manifest a laudable zeal to preserve them from immoralities,
and to furnish the children with the means of religious instruction."[38]
Indeed, the leaders of the new communities were as anxious as those in
the older ones to use religion as a means of control—but they first had to
be "saved" themselves.

Of the Rochester revival of 1831 Finney wrote, "it was soon seen
that the Lord was aiming at the conversion of the highest classes of
society." He noted that "my meetings soon became thronged with . . .
lawyers, physicians, merchants, and indeed most of the intelligent people. . . . The great majority of the leading men and women in the city
were converts . . . the most influential people. . . ."[39] As William G.
McLoughlin has noted, however, the "highest classes of society" in
Rochester were not like the wealthy of New York or Philadelphia. For
the most part, they were less educated and had no hereditary wealth. In

Rochester "the better people were simple sons and daughters of farmers" who had recently acquired wealth in the wake of the Erie Canal prosperity.[40] Finney's type of revivalism, unlike the traditional Reformed revivalism, made it possible for them to acquire the seal of social standing as rapidly as they had their wealth.

But western New York was not the only place where revivalism aided the social organization of relatively new communities. When the first minister came to Beach Island, South Carolina, in January 1826, there were only six professors of religion. The minister established Bible classes and regular preaching services. In this case the revival was closer to the established pattern and did not occur until August 1827, after a year and a half of religious instruction. Of the thirty-eight who "indulged a hope," eighteen were heads of families, two were superintendents of the Sunday school, and fourteen were Sunday school teachers. It was noted that "those who have been brought in, were, previous to the revival, among the regular attendants upon public worship."[41]

This same phenomenon also extended to the suburbs of the largest cities. James Patterson's church in the Northern Liberties section of Philadelphia regularly experienced revivals after 1816. This church was removed from the wealthy districts of Philadelphia and the revivals served to organize the local community leaders.[42] The Seventh Presbyterian Church in New York City also gave evidence of this principle. Organized as a "missionary" church and supported from outside, many who attended could not "afford to hire seats." A revival in 1821 brought many of these into church membership. The twenty-five converts were "generally persons in middle life: and what is remarkable, with but two exceptions, heads of families."[43]

In varying degrees, the revivalism that aided social organization and control in recently established communities necessitated adjustments in the traditional Reformed views of salvation. In villages or in the suburbs where the community leaders were not church members, it was impossible to think of a revival as a harvest of religiously trained youth. At the same time it was not likely that adults could be subjected to the same rigorous catechetical memorization and instruction deemed necessary for conversion. From the traditional Reformed perspective, the population had indeed already outgrown the means of religious instruction. In this context, ideas about salvation evolved from the concept emphasizing conversion as the work of God through the process of orthodox religious instruction to one featuring conversion as a human decision requiring little knowledge. In the point of philosophical consistency, this evolution followed the logic of the development in the doctrine of providence and thinking about social classes that had already transferred responsibility from God to man.

The theology of revivalism has been consistently associated with New

England in general and Nathaniel W. Taylor in particular. This need not be seriously disputed. In New England, Calvinism was considerably modified by Jonathan Edwards and Samuel Hopkins and by 1800 adherents to one or the other system of revivalistic theology outnumbered the old Calvinists. In the middle and southern states, on the other hand, theological development was less marked, and orthodox Calvinism remained the dominant theology. In the western areas the two traditions mixed freely as a result of the Plan of the Union of 1802 between the Congregationalists of New England and the Presbyterians. Certainly New England theological currents were influential.[44]

As connected with the new revivalism, however, the major theological statements seemed to have been made after the fact. Finney, for example, was a practitioner first and then a theoretician. Doctrine was tested by experience.[45] Finney's ideas did not appear in print and therefore did not furnish concrete data for theological debate until 1831 when Asa Rand published notes on Finney's sermon, *Sinners Bound to Change Their Own Hearts.*[46] By the same token, Nathaniel Taylor's best-remembered exposition, *Concio ad Clerum,* was not published until 1828, and the controversial sermon by Albert Barnes, *The Way of Salvation,* was preached in 1829.

The essence of the new theology was that man could obtain salvation through his own power of decision. The most significant debate among the Reformed of the middle and southern states centered around *The Way of Salvation.* In the course of a revival at Morristown, New Jersey, Barnes undertook to describe "the whole Christian plan of saving men" in a single sermon. He skirted the traditional doctrine of original sin but argued that "not one of all their descendants could escape the contagion to the end of time." All men sinned and God's atonement was extended to all men. "It is with peculiar interest," Barnes noted, "that we are permitted to proclaim that *all* that will believe, ALL, not a part, shall infallibly be saved.... *To All,* I say, if you believe the gospel, *heaven is yours.*" God had already done everything necessary for salvation. Every man's salvation depended on his own decision. "It is not that God is unwilling to save the sinner. It is simply because *you will not be saved.* You choose...."[47]

This sermon by Barnes confirmed all the suspicions the Old School Presbyterians had harbored about the heretical nature of the new revivalism. In 1826 the Presbytery of Oneida had written a defense of the revivals designed to make them appear acceptable on the Old School model,[48] but Barnes made a frontal attack.

In many ways Albert Barnes, friend of Finney and arch exponent of "Taylorism," became the symbolic target of the Old School. Barnes became pastor of the First Presbyterian Church in Philadelphia just after Finney had preached there. Presbyterians of Philadelphia were so opposed to any innovation in theology that they had classified Finney as a "crude Western exponent of Hopkinsianism," when in reality the Hopkinsians, although mildly revivalistic, likewise opposed the extremism of Finney. But in the center of conservative Presbyterianism, as Finney noted, "we are all hereticks, Alias Hopkintonians."[49] Coming into this situation, Barnes was immediately tried for heresy.

The formal charges brought against Barnes were strictly doctrinal in nature. He was charged on five counts. According to his Old School opponents, he was guilty of denying the doctrine of original sin. His doctrine of the atonement was perceived to be defective in three aspects by suggesting that Christ did not endure the penalty of the law, that the atonement itself did not secure the salvation of any, and that the atonement was general rather than particular. Barnes was further charged for stressing man's ability and for omitting the "doctrine of justification by the imputed righteousness of Christ." Finally it was alleged that Barnes gave no indication of his intention to accept the doctrinal standards of the Presbyterian church.[50]

The informal criticism of Barnes and of revivalism in general by the Old School, however, stressed the point of "knowledge." The section on revivalism in the pastoral letter of the General Assembly in 1827 stressed the need for Bible classes and Sunday schools. "Let the young know the Holy scriptures which are able to make them wise unto salvation."[51] In 1825 Chancy Webster, editor of the *Religious Monitor,* said that it was difficult for him to determine the authenticity of revivals by reading the accounts that came to him. This could only be done "by a close examination of the *knowledge* of the supposed subjects of grace, and an intimate acquaintance with their subsequent deportment." True believers "must possess a definite knowledge of the fundamental doctrines" of the Bible, for faith "in anything, of which we have vague notions" was "the absurdity of foolishness." For Webster, as for all the older Reformed, it was not enough to be "religious." To be saved one must have knowledge of the truth. The columns of the *Religious Monitor* consistently reflected this view of revivalism and conversion.[52]

Ashbel Green, one of Barnes's most forceful opponents, made his most perceptive analysis of the differences between the old and the new revivalism in December of 1827. Green had responded favorably to the account of the revivals given by the Presbytery of Oneida,[53] but a review of a sermon by Finney provoked Green's opposition. In his discussion of salvation Green emphasized method more than theology. There were three ways that "the Spirit of grace" gave "a saving efficacy to revealed truth," he said. "The first of these is, by mingling his holy influence, gently and yet powerfully, with the natural effects of a careful religious education." In this context, Green placed the emphasis on "natural." In some instances, however, religiously trained children resisted salvation and perhaps became wayward for a time. In later life these were prime candidates for a revival. Green was careful to note that "these revivals take place in congregations or places where the people have been well indoctrinated."

Green was fully aware, however, that every situation, particularly in the West, was not conducive to this process. "In revivals which take place under this last kind of instrumentality, great irregularities too often occur" because the people were "very imperfectly instructed in the great doctrines and principles of our holy religion." Green did not wish to oppose all such revivals, because if some were "not saved without a religious education . . . they must indubitably perish forever." The best security against such irregularities was that "preachers of the gospel, under whom revivals commence, should be men well informed, and well established in religion themselves." Green was primarily dissatisfied with Finney because he had attempted to justify these irregularities "on principle." These "errors and delusions," Green believed, were injurious to the cause of true religion.[54]

William Brownlee, editor of the *Magazine of the Reformed Dutch Church,* opposed the new revivalism on similar grounds. "Our Dutch people," he claimed, "make not that stir" when "a few dozen are melted down." Brownlee believed that the cause of religion would be better served if more time were given to the "examination of potential applicants" rather than to the writing of "bombastic, tedious, lucious narratives." He was a friend of revivals and had participated in a revival in which the pastor and elders spent three weeks examining the "applicants," many of whom "were put on a longer course of discipline, and preparation."[55]

The essence of the dispute, in spite of the theological complexities, was simple. The Old School viewed conversion as the result of education and did not connect it necessarily with any noticeable change in behavior. The New School viewed conversion as a matter of human decision that immediately affected behavior. Nathan S. S. Beman, the "war-horse of the New School" and one of the first to invite Finney to preach to his congregation, presented the new point of view to the General Assembly in 1832. He compared "apostolic" (New School) preaching with "modern" (Old School) preaching. Attacking intellectual and doctrinal preaching, Beman declared, "The apostles in their preaching, aimed at immediate success. . . . repentance of sin, and submission to the terms of salvation."[56] Albert Barnes summed up the differences between the growing factions more succinctly. In a sermon to the faculty and students of Princeton Theological Seminary in 1834, Barnes stated flatly, "Knowledge is good, but holiness is better."[57] The New School stressed the ability of the sinner to achieve immediate conversion and live a life of holiness by an act of will. The Old School continued to view conversion as an almost arbitrary act of the Holy Spirit operating through a correct apprehension of the "knowledge of the Lord."

This change in belief about conversion had rather extensive social implications. It made possible the conversion of the emerging elite in developing communities and the attending social organization. At the same time, and of greater significance, the new philosophy provided no easy or systematic method of keeping salvation from the masses. It could no longer be asked, as in the case of a Negro servant requesting baptism, "Does he know about Christian principles. . . . Can he read?"[58] In social terms, the new doctrine of the atonement was indeed "general" rather than "particular." It made possible again, for the first time since the breakdown of the household system, the conversion of the poor.

The same revivals that aided the conversion of the "nouveau riche" encouraged the salvation of "all classes." While the ministers, Finney in particular, prided themselves on the conversion of the "best people," one of the most consistent items in the accounts of revivals was that all classes were included among the converts. A report from Chenango County, New York, in 1817 specified that "all classes are subjects of this awakening:—the old and the young—the rich and the poor—the learned and ignorant—the lawyer, the farmer, and the mechanic. . . ."[59] This was also a common feature of all Finney revivals. At Utica, for example, the "sweet and saving influence" of the gospel fell "upon the rich and the poor, the ignorant and the learned."[60]

The report of the revivals by the Presbytery of Oneida contained specific accounts by location and concluded with a general summary, in which it was noted that "this revival has extended to all classes of society." According to the presbytery, this factor "should encourage ministers and churches to pray and labour for the salvation of *all men,* the high, and the low, the rich and the poor, the old and the young, the moral and the profane. . . ."[61] This very suggestion was evidence that the conversion of "all classes" marked a new departure.

There is some indication that the reaction to the new revivalism was in part based on class prejudice. This was true in the case of Lyman Beecher's early objections to Finney. Part of Finney's appeal to the new elite of the West and to the poorer classes was his consistent attacks on the very rich. This factor was evident in his *Lectures on Revivals of Religion.* It was no surprise, he contended, that the rich often were not "filled with the Spirit," because they were "so fond of dress, high life, equipage, fashion. . . ." For some the love of property and wealth actually made it impossible to "have the Spirit." Their eagerness for wealth led them to "grind" down the poor. Finney attacked the wealthy who paid large sums for charity balls, even though most who attended were "professors of religion." At one point Finney skillfully anticipated an objection. "You say, perhaps, 'I wish some of the rich churches could hear it!' Why, I am not preaching to them, I am preaching to you."[62]

Beecher and others objected to this kind of approach. He did not believe "that all men, because sinners, are therefore to be treated alike by ministers of the gospel without respect to age or station in society." This was particularly dangerous "in republican governments where public opinion is the only law." If the masses lost respect for their rulers, such a "leveling" certainly "would be the sure presage of anarchy and absolute destruction."[63]

Class prejudice was evident in the revivals in and around Albany in 1819 and 1820. In its incipient stages, the revival followed accepted norms. It started at Union College and "from the *college*, the *awakening* spread down into the city." When confined to the churches where there were prayer meetings and regular services and where "children are catechized weekly," there was no opposition. But when children and others from the "cotton factory" were saved, "some opposed the work in this place."[64] In 1824 "a revival of religion in a cotton manufactory" near Troy also provoked strong opposition.[65]

In general, the level of opposition to the new revivalism seemed to have a direct relationship to the social class of the converts. Even the General Synod of the Reformed Dutch Church—theologically conservative, strongly opposed to the new revivalism, and the most socially elite of the Reformed bodies—could accept revivalism if it produced wealthy converts. In its state of religion message in 1831, the synod was pleased "to learn that in the late revivals of religion in our land, and within the bounds of our own church, an unusual number of men have been gathered in—prominent men, men of wealth, of character, of high standing; and therefore likely to exert, a most happy influence upon the moral and religious interest of the church, and of the whole community."[66]

The new revivalism, however, was simply offensive to the higher classes. The emotional outpourings, the use of anxious benches, the speaking of women in "promiscuous assemblies," the exhorting of laymen, and the "ranting" of ministers offended accepted notions of what was proper. As one observer correctly discerned, "It is not to be questioned that the more staid and intelligent part of the community look upon them with distrust or contempt." The revivals with "all their low appliances" were "revolting to every sentiment of propriety."[67]

The class objections against the new revivalism transcended theological divisions in the society. An Arminian, Nathaniel Porter, for example, not only attacked Albert Barnes for still being a Calvinist but for undermining distinctions in society. According to Porter, the "various ranks and orders" demonstrated the sovereignty of God. Only a few were "called to rule a nation, and fill the various offices necessary to a well organized civil community." Porter, like most religious leaders, had no appreciation for the concept of government by the people. "If all were called to rule, where would be the ruled?" In God's order, "While some are elevated to rank, to wealth, and to honor, others are left to poverty and obscurity." Without these distinctions "anarchy and confusion

would be introduced into every department of society," and Porter
feared that Barnes's doctrine had these tendencies.[68]

The new revivalism, however, was not inherently democratic. The
revivalists had discovered something from their experience that was to
change the nature of religion in America. Revivals had proven to be the
most rapid and efficient mode of social control. The old method of
indoctrination was too slow, and it was an impossible task in light of the
rapid growth and diffusion of the American population. No one was
more aware of this than Charles Finney. He had heard "certain men tell
a wonderful deal about the necessity of 'indoctrinating the people.'" It
was his experience that when ministers "leave off laboring to convert
souls, for the purpose of 'indoctrinating' the young converts. . . . There
the revival stops." This was "absurd," he said. "Do they not know that a
revival indoctrinates the church faster than any thing else."[69] Nathan S.
S. Beman phrased it somewhat more accurately by declaring that "every
solitary conversion to God, and every powerful revival or religion . . .
impresses and controls society. . . ."[70]

The evangelists had discovered that a revival could accomplish quickly
the same goals pursued through the voluntary associations. Revivals,
moreover, were much more effective with adults. A revival could change
the characteristics of an entire village almost overnight. Again this phenomenon predated Finney. A revival in 1817 on Shelter Island, off the
east end of Long Island, produced a "great moral revolution." Before
the revival, "Profane language, drunkedness and Sabbath-breaking were
fearfully prevalent." Before the revival the population of three hundred
required "eleven hogsheads of rum" each year and "the inhabitants
spent the Sabbath on fishing, shooting, or their secular employments."
After the revival one hogshead of liquor supplied the entire island and almost everyone attended church. "This great change was produced by
the divine blessing on the united prayers and labors of a few pious persons. . . ."[71] In 1816 a revival in Franklin County, New York, which
affected "persons of all ages and descriptions," had similar results. The
revival "suppressed prophane swearing, Sabbath breaking, gambling,
and their accompanying evils, which are so disgraceful to society."[72]

What was already developed was brought to national attention by
Charles Finney and the revivals in western New York. Everywhere Finney preached there were observable differences in social behavior. After
the revival at Rome it was observed that "the Sabbath is more strictly
observed. Intemperance and profane swearing are checked." The revival at Utica "made 'new creatures' of gamblers and drunkards. . . ." In
the cotton factories, where revivalism had created opposition, salvation
seemed a particularly powerful agent of control. At Whitesborough,
where the superintendents "were among the first converts," the preachers were brought to the factories to evangelize the workers. The super-

intendents were said to have demonstrated "laudable zeal to preserve them from immoralities."[73] The new revivalism was simply a different form of social control. The other-worldly individual salvation offered by the evangelists became an instrument for the this-worldly collective salvation of American society. In 1826 the technique had been developed. By 1840 it would be the characteristic expression of American Protestantism.

The revivalists of the West, although educationally and socially inferior, had one argument that could not be denied—success. The majority of the Reformed in the East remained deeply suspicious, but a few recognized Finney and the new revivalism "as the last hope of the republic."[74]

Finney's first efforts in the urban centers of the East were not marked with the same success he had enjoyed in western New York. In 1827 Finney was invited by E. W. Gilbert to preach in his church in Wilmington, Delaware. It was soon obvious that there were vast differences between the two, but Finney succeeded in bringing Gilbert around to his views. From Wilmington Finney went to Philadelphia, where he faced strong opposition. He preached initially in James Patterson's church, which was a lower middle class church that had been built through the process of revivalism similar to that of Finney. When Finney went into the center of Philadelphia to the wealthier churches, however, the opposition was strong. Apparently Finney felt uncomfortable in this environment, and he retreated to Patterson's church for several weeks. Returning to the city, Finney went to the German Reformed Church. Although a large congregation, it had been torn and divided by language disputes. Unlike the other Reformed churches and partly because of the language problem, the members of this church were not among the socially elite. As a result, Finney was better received and was asked to remain as pastor.[75]

It remained for a group of laymen in New York to recognize the full potential of revivalism for the city. As in Philadelphia, the established ministers in New York were uniformly opposed to the new revivalism. The laymen, however, were much more concerned with social conditions than with theology or methods. Anson G. Phelps, David and William Dodge, and Lewis and Arthur Tappan were the most prominent of the group. These men, especially the Tappans, had worked earnestly to bring religious instruction to the poor of the city. These laymen quickly realized the potential that the new revivalism held for exerting influence on the urban masses, and in December of 1827 they began to seek Finney's support.

Nearly two years later Phelps rented a vacant church on Vandevanter Street and persuaded Finney to come to New York. After three months Phelps purchased a church on Prince Street, and in 1830 the First Free Presbyterian Church was established with Joel Parker as pastor. This was a significant event in the transition from indoctrination to salvation as a form of social control. The poor could now attend a Presbyterian church without paying pew rent, and the preaching encouraged them to claim salvation and turn from their wicked ways.[76]

Finney's work in New York was interrupted by his most successful revival in Rochester and a trip to Boston. The laymen in New York longed for his return and did everything possible to make the New York clergy more receptive of Finney. In March 1831, Lewis Tappan wrote Finney that "the tide of feeling is too strong in the churches . . . for the ministers to *oppose* you."[77] These laymen were primarily concerned about social order, but they now talked almost solely in the language of salvation. Tappan again wrote Finney in March 1832 that "this city must be converted or the nation is lost." After purchasing and remodeling the Chatham Street Theater, Tappan finally persuaded Finney to return to New York as pastor of the Second Free Presbyterian Church.[78]

The free church movement in connection with revivalism did not succeed in bringing religion to the poorest of the urban masses, but it had a significant effect on Reformed thinking about salvation and the social order. Most of the people who went to the free churches were from the lower middle and middle classes. These were people unable to cope with the elitism of the Presbyterian and Reformed churches or unable to pay the pew rent, but for the most part still classified as "decent people." Finney, for example, feared that "decent people" would not go to church in a theater.[79] As an example of Finney's preaching while in New York, the *Lectures on Revivals of Religion* clearly indicate, however, that Finney was preaching to "common" people and informing them that salvation was theirs for the taking.[80]

More significant than the work of Finney himself was the transition that occurred in the society movement as a result of the promise of revivalism as a successful form of social control. The same New York laymen who sought Finney's services were also influential in the society movement. The Tappans especially were gradually becoming the most forceful leaders in the societies. According to William McLoughlin, the Tappans "brought Finney a host of new allies from these enterprises as well as enlisting his followers in them."[81] Whitney Cross has called this "the wedding of humanitarian movements and revivalism."[82]

The amalgamation of revivalism with the voluntary associations was most evident in the evolution of the Sunday schools. In its early stages the Sunday school movement placed almost no emphasis on salvation. A large percentage of the Sunday school teachers were not themselves professing Christians. They were generally people from the "higher walks" of life who were concerned about the threat of poverty to the social order and who believed that religious education was the solution to that problem. In the late 1820s, however, it gradually became evident, as in the case of the western revivals, that religious salvation was a more effective form of social control than indoctrination. In this context, the Sunday school movement gradually altered its course and by the 1830s emphasized and pressed for conversions.

The character of the early Sunday school instruction in no way made personal religion necessary for the teacher. The students memorized previously prepared materials so "all that the *subordinate teachers,* at least, have to do, is to see that the scholars learn to repeat them correctly." This did not "involve the communication of religious instruction *as from themselves.*"[83] As late as 1825 the Philadelphia Association of Male Sunday School Teachers debated the question, "Is it proper to admit persons, as Teachers in our Sunday Schools, who do not give any evidence of an experimental acquaintance with religion?" There was some opposition, but the question was decided in the affirmative primarily because "thousands of students" would be without teachers if the practice were to be discontinued.[84]

Concern for social order was an acceptable motivation for teaching Sunday school. A writer for the *Evangelical Guardian* in 1818 insisted that teachers have "good motives" but believed that others than the "friends of God" could have adequate motivation. "Are you friends of social order?" he asked—"Engage in Sunday schools." Persons who were "patriots," who enjoyed "so many civil (not to say religious) rights and liberties" would also want to work in Sunday schools because "one of the best preservatives of those rights is the intelligence of the great mass of the people." Sunday schools provided "the stability of our times" and were to secure "the happiness, the safety, the glory of our nation." Sunday school teachers were not necessarily concerned for "souls" but for the welfare of the nation.[85]

The extent to which nonprofessing persons participated in the Sunday schools was evident by the large number of teachers who were converted. Almost all the early reports from local Sunday school unions reported the number of conversions, and invariably the number of teachers was greater than the number of scholars. This phenomenon was only slightly altered after the formation of the American Sunday School Union, which reported the conversion of 468 teachers and 532 scholars in 1826, 723 teachers and 758 pupils in 1827, and 1,269 teachers and 909 scholars in 1828.[86] The personal involvement in religious work apparently overcame the general reluctance of many to claim salvation. It was said that "a larger proportion of Sunday-school teachers, have become truly pious, within a few years, than of persons of any other class or description."[87]

The transition in the late 1820s from memorization to exposition partly reflected and certainly aided the larger evolution toward conversion as a means of social control. Around 1827 the salvation of Sunday school scholars began to receive considerable support. In January the *American Sunday School Magazine* printed an address to Sunday school teachers that pointed out that Sunday school instruction had ignored salvation. The author urged that this situation be corrected and pleaded with the teachers to seek their own salvation.[88] In September there was an account of two Sunday schools only four miles apart. The one stressed only indoctrination while the other pressed for the immediate conversion of the scholars. The latter method, it was argued, produced more visible changes in society.[89] In 1828 the magazine carried a number of articles with titles like "Efficacy of the Bible Class and Sunday School in Revivals" and "The Best Means to Promote the Conversion of Children."[90]

By 1829 the major question seemed to be decided. The New York Sunday school teachers discussed the question, "Why are there so few conversions in Sabbath-schools, and why are not revivals of religion more frequent in them; and what measures can be recommended to promote these objects?"[91] In the annual Sunday school address that year Edward D. Griffin accurately reflected the change. The Sunday school, Griffin declared, "avows its attachment to revivals of religion, and aims at nothing less than to make its pupils new born." No longer would the "old recitals of Scripture by rote" be adequate. Now "the teachers, by familiar questions" would "lead the children to think for themselves, and make close applications to their conscience and heart."[92]

It took some time to adjust the Sunday school machinery to the new approach. By 1831 the whole tone of the American Sunday School Union's annual report had changed. The movement toward revivalism was everywhere evident. The managers declared that "more personal, pointed spiritual instruction" would be expected from the teachers. "The conversion of children to God . . . is the object, more than ever before, of immediate and chief concern." Because of this change in tactic the managers would aid the teachers by changing the nature of Sunday school books. "Every book that leaves the press should be, in some measure, a help-meet for them in their work of faith and labour of love."[93] In 1832 the number of pupils converted rose to 6,444, double the number of teachers. In 1833 the managers went into great detail on the "new modes" to be used in the Sunday schools. The change could not be brought about rapidly enough. In 1834 the managers complained that "much of the instruction in our schools is deficient. . . . The pupil is not made to look upon *his own soul* as lost. . . ."[94] The transition to salvation as a means of social control was the most ingenious of the "engaging disguises."

The new policy of conversion was followed militantly. The major goals of the Sunday school movement had not changed, only the methods of achieving them had been altered. Sunday school supporters were still concerned about poverty and the preservation of "free institutions." In the context of revivalism, however, the verbalization of these goals diminished while religious salvational language increased. Through revivalism the religion of the rich now became also the religion of the poor. Salvation became the tool to "possess the land." As Stephen H. Tyng noted in the annual Sunday school sermon in 1837, "we wish thoroughly to Christianize the land in which we live, and to make the limits of the spiritual communion of the gospel co-extensive with the habitations of our people."[95] This was the way the ancient concept of the identity of religious belief and national citizenship was expressed in America in 1837.

At the same time the Sunday school movement made the transition from indoctrination to salvation it made a parallel transition that brought the movement even closer to revivalism. After 1825 the "rich" were increasingly encouraged to send their children to Sunday schools. This development was made necessary in order to secure the attendance of the children of the poor. One of the most fascinating facets of the literature of the early nineteenth century was its elite nature. In the journals and numerous pamphlets the elite discussed *their* problems openly and candidly, without fear that it would be read by the lower classes. Around 1825 it became obvious that the poor had somehow become aware of the Sunday school discussion and resented it. The elite responded by encouraging all parents to send their children to Sunday school.

The major arguments for the change appeared in the *American Sunday School Magazine* during 1825. In January, A. W. Leland of South Carolina submitted an article entitled "Sunday Schools not for the Poor Only." The Sunday schools were so associated with poverty, he argued, that "there has sometimes existed an idea of degradation and abandon connected with sending children to these blessed institutions." The Sunday schools should be for all children, not just for "the little outcasts of society, the idle, wretched wanderers in our streets and alleys."[96] In February, "J" from Philadelphia agreed that "the poverty of the children" was often referred to "in such a manner as to give offense to some parents."[97] Of several other articles during the year, only one argued that Sunday schools were only for the poor.[98]

The question was not entirely settled, but the problem had been posed and within several years the transition would be complete. A prize-winning essay by "Manville" in 1826 discussed the question of the nature and design of Sunday schools and "who ought to be admitted as scholars." "Manville" concluded that they were, in fact, "mainly" for the "poor" but that the "rich" should be allowed to attend.[99] In some places the practice was rapidly changed. An account of a Sunday school "celebration" in Washington, Pennsylvania, in 1826 emphasized that the "bare feet and coarse garments" of many of the children "bespoke that they were the children of poverty and wretchedness." Others "had the appearance of comfort and wealth."[100] By the 1830s the Sunday schools, originally for the poor, also served the rich, as salvation, formerly reserved to the rich, had come to the poor. The former, like the latter, however, was not inherently democratic. It was a necessary tactic to accomplish the goals of social control. In 1829 Samuel Miller urged the "rich" to send their children to Sunday school because "the example of the rich and pious" was "helpful."[101]

The other major societies also moved from indoctrination to salvation and merged with revivalism. The American Tract Society's earliest tracts either emphasized submission to authority and contentment with poverty or were heavily theological and the society served primarily as a printing and distribution center. As early as 1828 the managers began to stress the usefulness of tracts in revivals and for conversions.[102] By 1835 the American Tract Society had made the full transition. The managers took issue with those who "with strange inconsistency, contend that the mass of our countrymen are so besotted in sin, that *to labor for their salvation is hopeless.*" They had witnessed conversions with "their own eyes in the city of New York, among a population, they would fain believe, as hopeless and far from God, and in circumstances as unfavorable to piety, as can be found in our land." Thirty conversions among the poor of New York had been reported in a single month.[103]

The American Tract Society now employed agents who supervised "tract visitors." The cities were divided into wards and districts with the "visitors" assigned to specific areas. The visitors were to "endeavor to induce" the residents "immediately to give themselves to God." Like the "new Measures" of the new revivalism, the "visitors" were given detailed instructions on the most efficient means of securing an immediate decision. The American Tract Society went one step beyond the Sunday school unions that had ceased teaching writing. The "visitors" read the tracts to the poor who were unable to read for themselves. In 1836 the American Tract Society reported three hundred conversions among the poor of New York alone.[104]

Because of the functions of the American Home Missionary Society and the American Education Society, their merger with revivalism required fewer adjustments. Preachers could be educated and supported through the same means whether revivalistically oriented or not. Although Finney constantly criticized these societies for producing ministers who knew more about ancient languages than how to win souls for Christ, both reflected greater sympathy to revivalism. In 1829 the American Home Missionary Society began to stress the number of conversions under ministers supported by them, and by 1832 their report dwelt extensively on revivals.[105] The American Education Society also began to emphasize numbers of conversions, and in 1832 pointed out that reports from 92 former beneficiaries of the society indicated that they had been instrumental in 183 revivals and 20,000 conversions.[106]

The growing partnership between revivalism and the societies was evident in the temperance crusade. When the American Temperance Society was founded in 1826 the managers attempted with apparent success to secure support form all segments of the Reformed denominations. In the Rochester revivals of 1830 and 1831, Finney made a pledge for total abstinence synonymous with conversion. The two were so compatible that sometimes an emphasis on temperance was found to promote a revival. The Presbytery of Geneva, in its report of the revival, noted that "this effort in the cause of Temperance is regarded as holding an intimate relation to the revival in the subsequent stages of its progress. . . ."[107]

The most obvious indication of this change was the organization of the American Anti-Slavery Society in 1833. The older colonization society was a reflection of the former society leadership and by its very nature could not be changed, as in the case of the other societies, to fit the requirements of the new. The leaders of the American Anti-Slavery Society were all revival men. Arthur Tappan was the president, and his brother Lewis was influential in the organization of the society. Joshua Leavitt, avid abolitionist and editor of the *New York Evangelist,* had been trained at Yale by Nathaniel Taylor. Theodore Weld, a long-time associate of Finney, was the society's most vigorous agent.[108]

As early as 1827 the Presbyterian Synod of Indiana rejected the traditional Reformed position that the slaves were "not prepared for the enjoyment of civil liberty" because of a faulty religious education. In a memorial to the General Assembly the synod asked, "Can those who are *real* Christians offer such a plea?" Just as the new breed of Presbyterians demanded immediate surrender to God in the revivals, they demanded immediate abolition of a system that outraged alike "the laws of God, the spirit of the gospel, the dictates of humanity, and the principles of justice."[109] By the time the American Anti-Slavery Society was founded in 1833, the whole society movement had moved toward this point of view. Knowledge was good—but holiness was believed to be better.

The merger of the voluntary societies and revivalism was made complete by the withdrawal of nonrevivalistic or Old School members of the Reformed denominations. This trend was most marked among the Presbyterians. In the 1830s the revivalistic New School elements became the staunchest advocates of the voluntary societies while the Old School, responsible for initiating the societies, withdrew in favor of denominational boards. This was a major factor in the schism of 1837. In the smaller and more conservative Reformed denominations, there was less sympathy for revivalism and these denominations repeated the Old School process of forming denominational agencies and withdrawing from the voluntary associations.

The smaller and theologically more conservative Reformed denominations withdrew from the societies quickly without too much internal turmoil. Several members of the Associate Synod of North America began a sustained attack on the societies in the columns of the *Religious Monitor* in 1829. The editor affirmed that while the Associate church was not opposed to the "benevolent operations of the day," it was "bitterly . . . opposed to the unscriptural practices, and doctrines which the corrupters of God's word have introduced into these benevolent institutions."[110] At the meeting of the synod, committees were appointed to "consider and report on the propriety of forming a Bible Society with a view to distribute Bibles with Psalms in metre" and to suggest "measures for the circulation of Tracts on the peculiar principles of our witnessing profession." It was believed that the societies had become subversive of the denomination, and that the church itself should be the Bible society, the tract society, and the missionary society.[111] By 1834 the Associate Presbyterians "dissapproved of all other mission plans" except those conducted through the denomination.[112]

The Associate Reformed Synod of New York followed a similar course. In 1831 the editor of the denomination's *Christian's Magazine* wrote "An Apology for the Associate Reformed Church." Some had objected that the denomination did "not approve of the 'great movements' and benevolent operations of the day." The Associate Reformed, according to the editor, only objected to some of the "acts and measures."[113] In 1834 the synod formalized its withdrawal from the society movement with a resolution "that . . . we, as a denomination are imperiously called to arise in our strength. . . ."[114]

The Dutch Reformed also rapidly disengaged themselves from the society movement as it became New England-oriented and revivalistic. The General Synod refused to cooperate when the United Foreign Missionary Society was merged with the American Board of Commissioners for Foreign Missions. William Craig Brownlee explained that they declined "entering into the Eastern policy" because they were "strongly opposed to Hopkinsianism, and Independency. . . . We can never amalgamate with them." The Dutch had been second to none "in pecuniary contributions," but their generosity had been to their own detriment. As a result, Brownlee argued, "our hedges are being broken down, and the paths of the good old ways are being shut up. . . ."[115]

The Dutch Reformed involvement in the societies had been such that withdrawal was not easy, and there was considerable difference of opinion within the denomination. In 1827 Brownlee complained that not one in four of the communicating members supported the Missionary Society of the Reformed Dutch Church.[116] By 1829, however, the General Synod's committee on missions reported optimistically that "whatever may be the difference of opinion with regard to objects, not immediately connected with our own denomination," everyone agreed to support the denominational efforts.[117] The denomination was still divided in 1833 between supporters of the voluntary associations and those of denominational boards, as indicated by several close votes in the General Synod of that year.[118]

The trend, however, was clearly from associated to denominational activity. Early in 1828 the adherents of denominational boards formed the Sabbath School Union of the Reformed Dutch Church. The managers argued that many "baptized children of our churches" attended Sunday schools and ought to be taught the "truth" as contained in the catechisms of the church. They also objected to unconverted teachers.[119] Immediately after its organization, the society applied to the General Synod to be taken under its care. Sentiment was still such at this time that the synod believed it "inexpedient to legislate."[120] That same year a Board of Education for the Reformed Dutch Church was formed in New York. This move was supported by some of the more eminent members of the denomination, including Philip Milledoler, John Knox, Jr., Gerardus A. Kuypers, William C. Brownlee, and Thomas DeWitt. This board was not an official denominational organization but indicated the strong desire of many of the Dutch Reformed to withdraw from the society movement.[121] There was also strong support among the Reformed Dutch in 1828 to affiliate with the newly formed Presbyterian Foreign and Domestic Mission Board.[122] Brownlee and Eli Baldwin met with that board to discuss the possibilities of cooperation.[123]

By 1831 a majority in the General Synod favored denominational activity over associated activity. The voluntary education board requested that the General Synod take charge of its activities. The synod reappointed the existing officers as its own, and by 1833 the board of education was an integral part of the denomination.[124] It was more difficult to bring the independent Missionary Society of the Reformed Dutch Church under the control of the General Synod. A thriving organization since 1822, the society came into conflict with the Synod of Albany and in 1830 the synod's committee on missions expressed a desire to bring "the missionary operations of our church . . . under the control of General Synod." The independent society resisted and a second board of missions was established at Albany. In 1831 the General Synod proceeded to organize its own board of missions and in 1834 the independent society became auxiliary to the synod's board.[125] In 1832 the General Synod worked out an arrangement with the American Board of Commissioners for Foreign Missions whereby the synod could choose a missionary and the field of labor, and could control the churches formed. Thus they achieved effective denominational control without formally withdrawing from this one society. By 1836 several wished to discontinue this arrangement.[126] Thus, by around 1834 the Reformed Dutch had effectively withdrawn from the society movement, giving greater power within the societies to the supporters of revivalism.

It was not as easy for the Presbyterians to withdraw from the society movement as it merged with the new revivalism, because the denomination itself was seriously divided. The New School was sympathetic to New England theology and vigorously supported the new revivalism. The Old School continued to adhere to the Reformed tradition of the middle and southern states. This conflict has been extensively discussed and so there is no need to review the events at length. Members of the Old School, along with their Reformed allies, had clearly been the initiators of the society movement. After 1826 and the merger of the societies of the middle and southern states with those of New England and the influx of the new revivalism into the societies, these same leaders became the most ardent advocates of denominational as opposed to associated activity.

In 1828 a number of Old School ministers, including Ashbel Green and Jacob Janeway, presented an "Overture to the General Assembly of the Presbyterian Church on the Subject of Missions" in an attempt to strengthen the denominational board of missions by making foreign missions an integral part of its operations. Green argued that voluntary associations were contrary to Scripture, and that the church had made an error "through inattention." The "Overture" had repercussions beyond foreign missions, however, and the American Home Missionary Society sent a committee to confer with the Assembly. After extensive debate, the General Assembly decided that the board already had all the necessary powers and the subject was "indefinitely postponed."[127] In August the supporters of the denominational board sought a cooperative arrangement with the Missionary Society of the Reformed Dutch Church. This was a clear indication that the Old School was not opposed on principle to associated activity but to the new theology and new revivalism. The denomination was so divided on the question that agreement was impossible and in 1829 the General Assembly resolved "that the churches should be left entirely to their own unbiased and deliberate choice" between the voluntary associations and the denominational board.[128]

The result of the Old School dissatisfaction with the societies was a new conception of the denomination. The new theory was simple. In addition to its former functions, the denomination was to be considered as a "missionary society." The Old School Presbyterians generally credited this "discovery" to John Holt Rice. Rice held that the church ought to "consider herself as a great missionary society, instituted for the conversion of the world; and that henceforth she would make that her great object."[129] Whether Rice was the first Presbyterian leader to make this distinction or not, by 1830 it was becoming commonplace among supporters of the Old School. By 1831, Joshua Wilson, best known for his prosecution of Lyman Beecher, had elevated this idea to the status of religious orthodoxy. In *Four Propositions Sustained Against the Claims of the American Home Missionary Society,* Wilson held that the church was responsible to Christ for missions and that the Presbyterian church was already a missionary society while the American Home Missionary Society was "not an *ecclesiastical* but a *civil* Institution." Further, he contended that the American Home Missionary Society "disturbs the peace and injures the prosperity of the Presbyterian church."[130]

The new concept of the denomination actually was broad enough to include all functions of the societies, but since missions and ministerial education most affected the denomination they received the initial attention. Wilson's *Four Propositions* actually appeared just before a convention, scheduled for November in Cincinnati, which was to decide whether missions in the West would be carried out by the General Assembly or the American Home Missionary Society. The convention resulted in a total stalemate between Old School supporters of the new theory of the denomination and New School proponents of the idea that the only proper function of the denomination was internal government.[131]

After the schism of 1837 Presbyterianism in America was represented by two denominations, each with a different conception of what that meant. The New School continued to cooperate with voluntary societies in every function not related to its internal government. The Old School, operating on the idea that the denomination was a "missionary society," strengthened the board of home missions and the board of education and in 1837 established a board of foreign missions. But the new theory of the denomination went further. It included all those areas of labor previously performed by the societies. In 1838 the Old School organized a board of publication, thus becoming a "tract society" in addition to a "missionary" and "education" society.

The wholesale withdrawal of the Old School of all the Reformed denominations in the middle and southern states from the society movement greatly speeded up the transition to revivalism. The Presbyterian schism of 1837 marked the completion of that process, but it was nearly complete as early as 1834. This transition left all of the "national" machinery, so laboriously constructed by the Old School, in the hands of the friends of the new revivalism. This new evangelicalism, featuring social control through conversion, became the characteristic expression of American Protestantism.

The new revivalism did not substantially alter the Reformed national ideology. The alleged connection between religion and national prosperity, the necessity of religion to social order, and the special role of America in leading the world into the millennium continued to dominate thought about the nation. Only the method of achieving these goals was altered. In 1835 Finney argued that if American Christians worked hard enough in the cause of revivalism "the millennium may come in this country in three years."[132]

The most perceptive analysis of the social function of the new evangelicalism was presented in 1841 by Albert Barnes in his *Sermons on Revivals.* The specific purpose of the sermons was to demonstrate the adaptability of revivals to cities and large towns, but the analysis was applicable to the whole phenomenon. Revivals needed to be better understood, Barnes suggested, because they had "done more than any other single cause to form the public mind." Some still believed that revivalism was "fitted to influence only the weaker portions of the community," but they were of national significance and commanded the attention of "a Christian or a patriot." Wherever there was "reigning order, peace, and prosperity" in America, the influence of revivals was evident.[133]

Revivals successfully promoted social order, argued Barnes, because they were in harmony with the very structure of society. Communities were so organized that they were bound together by certain common beliefs and emotions. Rational and intellectual arguments were ineffective methods to unite community action on any object. "If you wish to spread any opinions and principles," Barnes contended, "you will not do it by appealing to individuals *as such,* you will call to your aid the power of the social organizations." Barnes acknowledged that this method could be "perverted to evil purposes" but believed that it was "stronger in favor of virtue than vice." In following this method, Barnes exhorted, "You will rouse men by their common attachment to country; you will remind them of dear-bought liberty; you will lay before them their common dangers; you will awaken a *common* feeling, and endeavor to lead them forth to the martial field together."[134]

Those who have identified revivalism with individualism have entirely ignored the contemporary discussions. Revivalism was much more concerned with exercising "an extensive influence . . . over a community" than with the salvation of individual souls. Barnes illustrated this feature by comparing revivals with the Milky Way. This heavenly phenomenon was made up of "single stars, each subject to its own laws, moving in its own sphere, glorious, probably in its own array of satellites; but their rays meet and mingle—not less beautiful because the light of millions is blended together." Revivals were very similar. A revival was nothing more than "a single true conversion" extended "to a community—to many individuals." In this way, conversion of individuals was the best method of influencing an entire community.[135]

Like the Old School leaders, Barnes was primarily interested in controlling public opinion. "Such is our freedom," he noted, that every man "may advance any sentiments he pleases." False opinion could be supported by the "power of argument," enforced by the "eloquence of persuasion," and promoted through "the power of the press." Such a situation was dangerous to the best interests of society and could only be controlled by extensive revivals. Barnes was particularly concerned about promoting revivals in the cities because "in this land and in all others the talent that most decidedly directs public opinion, and that acts with most power on the public mind" was concentrated in the cities. Frequently "men of influence, wealth, and power" from all over the nation came to the cities. These men should be evangelized because they controlled "the habits, or the fashions, or the religieus [sic] opinions" in their places of residence. These "respectable and influential merchants" were "moulding that vast population that is soon to give the nation its president, its great officers of government, and the laws...."[136]

The new revivalism, in fact, proposed to perform all the functions demanded by the Reformed view of what America should be like. If there were revivals, Barnes claimed, then "children would be taught; ... the Sabbath would return to bless.... Temperance would be promoted.... The houses of pollution and infamy would no more open.... The theatre would no more open its doors.... Sober industry would take the place of idleness ... plenty and comfort would succeed to want; decency of apparel to penury and rags...."[137] By 1841 in America, individual salvation was the means of promoting social order.

Conclusion

The success of the Reformed of the middle and southern states at shaping a distinctly American ideology of the relationship of religion and government was truly amazing. Unlike their New England counterparts, many of whom continued to enjoy some sort of establishment well into the nineteenth century, these Reformed entered the national experience with a backlog of experience in religious diversity and practical disestablishment, and even, in the South, as religious dissenters. They would have preferred a religious establishment that would have essentially recognized the validity of their understanding of Christianity. It was perhaps their own rigidity that caused them to fail in that attempt, especially in Virginia. But for such a rigid people, and they were rigid, they demonstrated a remarkable flexibility. When it became apparent that the American legal settlement would be one in which the state disengaged from the support of religion, the Reformed of the middle and southern states welcomed it and declared it to be the solution that would be most conducive to the spread and ultimate domination of Reformed Christianity. Unlike twentieth-century liberals, the Reformed interpreted disestablishment as the legal and official recognition of the twin Reformation doctrines of the priesthood of all believers and the absolute and unquestioned authority of the Christian Scriptures. And, to a very large degree, it was their definition, rather than the thinking of Jefferson and Madison, that captured the imagination of the American people and became the dominant popular opinion in the land.

But perhaps of even greater significance, the Reformed of the middle and southern states forged an ideology that ultimately based American national prosperity on national adherence to Reformed Christianity. Under the tutelage of John Witherspoon and Samuel Stanhope Smith, the Reformed captured the Enlightenment and brought it into the service of Reformed Christianity, altering traditional Calvinism in the process. Witherspoon and Smith, declaring that the truth of the law of nations could be devised by observation and reason alone, propounded a doctrine of natural law and political science that substantially reinforced the Calvinistic doctrine of providence in an era of skepticism and enlightenment. All history, they argued, proved beyond any reasonable doubt that those nations that adhered to the moral principles taught by Christianity had prospered and those that had taken a contrary route had fallen into ruin. The Reformed preachers of whatever denomination picked up this message and proclaimed it throughout the land. The United States, if it were to prosper, was required to be a Christian nation.

It was not merely national survival that was at stake, however, it was in fact all those things that were distinctly American—civil and religious liberty, and republican, if not democratic, government. With a stroke of genius, the Reformed blended the patriotic and nationalistic aspirations of their contemporaries with their own religious tradition and made them seem inseparable. America had become great in the world because of its Reformed Protestant nature, and it could remain so only to the degree it remained faithful to its Reformed Protestant heritage.

If the doctrine of providence, reshaped into natural law and nationalized, seemed to offer Americans a national formula for prosperity or doom, the doctrine of the millennium gave the Reformed community itself assurance of ultimate triumph and even more precise guidelines for the development of American society. The doctrine of providence served most powerfully to combat the secular enlightenment. The millennium was the supreme religious symbol of the Reformed community. As such, an analysis of that symbol gives greatest insight into the deepest desires of the Reformed.

As they interpreted the Bible, the Reformed sincerely believed that the millennium was at hand and that America was to play a decisive role in events leading to that glorious day. This, in effect, made them prime movers in the most significant events of all history. While they were, in their view, guaranteed success, their postmillennialism demanded of them extreme exertion. In the divine plan, they were charged with the responsibility of creating in America the millennial society.

The shape of the futuristic society, as delineated in the Reformed publications of the period, was surprisingly anachronistic. In tone, the various characteristics of the society ran from medieval to tribal with modern, more particularly American, developments lauded only as vehicles to achieve those ancient modes. Indeed, the Reformed of the early nineteenth century were experiencing an increasingly desacralized world, which, as Mircea Eliade has noted, "is a recent discovery in the history of the human experience," and they were attempting to make that world completely sacred again.

The central characteristic of millennial society was unity—conformity. The Reformed lived in perhaps the most highly diversified society on earth at the time. The United States featured a society diversified by occupation, social class, ethnicity, slavery, and, perhaps most importantly, religion. In this context the Reformed envisioned a society in which all would see "eye to eye." The American constitutional settlement that allowed religious liberty (i.e., diversity) would provide the way for perfect religious homogeneity. All secularists, irreligionists, and denominationalists of various views would unite in the Reformed camp. Unity would, of course, render somewhat obsolete American developments. Civil and religious liberty, however, were seen as essential to the development of unity. Under religious establishment, man had not been free to accept the truth. Once freed from the restraint of men and government, all would come to the truth. In the perfect millennial society, the national rulers would be "nursing fathers" to the church, much like Constantine, but the uniformity of society would be such that this would not be oppressive.

In social terms, however, the Reformed doctrine of the millennium called for few changes. The perfect society was not to be based on equality or democracy; society would still reflect a graded pattern. Some people would be rich and others would remain poor. There would be rulers and the ruled, presumably with the rich ruling, but all would be religious and fulfilling their appointed stations in conformity to the will of God. The rich magistrates would be kind, considerate, and fair while the poor would be industrious, honest, and content with their station in life.

In light of the millennial perception, it would never have occurred to the Reformed to raise questions about the validity or justice of their cause. Any consideration of the rights of others came in the context of temporaneity. Those who disagreed to whatever degree were simply misled. They would ultimately perceive the truth and acquiesce in it. The major concern of the Reformed, then, was how to achieve their goals.

To an amazing degree, the Reformed instinctively judged the degree to which the United States measured up to or fell short of their standards by reference to governments—increasingly in the nineteenth century, to the federal government. The failure of the federal government to explicitly recognize the providence of God bothered the Reformed immensely. That this may have been inconsistent with their glorification of "religious liberty" never occurred to the Reformed because religious liberty to them meant freedom to engage the truth, and the government, as well as individuals, had that freedom and responsibility. In spite of this defect, the Reformed would have been satisfied if the populace would have elected Christian officicals and they in turn would have enacted Christian laws.

Given the Reformed conception of the ideal, and given their basic satisfaction with that status quo, American society in the early part of the nineteenth century must have been far different than either liberal or conservative historians of the twentieth century have characterized it. While indeed different than the tribalized utopia of the Reformed, American society was more conservative, more elitist, more medieval, in fact more constant with its European heritage than all but a very few Americans have been willing to admit.

The Reformed vision came ultimately to be not so much how to change things but how to keep them the same. Some improvement, from their point of view, would, of course, be welcomed. But the fact was that the United States was growing rapidly, both in population and territory, and this very growth threatened not only the idealized future of the millennium, but the basically satisfactory present.

The Reformed perceived the major threat to American social order, and therefore the escatological significance of America, to come not so much from the essentially secularizing tendencies in American government as from the democratic tendencies. However much the Reformed might have opposed the secular enlightenment, or decried the election of Jefferson to the presidency, by the close of the War of 1812 these were essentially dead issues. Irreligion had assumed much more tangible form in the poverty and presumed lawlessness of the mass of American citizens. The rapid industrialization and urbanization of the United States, especially in the coastal regions of the middle states, had created for the Reformed the makings of a nightmare. Thousands of Americans who presumably had the power of electing government officials were beyond the control or even influence of organized religion, and these people were by definition and in reality the poor. At a later date the Reformed extended the area of their concern to include the people of the West, and their crusade to save America and in turn introduce the millennium came to focus on bringing these people, otherwise lowly and despised, under their control.

While it appeared self-evident to the Reformed that instruction in "the knowledge of the Lord" was the way to accomplish their goals, it was not at all clear what type of institution would best meet their needs. Given the historical development of mankind to that point, and the basic instincts of the Reformed, governments—local, state, and federal—always presented themselves as the most efficient. But the peculiarly American developments presented difficulties. In the United States, governments, beginning with the federal government, were gradually disengaging from the support and oversight of religion, and the trend proved to be irreversible.

The denomination was a likely candidate, but it too proved inadequate. In the first place, the conception of the denomination as an institution at the time of national independence was extremely narrow and presupposed a supportive government. The denomination as an institution was oriented toward the supervision of a homogeneous body of believers and could not easily be changed into an aggressive institution that could bring into its confines a heterogeneous and largely unwilling people. Beyond that, the denomination itself was a denial of the religious symbolism of the Reformed. It stood for fragmentation; they dreamed of unity. In the American system, it was relegated to nonsupport by the national government. This precluded the role of America as the vanguard of the millennium.

The institution that emerged as the most promising was the voluntary society. It could claim to be nonsectarian, even if it were not so in fact. At a minimum, the societies allowed for the cooperation of all the Reformed, who heralded them as forerunners of the millennial unity. On their own understanding of American religious liberty, the Reformed could solicit the aid of government for the societies in a way obviously inappropriate for the various denominations. Failing in official governmental support, they could at least utilize the aid of willing politicians and statesmen.

With all these assets, the voluntary societies from the earliest local urban beginnings to the great national conglomerates, could concentrate their efforts on the greatest threat to American society—the poor. The societies attacked the problem of poverty not by attempting to eliminate it, but my making the poor conform to satisfactory standards of behavior. Indeed, poverty was such an accepted and established condition of social existence that it was probably impossible for them to have done otherwise. But the poor, who would even persist into the millennium, must be made to behave according to Christian (Reformed) norms or the prosperity and future of the nation, indeed of the world, was threatened. The societies thus sought to render the poor honest, industrious, frugal, sober—and content.

The Reformed scheme to conquer America through indoctrination ultimately failed, not because it was deemed improper, un-American, or even illegal (although the legislature of Pennsylvania certainly raised that issue), but because it was too slow, too awkward, and too identifiably elitist. Revivalism, after tentative forays in the 1740s and at the turn of the century, emerged as the distinctively American mode for promoting social order through religion. Revivalism certainly conformed more closely to the American ethos. It could appear democratic and individualistic while remaining in fact elitist and collective. It eschewed reason and embraced emotion. It was, in fact, a nearly perfect vehicle for the transmission of the ancient notions of the interrelatedness of religious observance and national prosperity to a sprawling, incipient industrial nation. For although the promoters of revivalism introduced methods alien and abominable to the rigid Reformed who were now labeled "Old School," they maintained intact and promoted with vigor the ideology of religion and national prosperity so carefully constructed by that very same "Old School."

This most significant development of the nineteenth century decided the course of development in American religion in several areas. In the first place, American religion was to be salvational as opposed to civil. The "Old School" had offered a civil religion—a religion of and for the republic that would promote its interests and prosperity. But that religion was rejected in favor of one that offered salvation both for the individual and the republic. The heyday of American civil religion was the 1820s rather than the 1950s. Salvational and civil religion were so entwined that it required the analytic genius of a generation of scholars in the 1960s and 1970s to attempt, unsuccessfully, to disengage it.

A second consequence of the triumph of revivalism was to move the national significance of religion in America once and for all beyond the dominance of any conglomerate of institutions. Religion, and, at least for the time being, Protestant religion, became the pervasive influence in American culture. Institutional expression of that religion, whether through declining voluntary societies or through the denomination with its enlarged conception, became secondary to the pervasiveness of religion—not quite yet if it indeed ever has become religion in general—to that culture. The resurgence of religion in the 1970s in its multi-institutional form certainly should cause concern among those who have rushed from "post-Protestant" to "post-Christian" as an adequate characterization of the American scene.

Finally, the coincidence of purpose and ideology from the "Old School" to the revivalists should cause some reflection on the nature of "social" Christianity. Revivalism quickly moved beyond the phase of aggressive social reform that it reflected in the 1840s and 1850s to become the recognized protector of the status quo. It did this essentially by ignoring "social" issues and concentrating on "religion." By contrast, the proponents of the so-called "Social Gospel" appeared to be something new on the American scene, when they were in fact the latter-day exponents of the "Old School."

Notes

INTRODUCTION

1. Carl Bridenbaugh, *Mitre and Sceptre: Transatlantic Faiths, Ideas, Personalities, and Politics 1689–1775* (New York: Oxford University Press, 1967); Alan Heimert, *Religion and the American Mind from the Great Awakening to the Revolution* (Cambridge: Harvard University Press, 1966).

2. Robert Ellis Thompson, *A History of the Presbyterian Churches in the United States*, vol. 6 of *The American Church History Series*, ed. Philip Schaff et al., 13 vols. (New York: Christian Literature Co., 1893–1898); Leonard J. Trinterud, *The Forming of An American Tradition: A Re-examination of Colonial Presbyterianism* (Philadelphia: Westminster Press, 1949); Lefferts A. Loetscher, *The Broadening Church: A Study of the Theological Issues in the Presbyterian Church Since 1869* (Philadelphia: University of Pennsylvania Press, 1954); George M. Marsden, *The Evangelical Mind and the New School Presbyterian Experience: A Case Study of Thought and Theology in Nineteenth-Century America* (New Haven: Yale University Press, 1970); William Warren Sweet, *The Presbyterians, 1783–1840: A Collection of Source Materials*, vol. 2 of *Religion on the American Frontier* (New York: Harper and Brothers, 1936); Walter Brownlow Posey, *The Presbyterian Church in the Old Southwest, 1778–1883* (Richmond: John Knox Press, 1952); Ernest Trice Thompson, *Presbyterians in the South, Volume One: 1607–1861* (Richmond: John Knox Press, 1963); L. C. Rudolph, *Hoosier Zion: The Presbyterians in Early Indiana* (New Haven: Yale University Press, 1963); Robert Hastings Nichols, *Presbyterianism in New York State: A History of the Synod and Its Predecessors,* ed. and completed by James Hastings Nichols (Philadelphia: Westminster Press, 1963).

3. Edwin Scott Gaustad, *Historical Atlas of Religion in America* (New York: Harper and Row, 1962), pp. 4, 43.

4. Charles Beecher, ed., *Autobiography, Correspondence, etc., of Lyman Beecher, D. D.*, 2 vols. (New York, 1864–1865), 2:423.

5. Winthrop Hudson, *American Protestantism* (Chicago: University of Chicago Press, 1961), pp. 51, 60.

6. Gaustad, *Historical Atlas,* p. 26.

7. John B. Boles, *The Great Revival, 1787–1805: Origins of the Southern Evangelical Mind* (Lexington: University Press of Kentucky, 1972). The argument that the early nineteenth-century revivals produced a distinctive southern religion is not convincing. Boles makes two fundamental errors at this point. He does not demonstrate that revivalism in the South differed substantially from that of other sections. This would be essential to demonstrate that ensuing southern religion was distinctive. In the second place, Boles ignores major segments of the southern religious community. The major Presbyterian revivalists in Kentucky were forced out of the denomination that never accepted their brand of revivalism and that continued to flourish. Boles makes no mention of John Holt Rice, who was perhaps the major Presbyterian minister of the South and who was the foremost supporter of southern religious institutions. Many of the Baptists also remained aloof from the revival. Of these Boles makes no mention. The largest Baptist group in Kentucky, the Elkhorn Association, excommunicated

four members for every new one baptized during the period from 1803 to 1805. Obviously these significant groups must be accounted for in the development of southern religion. See E. T. Thompson, *Presbyterians in the South*, 1:126–79, 276–79; Richard Carwardine, "The Second Great Awakening in the Urban Centers; An Examination of Methodism and the 'New Measures,'" *The Journal of American History* 59 (September 1972): 327–40; William L. Lumpkin, *Baptist Foundations in the South* (Nashville: Broadman Press, 1961), pp. 1–23, 133; Catharine C. Cleveland, *The Great Revival in the West, 1779–1805* (Chicago: University of Chicago Press, 1916), pp. 37–43; William Warren Sweet, *The Baptists, 1783–1830*, vol. 1 of *Religion on the American Frontier* (New York: Harper and Brothers, 1931), pp. 50–53, 498–509; James Edward Humphrey, "Baptist Discipline in Kentucky, 1781–1860," (Th.D. diss., Southern Baptist Theological Seminary, 1959), p. 291.

8. E. T. Thompson, *Presbyterians in the South*, pp. 530–71; James W. Silver, *Confederate Morale and Church Propaganda* (University, Alabama: University of Alabama Press, 1957).

CHAPTER 1

1. James D. Richardson, ed., *A Compilation of the Messages and Papers of the Presidents* (Washington, D.C.: Bureau of National Literature, 1904), 1:216–18.

2. Ibid., p. 221.

3. Ibid.; Horace Binney, *An Inquiry into the Formation of Washington's Farewell Address* (Philadelphia, 1859), p. 201.

4. Letter from George Washington to William Pearce, May 25, 1794, quoted in Norman Cousins, ed., *"In God We Trust," The Religious Beliefs and Ideas of the American Founding Fathers* (New York: Harper and Row, 1958), p. 68.

5. George Washington, General Order, Cambridge, July 4, 1775, quoted in ibid., p. 50.

6. Ibid., pp. 51–56.

7. Binney, *Washington's Farewell Address*, p. 177.

8. Ibid., p. 201.

9. John C. Hamilton, *Alexander Hamilton: Portrait in Paradox* (New York: Harper and Row, 1959), pp. 7–9; Broadus Mitchess, *Alexander Hamilton: Youth to Maturity, 1755–1788* (New York: MacMillan, 1957), pp. 39–43.

10. John Maclean, *History of the College of New Jersey, From Its Origin in 1746 to the Commencement of 1854*, 2 vols. (Philadelphia, 1877), 1:337, 2:127.

11. *Memoirs of William Graham, First President of Washington College, Virginia*, Manuscript, Princeton Theological Seminary Library (n.p., n.d.); James Carnahan, ed., *The Autobiography and Ministerial Life of the Rev. John Johnston* (New York, 1856), p. 28.

12. Lyman Henry Butterfield, *John Witherspoon Comes to America: A Documentary Account Based Largely on New Materials* (Princeton: Princeton University Press, 1953), p. xiii.

13. John Sanderson et al., *Biography of the Signers of the Declaration of Independence* (Philadelphia, 1820–1827) 5:115, quoted in ibid.

14. Varnum Lansing Collins, *President Witherspoon: A Biography*, 2 vols. (Princeton: Princeton University Press, 1925), 1:117.

15. Ibid., p. 113; *The Works of John Witherspoon,* 4 vols. (Philadelphia, 1801), 4:213.

16. Witherspoon, *Works,* 2:407.

17. Collins, *President Witherspoon,* 1:65.

18. Witherspoon, *Works,* 2:407.

19. Quoted in David Walker Woods, Jr., *John Witherspoon* (New York: F. H. Revell, Co., 1906), pp. 128, 231.

20. For biographical information on Witherspoon see Collins, *President Witherspoon;* Maclean, *History of the College of New Jersey.*

21. Dumas Malone, ed., *Dictionary of American Biography,* 22 vols. (New York, 1936), 10: pt. 2, p. 438.

22. Quoted in Collins, *President Witherspoon,* 1:112; Maclean, *History of the College of New Jersey,* 1:357–63, 402; 2:113–17. Maclean analyzed the offices held by the graduates during this period, giving Witherspoon credit for all attending during his presidency. The following list reflects Maclean's analysis with the numbers in parenthesis representing those actually receiving their major instruction from Smith. Witherspoon: one president; one vice-president; six members of the Continental Congress; twenty (eleven) senators; twenty-three (eighteen) representatives; thirteen (six) governors; three (two) judges of the Supreme Court; twenty "or *more*" officers in the American Revolution; thirty "at least, became distinguished"; nineteen (eight) presidents or professors. Smith: twenty-one presidents or professors; one vice-president; two presidents pro tem. of the Senate; nine senators; twenty-five representatives; four cabinet members; six ministers to foreign nations; thirteen judges of the United States Supreme and district courts; eight governors; twenty-four "held high state judicial posts"; four state attorneys-general; thirty-three "were men of note." On the basis of students actually taught, then, Smith emerges as the teacher of the greater number of statesmen.

23. Samuel Stanhope Smith, *The Lectures . . . on the Subjects of Moral and Political Philosophy,* 2 vols. (New York, 1812), 2:306; idem, *On the Love of Praise* (New Brunswick, 1810), pp. 25–26, 29.

24. Biographical information on Smith may be found in William B. Sprague, ed., *Annals of the American Pulpit,* 7 vols. (New York, 1857–1861), 3:335–45; an anonymous memoir in *Sermons of Samuel Stanhope Smith,* ed. Frederick Beasley, 2 vols. (Philadelphia, 1821), 1:3–50; Maclean, *History of the College of New Jersey,* 2:122–46; Samuel Holt Mark, "Samuel Stanhope Smith (1751–1819): Friend of Rational Liberty," in William Thorp, ed., *The Lives of Eighteen from Princeton* (Princeton: Princeton University Press, 1946), pp. 86–110; William H. Hudnut III, "Samuel Stanhope Smith: Enlightened Conservative," *Journal of the History of Ideas* 17 (1965):540–52.

25. *Encyclopedia Britannica* (Chicago, 1968), 6:166–67.

26. James McCosh, *Scottish Philosophy* (New York, 1884), p. 9. For a detailed explication see Selwyn A. Graves, *The Scottish Philosophy of Common Sense* (Oxford: Clarendon Press, 1960); Paul Edwards et al., *The Encyclopedia of Philosophy,* 5 vols. (New York: MacMillan, 1967), 2:155–59.

27. Maclean, *History of the College of New Jersey,* 1:189.

28. For a discussion of the influence of the Scottish philosophy on American

theology see Sydney E. Ahlstrom, "The Scottish Philosophy and American Theology," *Church History* 24 (September 1955):262–66.

29. For the dynamic aspect of New England theology see Joseph Haroutunian, *Piety Versus Moralism: The Passing of New England Theology* (New York: Henry Holt and Co., 1932).

30. Sydney E. Ahlstrom, "Theology in America: A Historical Survey," in *The Shaping of American Religion,* vol. 1 of *Religion in American Life,* 4 vols., ed. James Ward Smith and A. Leland Jamison (Princeton: Princeton University Press, 1961), p. 267.

31. John Witherspoon, *Lectures on Moral Philosophy,* ed. Varnum Lansing Collins (Princeton: Princeton University Press, 1912), pp. 1–2. I have used this critical edition throughout.

32. Ibid., pp. 17–18.

33. Ibid., pp. 28–30.

34. James L. McAllister, "John Witherspoon: Academic Advocate for American Freedom," in *A Miscellany of American Christianity,* ed. Stuart C. Henry (Durham: Duke University Press, 1963), pp. 218, 222.

35. S. S. Smith, *Moral and Political Philosophy,* 1:12.

36. Paul Russell Anderson and Max Harold Fisch, *Philosophy in America from the Puritans to James, With Representative Selections* (New York: D. Appleton-Century Co., 1939), p. 297. Anderson contends that Smith was a more representative figure than Witherspoon.

37. S. S. Smith, *Moral and Political Philosophy,* 1:14–15.

38. Ibid., pp. 19–23.

39. John Rodgers, *The Faithful Servant Rewarded* (New York: 1795), p. 33; Collins, *President Witherspoon,* 2:14.

40. S. S. Smith, *Moral and Political Philosophy,* 1:12.

41. Samuel Stanhope Smith, *Lectures on the Evidences of the Christian Religion* (Philadelphia, 1809), p. 322.

42. Samuel Stanhope Smith, *An Essay on the Causes of the Variety of Complexion and Figure in the Human Species,* 2nd ed. (New Brunswick, 1810), pp. 4–5.

43. Witherspoon, *Works,* 2:452–75.

44. Witherspoon, *Moral Philosophy,* pp. 110–13.

45. S. S. Smith, *Moral and Political Philosophy,* 1:25. It may be an injustice to extract and rearrange such small segments of his work. He was, more than most, committed to a "system," and his work, though overlooked, seems important enough to receive treatment as such. See for example his *A Comprehensive View of the Leading and Most Important Principles of Natural and Revealed Religion* (New Brunswick, 1815).

46. S. S. Smith, *Moral and Poltitical Philosophy,* 2:280.

47. Ibid., 1:93–94; 2:238.

48. Ibid., 2:93.

49. Ibid., pp. 10–11.

50. Ibid., p. 56.

51. Ibid., pp. 323–24.

52. Ibid., p. 309.

53. Ibid., pp. 95, 227, 314.

54. Ibid., pp. 112–13. Cf. pp. 95, 107, 142.

55. Ibid., pp. 107–09.

56. Ibid., p. 99.

57. Ibid., pp. 110–11.

58. Ibid., p. 24.

59. Robert Smith, *The Obligations of the Confederate States of North America to Praise God* (Philadelphia, 1782), p. 4.

60. S. S. Smith, *Moral and Political Philosophy,* 2:300–05.

61. Ibid., p. 146. While Smith said at one point that "there is no exercise of the human faculties more favorable to virtue, than the humble, patient, and diligent cultivation of the intellectual powers," he thought of education primarily in the moral sense. Pursuit of liberal arts was only for those who had "inclination and leisure to pursue them." Ibid., pp. 77, 306.

62. Ibid., pp. 142–58, 226, 306.

63. Ibid., p. 156.

64. Ibid., p. 59.

65. Ibid., 1:34–35.

66. Ibid., p. 146.

67. Ibid., pp. 60–64.

68. Ibid., 2:313.

69. Ibid., 1:74.

70. Ibid., p. 70.

71. Ibid., 2:315–17. Smith also favored internal improvements and state magnificence in buildings, statues, and monuments, or "public magnificence with private simplicity."

72. Ibid., 1:72–73.

73. Ibid., 2:277.

74. Witherspoon, *Moral Philosophy,* pp. 87–90.

75. S. S. Smith, *Moral and Political Philosophy,* 1:86.

76. Ibid., 2:306, 313.

77. Ibid., p. 280.

78. Ibid., pp. 291–99.

79. Ibid., p. 293.

80. Ibid., pp. 280, 313.

81. Ibid., p. 310.

82. Ibid., pp. 308–12.

CHAPTER 2

1. Paul K. Conkin, *Puritans and Pragmatists: Eight Eminent American Thinkers* (New York: Dodd, Mead and Co., 1968), p. 118.

2. Charles Evans, ed., *American Bibliography,* 12 vols. (New York: Peter Smith, 1941–1942). A brief glance at this comprehensive bibliography of works printed in America before 1800 easily demonstrates the abundance of religious materials.

3. Cousins, *"In God We Trust,"* pp. 217–94.

4. For a discussion of the development of federal theology in New England see

Perry Miller, *Errand Into the Wilderness* (Cambridge: Belknap Press, 1956), pp. 89–98.

5. For Calvin's views on providence see John Calvin, *A Compend of the Institutes of the Christian Religion,* ed. Hugh T. Kerr (Philadelphia: Westminster Press, 1964), pp. 34–37.

6. Perry Miller, "From Covenant to the Revival," in *The Shaping of American Religion,* vol. 1 of *Religion in American Life,* ed. Smith and Jamison, pp. 327–58.

7. William Gribbin, "The Covenant Transformed: The Jeremiad Tradition and the War of 1812," *Church History* 40 (September 1971):297–305. Gribbin builds on Miller's basic thesis without examining it critically.

8. Melancthon Glasgow, *History of the Reformed Presbyterian Church in America* (Baltimore, 1888).

9. James M'Chord, *National Safety* (Lexington, 1815), p. 6.

10. Gaillard Hunt, ed., *Journals of the Continental Congress, 1774–1789* (Washington, D.C.: Government Printing Office, 1922), 25:699–700.

11. Witherspoon, *Works,* 2:455.

12. George Duffield, *A Sermon . . .* (Boston, 1784), p. 18.

13. John Rodgers, *The Divine Goodness Displayed in the American Revolution* (New York, 1784), p. 20.

14. Witherspoon, *Works,* 2:451–75.

15. Duffield, *A Sermon,* p. 1.

16. Witherspoon, *Works,* 2:454–75.

17. See Samuel Stanhope Smith, *The Divine Goodness to the United States of America* (Philadelphia, 1795); idem, *A Discourse on the Nature and Reasonableness of Fasting* (Philadelphia, 1795); idem, *Sermons,* 1:19–38, 51–66.

18. S. S. Smith, *Sermons,* 2:314–36.

19. For Smith's position see his *Moral and Political Philosophy,* 2:120; Hudnut, "Enlightened Conservative," p. 546.

20. Hudnut, "Enlightened Conservative," pp. 551–52; Archibald Alexander, *A Sermon Delivered at the Opening of the General Assembly* (Philadelphia, 1808), p. 25.

21. William Linn, *The Blessings of America* (New York, 1797), pp. 23–24.

22. John B. Johnson, *The Dealings of God with Israel and America* (Albany, 1798), pp. 14–17.

23. Eliphalet Nott, *A Discourse Delivered in the Presbyterian Church, in Albany, the Fourth of July, A.D. 1801* (Albany, 1801), pp. 9–23.

24. John M. Bradford, *The Fear of the Lord, the Hope of Freedom* (Albany, 1814), pp. 8–27. For other examples see George S. Boardman, *A Sermon . . .* (Sacket's Harbor, New York, 1824); Joseph Clark, *A Sermon . . .* (New Brunswick, 1812); George Bush, *Lack of Vision the Ruin of the People* (Indianapolis, 1826); William Linn, *A Discourse on National Sins* (New York, 1798); James Muir, *A Sermon . . .* (Philadelphia, 1798); Symmes C. Henry, *An Oration Delivered by Appointment Before the Cincinnati Society of New Jersey* (Trenton, 1824).

25. Ashbel Green, *Obedience to the Laws of God, the Sure and Indispensable Defense of Nations* (Philadelphia, 1798), pp. 39–40.

26. Ibid., pp. 19, 40.

27. Alexander McClelland, *Sermons by the Late Alexander McClelland, D.D.,* ed. Richard W. Dickinson (New York, 1867), pp. 1–17.

28. For additional insight into this phenomenon see John G. Dreyer, *Concord and Religion: The Principle Sources of Civil Prosperity* (New York, 1812), p. 12; Seth Williston, *A Fast Sermon, on the National Profanation of the Sabbath* (Albany, 1825), p. 7; David M'Conaughy, *The Duties and Dangers of Prosperity* (Gettysburg, 1817), p. 14; John B. Romeyn, *Sermons*, 2 vols. (New York, 1816), 2:313; Alexander M'Leod, *Messiah, Governor of the Earth: A Discourse* (Glasgow, Scotland, 1804), p. 39; *Christian Advocate* 1 (1823):3. This rational view of providence began to recede in the late 1820s as ministers generally became less educated and social conditions favored more "enthusiasm" in religion. See for example Alexander Mitchell, *A Serious Letter to a Friend on the Influence of Providence, the Efficacy of Prayer, and on Universalism* (Eaton, Ohio, 1829), p. 7.

29. M'Chord, *National Safety*, pp. 4–17.

30. James Wilson, *The Utility of the Scriptures of the Old Testament*, (Alexandria, 1798), pp. 16, 22.

31. Samuel Miller, *A Sermon* ... (New York, 1798), pp. 23–26.

32. Samuel Miller, *A Sermon* ... (New York, 1799), pp. 22–25.

33. Examples of such events were a fire in Richmond, Virginia, in 1812; an epidemic of yellow fever in 1822; a cholera epidemic in 1832; and a fire in New York in 1835. For examples of how these were treated in sermons of the day see Ichabod Spencer, *The Conflageration in the City of New York* (New York, 1836); James H. Willson, *Tokens of the Divine Displeasure in the Late Conflagerations in New York, and Other Judgements Illustrated* (New Burch, New York, 1835); Paschal N. Strong, *The Pestilence, A Punishment for Public Sins* (New York, 1822); *Christian Advocate* 1 (October 1823):484.

34. Samuel Miller, *A Sermon* ... (New York, 1812).

35. Archibald Alexander, *A Discourse Occasioned by the Burning of the Theater in the City of Richmond* (Philadelphia, 1812), pp. 18–22.

36. For the millennial interpretation see Samuel Fisher, *Two Sermons* ... (Morristown, New Jersey, 1814); James Muir, *Ten Sermons* (Alexandria, 1812), pp. 15–20; idem, *Repentance, or Richmond in Tears* (n.p., n.d.). Muir listed all the printed sermons on the event and gave a brief characterization of each. See also S. Miller, *A Sermon* ... , 1799, pp. 26–27.

37. Andrew Wylie, *Godliness the Nation's Hope* (Washington, Pennsylvania, 1828), pp. 7–11.

38. Presbyterian Church in the United States of America, *Minutes of the General Assembly* (Philadelphia, n.d.), 1:485. Cited hereafter as *MGA*.

39. James Inglis, *A Sermon* ... (Baltimore, 1808), p. 10.

40. J. Clark, *A Sermon*, p. 11.

41. Stephen N. Rowan, *The Sin and Danger of Insensibility under the Calls of God to Repentance* (New York, 1812), p. 18. See also Dreyer, *Concord and Religion*, p. 7.

42. John E. Latta, *A Sermon* ... (Wilmington, 1815), p. 18.

43. M'Conaughy, *Duties and Dangers of Prosperity*, p. 18.

44. *MGA*, 1:515–16.

45. Strong, *The Pestilence*, p. 17; David M'Conaughy, *The Nature and Origin of Civil Liberty, With the Means of its Perpetuation* (Gettysburg, 1823), p. 16.

46. Nicholas Murray, *A Sermon* ... (Elizabethtown, New Jersey, 1838), p. 16; Jacob Brodhead, *A Sermon* ... (New York, 1831), p. 21; Cornelius C. Cuyler, *The Signs of the Times* (Philadelphia, 1839), pp. 97–98; George W. Bethune, *A*

Sermon ... (Philadelphia, 1839), pp. 14–18; Daniel D. Barnard, *A Discourse on the Life, Services and Character of Stephen Van Rensselaer* (Albany, 1839), p. 36.

47. John Winthrop, "Christian Charities. A Modell Hereof," in H. Sheldon Smith, Robert T. Handy, and Lefferts A. Loetscher, *American Christianity: An Historical Interpretation with Representative Documents,* 2 vols. (New York: Charles Scribner's Sons, 1960–1963), 1:98.

48. Philip Milledoler, *A Discourse* ... (New York, 1806), p. 6.

49. Jacob Brodhead, *A Plea for the Poor* (Philadelphia, 1815), pp. 10–11.

50. David J. Rothman, *The Discovery of the Asylum: Social Order and Disorder in the New Republic* (Boston: Little, Brown and Co., 1971), pp. xix, 3–12.

51. Jacob Janeway, *The Blessedness of the Charitable* (Philadelphia, 1812), p. 12.

52. John Frederick Schroeder, *Plea for the Industrious Poor and Strangers, in Sickness* (New York, 1830), p. 3.

53. New York Society for the Prevention of Pauperism, *Report of a Committee on the Subject of Pauperism* (New York, 1818), p. 12; Ward Stafford, *New Missionary Field: A Report to the Female Missionary Society for the Poor of the City of New York, and Its Vicinity* (New York, 1817), p. 41; Union Benevolent Association, *Constitution and Report Explanatory of Its Object* (Philadelphia, 1831), p. 4; Female Domestic Missionary Society of Philadelphia, *First Annual Report of the Managers* (Philadelphia, 1817), p. 6.

54. Stafford, *New Missionary Field,* p. 30.

55. Archibald Alexander, *The Pastoral Office* (Philadelphia, 1834), p. 20.

56. Ibid.

57. James Spencer Cannon, *Lectures on History and Chronology Introductory to the Reading of Ancient, Sacred, and Profane History* (New Brunswick, 1830), pp. 7–10.

58. Joseph Warren Scott, *An Oration, Delivered on the Twenty-Second Anniversary of American Independence,* July 4, 1798 (New Brunswick, 1798), p. 7.

59. Jedidiah Morse, *A Sermon, Exhibiting the Present Dangers, and Consequent Duties of the Citizens of the United States of America* (New York, 1799), p. 20.

60. For additional examples of the use of Greece and Rome as illustrations of the doctrine of providence, see Williston, *A Fast Sermon,* p. 34; John McDonald, *Sermon, Delivered in the Capitol, July 4, 1814* (Albany, 1814), pp. 32–33; Gideon Starr, *An Oration, Delivered in the Dutch Church, in the City of Schenectady, on the Fourth of July, 1801* (Albany, 1801), pp. 7–10; John Matthews, *Memorial of Independence* (Baltimore, 1815), p. 21; Romeyn, *Sermons,* 1:99; Smith, *Sermons,* 2:27; James Abercrombie, *Two Sermons* ... (Philadelphia, 1812), pp. 7–10; William T. Hamilton, *Grounds for Thanksgiving* (Newark, 1832), p. 10.

61. William Linn, *Discourses on the Signs of the Times* (New York, 1793), pp. 11–19; Solomon Froeligh, *Republican Government Advocated* (Elizabethtown, New Jersey, 1794), p. 15; Samuel Miller, *Christianity the Grand Source, and the Surest Basis, of Political Liberty* (New York, 1793), p. 31.

62. Eliphalet Nott, *The Addresses, Delivered to the Candidates for the Baccalaureate at the Anniversary Commencements in Union College* (New York, 1814), pp. 12–13.

63. Dreyer, *Concord and Religion,* pp. 8–9.

64. Matthews, *Memorial of Independence,* pp. 21–23.

65. Tyson Edwards, *Reasons for Thankfulness* (Rochester, New York, 1837), p. 7.

66. P. Miller, "From Covenant to Revival," p. 354.

67. Herbert M. Morais, *Deism in Eighteenth-Century America* (New York: Russell and Russell, 1960), p. 128. See pp. 120–30 for an account of militant deism.

68. A. Green, *Obedience to the Laws of God*, pp. 45–46.

69. Ibid., pp. 7–8, 21, 44–45.

CHAPTER 3

1. John Breckinridge, *An Address, Delivered July 15, 1835, Before the Eucleian and Philomothean Society of the University of the City of New York* (New York, 1836), p. 34.

2. John F. Wilson, ed., *Church and State in American History* (Boston: D. C. Heath and Co., 1965), p. xi.

3. James Fulton Maclear, "'The True American Union' of Church and State: The Reconstruction of the Theocratic Tradition," *Church History* 28 (March 1959):53–56.

4. Sidney E. Mead, "Neither Church nor State: Reflections on James Madison's 'Line of Separation,'" *A Journal of Church and State* 10 (Autumn 1968):349–64.

5. Hooper Cumming, *An Oration* . . . (Newark, 1823), p. 8; Cyrus Gildersleeve, Centurial *Jubilee, A Sermon Preached at Bloomfield, N.J., Oct. 31, 1817* (Newark, 1817), p. 8.

6. Breckinridge, *An Address*, p. 7.

7. Edward D. Griffin, *Sermons of Edward D. Griffin, to which Is Prefixed a Memoir of His Life*, ed. William B. Sprague, 2 vols. (New York, 1839), 1:166; Gardiner Spring, *A Tribute to New England* (New York, 1821), pp. 16–17, 35.

8. Henry, *An Oration*, p. 7.

9. Eliphalet Nott, *Miscellaneous Works* (Schenectady, 1810), p. 152. For further illustrations of the elision of the Reformation, Puritanism, and the American Revolution see J. B. Johnson, *Dealings of God;* McDonald, *Sermon;* Nott, *A Discourse;* John Knox, Jr., *An Essay on the Appreciation of Reformation Principles in the American Government* (Philadelphia, 1833); M'Conaughy, *Nature and Origin of Civil Liberty;* John C. Smith, *The Religion and Patriotism of '76* (Washington, 1844); Melancton B. Williams, *An Oration, Delivered at Springfield, N.J., on the Fortieth Anniversary of American Independence* (Newark, 1815); Albert Barnes, *An Address, Delivered July 4th, 1827, at the Presbyterian Church in Morristown* (Morristown, New Jersey, 1827); Nathan S. S. Beman, *The Western Continent: A Discourse, Delivered in the First Presbyterian Church, Troy, July Fourth, 1841* (Troy, New York, 1841).

10. Morse, *A Sermon*, pp. 8–9.

11. John Holt Rice, *An Inaugural Discourse, Delivered on the First of January, 1824* (Richmond, 1824), p. 7.

12. Joshua Moore, *A Discourse, Delivered at the Council House, Detroit, Before the Legislative Council of Michigan Territory, June 21, 1824* (Detroit, 1824), p. 14.

13. M'Conaughy, *Duties and Dangers of Prosperity*, p. 8. See also the periodicals *Christian Messenger* 2 (November 1817):3 and *Evangelical Witness* 1 (1822):166–68; and see Spring, *Tribute to New England*, pp. 16–17, 35.

14. Nott, *Miscellaneous Works*, pp. 21–22.

15. Asa Hillyer, *A Sermon* . . . (Newark, 1823), p. 8.

16. James Richards, *A Sermon* . . . (Newark, 1823), p. 14.

17. Ezra Stiles Ely, *A Sermon for the Rich to Buy, that They May Benefit Themselves and the Poor* (New York, 1810), p. 21. For other examples of the definition of

religious liberty as a positive religious concept see Linn, *Blessings of America,* pp. 21–22; J. O. Choules, *An Oration . . .* (New York, 1826), p. 10; Henry, *An Oration,* p. 31; Matthews, *Memorial of Independence,* pp. 13–16; Beman, *Western Continent,* pp. 16–19; John M'Knight, *The Divine Goodness to the United States of America* (New York, 1795), pp. 15–16.

18. Froeligh, *Republican Government Advocated,* p. 12.

19. E. P. Smith, *A Sermon . . .* (n.p., 1825), p. 17.

20. Romeyn, *Sermons,* 2:355–56.

21. John Holt Rice, *The Power of Truth and Love* (Boston, 1828), pp. 12–13. This sermon contains an excellent statement of the entire position. See also John Webb Pratt, *Religion, Politics, and Diversity: The Church-State Theme in New York History* (Ithaca: Cornell University Press, 1967), pp. 101–13.

22. Memorial from the Presbytery of Hanover to the General Assembly of Virginia, June 3, 1777. Reproduced in Charles R. James, *Documentary History of the Struggle for Religious Liberty in Virginia* (Lynchburgh: J. P. Bell Co., 1900), p. 226. The often-cited memorial of this presbytery in 1776 was only one of several petitions sent to the General Assembly. Most of the others were much more reflective of actual Presbyterian thought on the subject of disestablishment. See Fred J. Hood, "Revolution and Religious Liberty: Conservation of the Theocratic Concept in Virginia," *Church History* 40 (June 1971):170–81.

23. Presbyterian Church in the United States of America, *The Constitution* (Philadelphia, 1797), pp. 96–98, 371–72.

24. J. Knox, *Reformation Principles,* p. 9; Matthews, *Memorial of Independence,* pp. 13–14; M'Conaughy, *Nature and Origin of Civil Liberty,* pp. 9–10.

25. See Ray Allen Billington, *The Protestant Crusade, 1800–1860: A Study of the Origins of American Nativism* (Chicago: Quadrangle Paperback, 1964), pp. 32–75.

26. Witherspoon, *Moral Philosophy,* pp. 110–12.

27. Edward Tanjore Corwin, *A Digest of the Constitutional and Synodical Legislation of the Reformed Church in America* (New York, 1906), pp. 200–02.

28. William Craig Brownlee, *Popery, An Enemy to Civil and Religious Liberty; and Dangerous to Our Republic* (New York, 1836), pp. 45–46. See also his *Letters in the Roman Catholic Controversy* (New York, 1834). Brownlee was also editor of the anti-Catholic magazine, *The Protestant.* See Billington, *Protestant Crusade,* p. 55.

29. John Breckinridge, *An Address.* The literature on this subject is voluminous. For some examples see also Edward N. Kirk, *An Oration, Delivered July 4, 1836 at the Request of the Common Council, Civil Societies, Military Associations, etc.* (Albany, 1836); C. W. Musgrave, *A Vindication of Religious Liberty; or, the Nature and Efficiency of Christian Weapons* (Baltimore, 1834); Richard Dickenson, *A Sermon Preached in the Canal Street Presbyterian Church* (New York, 1843).

30. Witherspoon, *Moral Philosophy,* pp. 110–12.

31. The memorial is cited in full in William Henry Foote, *Sketches of Virginia: Historical and Biographical,* 2nd ed. (Richmond: John Knox Press, 1966), pp. 336–38. The best statement of the Reformed position in this period is found in Thomas Reese, *An Essay on the Influence of Religion in Civil Society* (Charleston, 1783).

32. Sidney E. Mead, *The Lively Experiment: The Shaping of Christianity in America* (New York: Harper and Row, 1963), pp. 38–63; Hood, "Revolution and Religious Liberty," pp. 170–81.

33. Linn, *Signs of the Times*, p. 23.

34. Ibid., pp. 50–56, 82, 110–12; S. S. Smith, *Divine Goodness*, p. 29; J. H. Rice, *Power of Truth and Love*, p. 12; Amzi Armstrong, *A Syllabus of Lectures on the Visions of the Revelation* (Morristown, New Jersey, 1815), pp. 139–40.

35. Linn, *Signs of the Times*, p. 110.

36. Romeyn, *Sermons*, 1:15; John D. Blair, *Sermons Collected from the Manuscripts of the Late Rev. John D. Blair* (Richmond, 1825), p. 237.

37. Hillyer, *A Sermon . . .* (1823), p. 8; Linn, *Signs of the Times*, p. 82; *Christian Advocate* 2 (August 1824):384.

38. M'Conaughy, *Duties and Dangers of Prosperity*, p. 8.

39. Quoted in William Maxwell, *A Memoir of the Rev. John H. Rice, D.D.* (Philadelphia, 1835), p. 18.

40. John Holt Rice, *Historical and Philosophical Considerations on Religion* (Richmond, 1832), pp. 3–4.

41. James W. Alexander, *The Life of Archibald Alexander, First Professor in the Theological Seminary, at Princeton, New Jersey* (New York, 1854), p. 481.

42. J. H. Rice, *Considerations on Religion*, pp. 50–54.

43. Ibid., pp. 54–62, 73.

44. Ibid., pp. 74–79.

45. Ibid., pp. 68–74.

46. Ibid., pp. 65–68.

47. John Holt Rice, *The Importance of the Gospel Ministry* (Richmond, 1817), pp. 8–9; idem, *Considerations on Religion*, pp. 79–88. This was a common sentiment among the Reformed. See *Magazine of the Reformed Dutch Church* 1 (December 1826):281.

48. J. H. Rice, *Considerations on Religion*, pp. 89–97.

49. Ibid., p. 91.

50. George Washington Bethune, *Our Liberties: Their Danger, and the Means of Preserving Them* (Philadelphia, 1835), p. 11.

51. M'Conaughy, *Nature and Origin of Civil Liberty*, pp. 11–12.

52. Theodore Frelinghuysen, *An Address, Delivered Before the Philoclean and Peitessophian Societies of Rutgers College* (New Brunswick, 1831).

53. Daniel D. Barnard, *An Oration . . .* (Albany, 1835), p. 7.

54. S. Miller, *Christianity the Grand Source of Political Liberty*, pp. 7–23.

55. Ibid.

56. Froeligh, *Republican Government Advocated*, pp. 6–7.

57. Gardiner Spring, *Memoirs of the Rev. Samuel J. Mills* (New York, 1820), pp. 106–7.

58. G. W. Bethune, *Our Liberties*, p. 7.

59. Matthews, *Memorial of Independence*, p. 22.

60. Muir, *A Sermon*, p. 11.

61. Elisha P. Swift, *A Sermon . . .* (Pittsburgh, 1825), p. 17.

62. It was this position that was rejected by those Presbyterians who became advocates of immediate emancipation. See for example the "Records of the Synod of Indiana," *Journal of the Presbyterian Historical Society* 34 (December 1956): 266–71.

63. Samuel Miller, *A Sermon . . .* (Trenton, 1823), pp. 7–9, 14, 21. While Miller held the same idea to be true of all men, and thus his outlook here was consistent

with this total philosophy, there was an inconsistency in his approach to slavery that should be pointed out. He favored colonization, and one of the arguments he used to support that scheme was that the "Christianized" Negroes sent there would evangelize the continent of Africa. These supposedly were the same individuals who would have a degrading effect on American society. Miller's sermon has been selected as representative. For other examples see William T. Hamilton, *A Word for the African* (Newark, 1825), p. 23; Edward D. Griffin, *A Plea for Africa* (New York, 1817), pp. 15–30; Joseph Tracy, *Natural Equality* (Windsor, Vermont, 1833), pp. 10–15; Theodore Frelinghuysen, *An Oration Delivered at Princeton, New Jersey, Nov. 16, 1824, Before the New Jersey Colonization Society* (Princeton, 1824), p. 9; Ralph Randolph Gurley, *A Discourse Delivered on the Fourth of July, 1825, in the City of Washington* (Washington, D.C., 1825), pp. 14–17.

64. M'Conaughy, *Nature and Origin of Civil Liberty*, p. 4.

65. Matthews, *Memorial of Independence*, p. 5. See also Scott, *An Oration;* Starr, *An Oration*, p. 4; Solomon Froeligh, *A Discourse* . . . (Montgomery, 1813), p. 5; M'Conaughy, *Nature and Origin of Civil Liberty*, p. 3; Cumming, *An Oration*, p. 19; Henry, *An Oration*, p. 11; Kirk, *An Oration*, p. 7; Choules, *An Oration*, p. 5; William B. Sprague, *Religious Celebration of Independence* (Hartford, 1827), pp. 3–4.

66. A. Wylie, *Godliness*, p. 12.

67. Smith, *Sermons*, 2:20–25, 30.

68. G. W. Bethune, *Our Liberties*, p. 5.

69. Cumming, *An Oration*, pp. 5–7.

70. Barnes, *An Address*, pp. 15–17. See also J. C. Smith, *Religion and Patriotism*, pp. 8–9; *Christian Monitor* 1 (December 1815):181; 2 (April 1817):248.

71. J. Blair, *Sermons*, p. 5.

72. McKnight, *Divine Goodness*, pp. 19–20.

73. Romeyn, *Sermons*, 1:70, 81.

74. Quoted in Bible Society of Philadelphia, *Sixth Report* (Philadelphia, 1814), p. 41.

75. George Potts, *An Address* . . . (Philadelphia, 1826), pp. 31–32.

76. Ibid., pp. 3, 12. See also *Christian Advocate* 4 (April 1826):174–77; (December 1826):536; 5 (October 1827):461.

CHAPTER 4

1. Jonathan Edwards, *History of the Work of Redemption*, vol. 3 in *The Works of President Edwards*, 8 vols. (New York, 1830).

2. Alan Heimert, *Religion and the American Mind*, pp. 38, 61.

3. James M'Chord, *The Morning Star or Precursor of the Millennium* (Lexington, 1813), p. 8.

4. Enoch Shepard, *Thoughts on the Prophecies; Applicable to the Times* (Marietta, Ohio, 1812); [Elias Boudinot], *Second Advent, or Coming of the Messiah in Glory, Shown to Be a Scripture Doctrine, and Taught by Divine Revelation, from the Beginning of the World, by an American Layman* (Trenton, 1815).

5. *Presbyterian Magazine* 2 (1822):552; *Evangelical Witness* 1 (1822):348; American Bible Society, *Extracts of Correspondence* (May 1823), pp. 1–3.

6. Thomas DeWitt, *The Gospel Warbest and the Christian's Duty* (Boston, 1831), p.

17; Ernest Lee Tuveson, *Redeemer Nation: The Idea of America's Millennial Role* (Chicago: University of Chicago Press, 1968), pp. 52–53; Leroy Froom, *The Prophetic Faith of our Fathers: The Historical Development of Prophetic Interpretation*, 4 vols. (Washington, D.C.: Review and Herald, 1946). Volume 4 contains an extensive bibliography of works on the millennium and illustrates profoundly the extensiveness of millennialism in nineteenth-century America. .

7. John Blair Smith, *The Enlargement of Christ's Kingdom* (Schenectady, New York, 1797), p. 31.

8. Linn, *Signs of the Times,* p. 154.

9. Alexander M'Leod, *Lectures Upon the Principal Prophecies of the Revelation* (New York, 1814), p. 325.

10. Linn, *Signs of the Times,* p. 160.

11. S. Miller, *A Sermon,* 1798, p. 10.

12. Henry Kollock, *Sermons on Various Subjects,* 4 vols. (Savannah, 1822), 4:124, 175–77.

13. The terms "premillenarianism," "premillennialism," and "postmillennialism" were not in use during this period. "Millenarian" was used to describe what is now called "premillennialism" and "premillenarianism," and the postmillennial position was without a specific designation since it was the majority position and there was little controversy. After the 1820s, when there was a significant increase of militant "millenarianism," a distinction was made between the "premillennial" and "postmillennial" return of Christ. This distinction formed the basis of the contemporary terms "premillennialism" and "postmillennialism," which came into common usage during the 1850s. In the transitional period of the 1830s and 1840s postmillennialism was frequently referred to as "Whitbyanism," or the "temporal" or "spiritual millennium," while "millenarianism" continued to be used with reference to premillennialism. "Chiliasm" has always been a proper synonym for "millenarianism" or "premillennialism." Thus, while any use of the terms "premillenarianism," "premillennialism," and "postmillennialism" with reference to this period is anachronistic, the usage I have employed is consistent with the historical definitions of those terms. See D. T. Taylor, *The Voice of the Church on the Coming and Kingdom of the Redeemer,* rev. and ed. H. L. Hastings (Peace Dale, Rhode Island, 1855); "A Congregationalist," *The Time of the End* (Boston, 1856); George Duffield, *Millenarianism Defended* (New York, 1843); John McDowell, *Fifty Years a Pastor* (Philadelphia, 1855); John Lillie, *Millenarianism Tried by the Standards of the Westminster Assembly of Divines* (Philadelphia, 1843).

14. This point was verified by the history of the disputes between premillennialists and postmillennialists in nineteenth-century America. For some specific insight into this by a premillennialist see S. M. M'Corkle, *Thoughts on the Millennium, Comments on the Revelations: Also a Few Remarks on Church Government* (Nashville, 1830), pp. 6, 32.

15. Amzi Armstrong, *A Syllabus of Lectures on the Visions of the Revelation* (Morristown, New Jersey, 1815), pp. 3, 237–38.

16. Amzi Armstrong, *The Last Trumpet* (New York, 1824), p. 17.

17. A. Alexander, *Pastoral Office,* p. 23.

18. Lillie, *Millenarianism Tried,* pp. 4–9.

19. John M'Farland, *The Signs of the Times* (Paris, Kentucky, 1821), p. 4.

20. William Miller was the best known of the premillennialists. There was little new in his work on the millennium, except the physical premillennial return of Jesus, which did have some advocates earlier. That number was growing in the 1830s. Miller's date of 1843 was a standard chronology for those who made calculations by the Jewish calendar. See William Miller, *Evidence from Scripture and History of the Second Coming of Christ About the Year 1843* (Troy, New York, 1838); Whitney R. Cross, *The Burned-Over District: The Social and Intellectual History of Enthusiastic Religion in Western New York, 1800–1850* (Ithaca: Cornell University Press, 1950), pp. 287–321. For some earlier premillennialist works see Robert Reid, *The Seven Last Plagues; or the Vials of the Wrath of God* (Pittsburg, 1838); James A. Begg, *The Scriptural Argument for the Coming of the Lord at the Commencement of the Millennium Revived from the Literal Fulfillment of Prophecy, and the Views Held in the Apostolic Age Concerning the Millennial Kingdom* (Pittsburgh, 1832); Brian Bowman, *The Saw: or the Truth of Scripture, Being a Calculation of the Second Coming of Christ* (n.p., 1830). There were a number of refutations of Miller. See W. H. Coffin, *The Millennium of the Church, to Come Before the End of Time* (Baltimore, 1843); John Dowling, *An Exposition of the Prophecies, Supposed by William Miller to Predict the Second Coming of Christ in 1843* (New York, 1840). In the 1830s other ideas of the millennium were also espoused. George Bush, *A Treatise on the Millennium; in which the Prevailing Theories on that Subject Are Carefully Examined; and the True Scriptural Doctrine Attempted to Be Elicited and Established* (New York, 1832), argued that the millennium was already in the past.

21. There seems to be some imprecision in Alan Heimert's use of the term "premillenarianism." Apparently he uses "premillenarianism" to indicate the belief that calamity would accompany the introduction of the millennium rather than the usual employment of the word to designate the return of Christ before the millennium. He mentions that one of the factors in the rise of a "Calvinist Frederalism" was "a return to premillenarianism among clergymen perplexed and then frightened by the course of the French Revolution." Presumably Samuel Hopkins is included in this category, as his name occurs in the same sentence and he is often designated by Heimert as a Federalist. Hopkins, however, was a postmillennialist in the same sense as contemporary Presbyterians to the south. See Heimert, *Religion and the American Mind,* pp. 64–65, 71, 113–14, 117, 489, 496, 535. For Hopkins's understanding of the second advent as following the millennium see Samuel Hopkins, *A Treatise on the Millennium* (Boston, 1793), pp. 42–55.

22. Heimert, *Religion and the American Mind,* pp. 113–14.

23. *Christian Advocate* 3 (1825):vi.

24. Romeyn, *Sermons* 1:182. For a similar description see S. Miller, *A Sermon,* 1799, pp. 26–27.

25. James Richards, *The Spirit of Paul the Spirit of Missions* (Boston, 1814), p. 23; Edward D. Griffin, *A Sermon . . .* (New York, 1819), pp. 7–8.

26. John McKnight, *A View of the Present State of the Political and Religious World* (New York, 1802), pp. 20–23; S. Miller, *A Sermon,* 1799, p. 27.

27. James Blythe, *A Portrait of the Times* (Lexington, Kentucky, 1814), p. 30. For similar opinions see Richards, *Spirit of Paul,* p. 23; E. Griffin, *A Sermon,* p. 23; T. Edwards, *Reasons for Thankfulness,* p. 14.

28. *Magazine of the Reformed Dutch Church* 2 (December, 1827):266–67.

29. Fisher, *Two Sermons,* p. 39; John E. Latta, *A Sermon* . . . (Wilmington, 1808), p. 23; S. Miller, *A Sermon,* 1798, pp. 29–30. Henry Kollock expressed the conviction that Africa and Asia would share America's exemption. See his *Sermons* 4:114, 136–138.

30. M'Leod, *Lectures Upon Revelation,* pp. 331, 344.

31. William C. Davis, *The Millennium, A Short Sketch on the Rise and Fall of Antichrist* (Salisbury, South Carolina, 1811), p. 46.

32. Nott, *Miscellaneous Works,* pp. 29–32.

33. Simeon H. Calhoun, *An Oration Delivered July 4, 1829, Before the Faculty and Students of Williams College* (Williamsburg, 1829), p. 25. Although this study emphasizes the domestic features, the theme of expansion has been treated somewhat extensively by Tuveson in *Redeemer Nation.* For some contemporary statements of this position see Matthews, *Memorial of Independence,* pp. 18–19; Thomas Rhett Smith, *An Oration Delivered in St. Michael's Church, Before the Inhabitants of Charleston, South Carolina* (Charleston, 1802), p. 16; Beman, *Western Continent,* pp. 7–12; John Woodbridge, *A Sermon Preached in the Bowery Presbyterian Church* (New York, 1835), p. 16.

34. Blythe, *Portrait of the Times,* pp. 5–9.

35. *The Writings of John M. Mason,* ed. Ebenezer Mason, 5 vols. (New York, 1832), 1:150.

36. Kollock, *Sermons,* 4:166–67.

37. H. Sheldon Smith, *Changing Conceptions of Original Sin: A Study in American Theology Since 1750* (New York: Charles Scribner's Sons, 1955), pp. 1–9, 125–26.

38. Samuel Miller, *A Sermon* . . . (Boston, 1822), pp. 6–7.

39. For various usages see Samuel E. M'Corkle, *A Charity Sermon* (n.t.p., 1793 [?]), p. 53; Moore, *A Discourse,* p. 6; John B. Romeyn, *A Sermon* . . . (Philadelphia, 1808), p. 22; J. Mason, *Writings* 1:144–48; Archibald Alexander, *Objections Obviated, and God Glorified* (Boston, 1830), pp. 10–13; idem, *An Inaugural Discourse* (Princeton, 1812), p. 60. Alexander argued that the alphabet was given by divine miracle, perhaps to Moses. Such a phenomenon "was no invention of man but a revelation from God."

40. S. Miller, *A Sermon,* 1799, pp. 27–28; Samuel Miller, *A Brief Retrospect of the Eighteenth Century,* 2 vols. (New York, 1803), 2:295–302; Romeyn, *Sermons* 1:1–2, 60.

41. Philip Lindsly, *An Address* . . . (Nashville, 1825), pp. 4–7.

42. *Christian Advocate* 3 (May 1825):224; 4 (July 1826):302–07.

43. Romeyn, *Sermons,* 1:126–32.

44. *New York Missionary Magazine, and Repository of Religious Intelligence* 1 (1800):370.

45. Ashbel Green, *Discourses Delivered in the College of New Jersey* (Philadelphia, 1822), p. 9.

46. *Magazine of the Reformed Dutch Church* 1 (April 1826):23; see also DeWitt, *Gospel Warbest,* p. 10; James F. Hurley and Julia Goode Eagan, *The Prophet of Zion-Parnassus: Samuel Eusebius McCorkle* (Richmond: Presbyterian Committee of Publication, 1934), p. 92.

47. S. Miller, *A Brief Retrospect,* 1:xii–xiii.

48. Ashbel Green was also willing to admit that impious but learned persons had "occasionally appeared." See A. Green, *Discourses,* p. 9.

49. S. Miller, *A Sermon,* 1798, pp. 16–18.

50. Archibald Alexander, "Essay on the Nature of Vital Piety," introductory essay in Jared Waterbury, *Advice to a Young Christian* (New York, 1843), p. 8.

51. A. Green, *Discourses,* pp. 6–12; J. Blair, *Sermons,* p. 95.

52. Nott, *Miscellaneous Works,* pp. 3–6, 25–32.

53. Daniel Dana, *A Sermon . . .* (Andover, 1817), p. 3.

54. Joseph Clark, "The True and False Grounds of Religion," in *The New Jersey Preacher,* ed. George S. Woodhull and Isaac V. Brown (Trenton, New Jersey, 1813), p. 263.

55. Enoch Burt, "The Excellence of the Knowledge of Christ," in *The New Jersey Preacher,* ed. Woodhull and Brown, p. 361.

56. For various treatments of this subject see John Chester, *A Sermon . . .* (Hudson, New York, 1813); Samuel Taggart, *Knowledge Increased by Travelling to and fro, to Preach the Gospel* (Northampton, Massachusetts, 1807); Ashbel Green, "The Efficacy of Divine Truth," *The National Preacher* 3 (July 1828):17–28; Burt, "Excellence of the Knowledge"; Romeyn, *Sermons,* 1:397–420.

57. E. Griffen, *Sermons,* 1:274.

58. Kollock, *Sermons,* 4:300.

59. Ibid., 2:450; 4:198–200. See also his discussion of regeneration, 2:154–59.

60. Samuel Miller, *The Duty of the Church to Take Measures for Providing an Able and Faithful Ministry* (New York, 1812), p. 21.

61. *Presbyterian Magazine* 1 (March 1821):101–04.

62. Chester, *A Sermon,* p. 12. The best full-length statement of this position was that of Samuel Stanhope Smith, "The Connexion of Principle with Practice, or the Duty of Maintaining Sound Evangelic Principles in the Church," appended to *A Comprehensive View,* pp. 519–43.

63. S. S. Miller, *A Sermon,* 1798, p. 42.

64. A. Green, "Efficacy of Divine Truth," pp. 18, 22.

65. Arthur J. Stansbury, *The Christian Duty of Spreading the Scriptures* (New York, 1814), p. 10.

66. DeWitt, *Gospel Warbest,* p. 21.

67. For examples of a belief in the close relationship between the progress of education and the advancement of the millennium see Samuel B. How, *A Sermon . . .* (Savannah, 1825), pp. 19–20; Bush, *Lack of Vision,* p. 16; Blythe, *Portrait of the Times,* p. 28; Hillyer, *A Sermon,* pp. 11–12; Romeyn, *Sermons,* 1:7–10.

68. A. Green, *Discourses,* p. 17; Ashbel Green, *Lectures on the Shorter Catechism* (Philadelphia, 1805), pp. 6–8.

69. Taggart, *Knowledge Increased,* p. 20. This discussion emphasizes the educational aspect of the ministry more than has usually been done in more general treatments. Sidney Mead, for example, says of this period, "Chief among the activities of the church which defined the common ground of the ministry was the conversion of souls." The difficulty with attempting to place the Reformed of the middle and southern states in this category, at least prior to 1826, is illustrated by the fact that Mead cites no sources from these groups for the early period, although there is probably more Presbyterian literature on this subject than on any other. See Mead, "The Rise of the Evangelical Conception of the Ministry in America: 1607–1850," in *The Ministry in Historical Perspectives,* ed. H. Richard Niebuhr and Daniel D. Williams (New York: Harper and Brothers, 1956), pp.

207–49, 310–14. See also Elwyn Allen Smith, *The Presbyterian Ministry in American Culture: A Study in Changing Concepts, 1700–1900* (Philadelphia, 1962), pp. 138–61.

70. S. Miller, *A Sermon*, 1798, p. 33.

71. Nott, *Miscellaneous Works*, p. 159.

72. *Evangelical Witness* 1 (1822):348.

73. M'Leod, *Lectures Upon Revelation*, pp. 42, 47.

74. Kollock, *Sermons*, 4:123. Very few of the Reformed followed the more nationalistic interpretation of the latter passage, which identified the United States as the child born to the woman who fled into the wilderness. See David Austin, *The Millennium* (Elizabethtown, New Jersey, 1794), p. 392.

75. M'Leod, *Lectures Upon Revelation*, p. 296. The theocratic emphasis throughout M'Leod's work is very strong. See also pp. 200–10, 240–45, 252, 295, 342–44. Robert T. Handy, *A Christian America: Protestant Hopes and Historical Realities* (New York: Oxford University Press, 1971), argues that the Protestant vision was not theocratic in nature. In terms of the present it was not, but in millennial terms it was decidedly theocratic.

76. Romeyn, *A Sermon*, p. 15.

77. Linn, *Signs of the Times*, pp. 11–12, 19.

78. McKnight, *Divine Goodness*, pp. 4–5, 11–12; idem, *A View of the Present State*, pp. 22–23.

79. Jonathan Freeman, *A Sermon . . .* (New Windsor, 1799), p. 18; M'Leod, *Lectures Upon Revelation*, p. 217; Morse, *A Sermon*, pp. 16–22.

80. Blythe, *Portrait of the Times*, pp. 21–22.

81. S. Miller, *A Sermon*, 1798, pp. 27, 33.

82. For examples of usage of this passage see Blythe, *Portrait of the Times*, p. 21; Archibald Alexander, *A Missionary Sermon . . .* (Philadelphia, 1814), p. 29; How, *A Sermon*, p. 11.

83. Spring, *Memoirs of Samuel J. Mills*, p. 246.

84. Romeyn, *Sermons*, 1:157–59.

85. J. H. Rice, *Importance of Gospel Ministry*, p. 6.

86. How, *A Sermon*, p. 17.

87. Romeyn, *Sermons*, 1:151, 154.

88. Ibid., pp. 149–50.

89. *Latter Day Luminary* 1 (May 1818):74.

90. Alexander Proudfit, *The Agency of God in the Elevation of Man* (Salem, New York, 1828).

91. *Christian's Magazine* 1 (1832):29.

92. Blythe, *Portrait of the Times*, pp. 34–35.

93. See Chester, *A Sermon*, pp. 25–26; S. Miller, *A Sermon*, 1823, p. 24; E. Griffen, *A Plea for Africa*, pp. 32–34. For a recent historical account of the Presbyterian relationship to the Negro see Andrew Murray, *Presbyterians and the Negro—a History* (Philadelphia: Presbyterian Historical Society, 1966).

94. For some insight into this see the statement of DeWitt Clinton in *The Religious Monitor* 1 (1824–1825):73.

95. S. Miller, *A Sermon*, 1822, p. 27. See Nott, *Miscellaneous Works*, p. 158; Romeyn, *Sermons*, 1:148–50. Some of the Reformed believed that there would be different degrees of honor and happiness in heaven in proportion to the amount

of piety and good works in this life. Faithful ministers would receive the places of greatest glory. Kollock, *Sermons*, 4:48–49; Ezra Stiles Ely, *Retrospective Theology, or the Opinions of the World of Spirits* (Philadelphia, 1825), p. 8.

96. Romeyn, *Sermons*, 1:145–47.

97. Ibid., p. 148.

98. See Ibid., pp. 148–50; S. Miller, *A Sermon*, 1822, p. 21; Samuel Miller, *The Earth Filled with the Glory of the Lord* (Boston, 1835), p. 7; Matthew LaRue Perrine, *The Nature and End of the Gospel Dispensation* (New York, 1816), pp. 12–13, 20–23; Isaac V. Brown, *First Principles, or Hints to Suit the Times, and Calculated to Promote Ecclesiastical Union* (Trenton, New Jersey, 1821), pp. 3–4.

99. *Religious Monitor* 2 (1825–1826):289–91.

100. A. Green, *Lectures on the Shorter Catechism*, p. 13.

101. Blythe, *Portrait of the Times*, p. 40.

102. Ibid., p. 40. The interdenominational institutions with which the Reformed associated were in fact committed to the Reformed tradition.

103. Philip Milledoler, *Discourses Delivered by Appointment of the General Synod of the Reformed Dutch Church* (New York, 1824), p. 11. See also Philip Milledoler, *Concio Ad Clerum* (New York, 1823), pp. 3–4; *Magazine of the Reformed Dutch Church* 2 (1827–1828):37.

104. For an example of this practical side of unity see Muir, *Ten Sermons*, p. 7. For the effect of millennial study in the promotion of unity see Kollock, *Sermons*, 4:13.

CHAPTER 5

1. Witherspoon, *Moral Philosophy*, pp. 115–17.

2. Leo Pfeffer, *Church, State, and Freedom*, rev. ed. (Boston: Beacon Press, 1967), pp. 270–73.

3. *The Works of James Wilson*, ed. James DeWitt Andrews, 2 vols. (Chicago, 1793) 1:13–14.

4. Ibid., p. 14.

5. Ibid., pp. 15, 19.

6. Ibid., pp. 23–25.

7. Ibid., pp. 206–52.

8. Ibid., p. 208.

9. Ibid., pp. 110–21.

10. Ibid., pp. 121–22.

11. Ibid., pp. 122–26.

12. Ibid., pp. 91–94.

13. Ibid., p. 211.

14. David Hoffman, "A Lecture, Introductory to a Course of Lectures, Now Delivering in the University of Maryland," in Perry Miller, ed., *The Legal Mind in America, From Independence to the Civil War* (Ithaca: Cornell University Press, 1969), pp. 89–91.

15. James Kent, *Commentaries on American Law*, 13th ed., 4 vols. (Boston, 1884), 1:2–20.

16. James Kent, "A Lecture, Introductory to a Course of Law Lectures in Columbia College," in P. Miller, *Legal Mind in America*, pp. 95–97.

17. Joseph Story, "Discourse Pronounced Upon the Inauguration of the Author, as Dane Professor of Law in Harvard University," in P. Miller, *Legal Mind in America,* pp. 178–86.

18. St. George Tucker, ed., *Blackstone's Commentaries,* 5 vols. (Philadelphia, 1803), 1:xvii, 38–61; 2: Appendix, 7; 5:59.

19. William Craig Brownlee, *A Dissertation on the Nature, Obligations, and Form of a Civil Oath* (New York, 1825).

20. Jackson v. Gridley, 18 Johnson (New York) 98–105 (1820).

21. Butts v. Swartwood, 2 Cowen (New York) 431–36 (1823).

22. Noble v. People, 1 Illinois 54 (1822).

23. Wakefield v. Ross, Fed. Case No. 17,050, 5 Mason 16 (1827).

24. Leonard v. Manard, 1 Hall (New York Super) 200 (1828).

25. M'Clure v. State, 9 Tennessee (1 Yerger) 207 (1829).

26. People v. Ruggles, 8 Johnson (New York) 290 (1811).

27. Updegraff v. Commonwealth of Pennsylvania, 11 Serge and Rawle, 394 (1824). In State v. Chandler, 2 Herrington (Delaware) 553 (1839), the Superior Court of Delaware, through the opinion of Chief Justice John M. Clayton, declared that Christianity was part of the common law of that state. That position was verified by the Supreme Court in Vidal v. Mayor, Aldermen, and Citizens of Philadelphia, 43 U.S. 127, 2 How. 127, 11 L.Ed. 205 (1844).

28. *The Statutes at Large of Pennsylvania from 1682 to 1801* (Harrisburg, 1911), 16:106–08.

29. *Laws of the Commonwealth of Pennsylvania* (Philadelphia, 1822), 7:660–61.

30. Ibid., 6:432; 7:155, 244, 489, 604–06.

31. Shepherd Knapp, *A History of the Brick Presbyterian Church in the City of New York* (New York: Trustees of the Church, 1909), pp. 6, 13–14.

32. *Acts and Proceedings of the General Synod of the Reformed Dutch Church in North America* (New York, October 1780), pp. 83–84. Cited hereafter as *APGS.*

33. Ibid., October 1782, p. 98.

34. Ibid., pp. 103, 143, 167, 183, 226, 407, 408; Synod of New York and New Jersey, *Extracts from the Minutes* (Elizabethtown, New Jersey, 1809), pp. 6, 13–14; *Evangelical Witness* 3 (1825):156–69; *Magazine of the Reformed Dutch Church* 2 (1827):53–54; Matthews, *Memorial of Independence,* pp. 19–20; Williston, *A Fast Sermon,* p. 19; M'Chord, *National Safety,* pp. 28–29.

35. Synod of New York and New Jersey, *Extracts from the Minutes,* 1811, p. 40.

36. McDonald, *Sermon,* pp. 36–39.

37. Nathaniel S. Prime, *An Address to the Cambridge Branch of the Moral Society of the County of Washington* (Albany, 1815), pp. 9, 20–21.

38. Quoted in Anson Phelps Stokes, *Church and State in the United States,* 3 vols. (New York: Harper and Brothers, 1950), 2: p. 13.

39. R. Douglas Brackenridge, "The Development of Sabbatarianism in Scotland, 1560–1650," *Journal of Presbyterian History* 42 (September 1964):149–65.

40. *MGA,* 1:566.

41. Synod of Pittsburgh, *Records* (Pittsburgh, 1852), p. 74.

42. Quoted in Stokes, *Church and State,* 2:13.

43. *MGA,* 1:485.

44. Ibid.

45. J. Clark, *A Sermon,* pp. 12–13.

46. Arthur J. Stansbury, *God Pleading with America* (Goshen, New York, 1813), pp. 14–15.

47. Romeyn, *Sermons*, 2:345–47.

48. John E. Latta, *A Sermon* ... (Wilmington, 1812), p. 21. See also Nathan Perkins, *The National Sins and National Punishment in the Recently Declared War* (Hartford, 1812), p. 11; Rowan, *Sin of Insensibility*, p. 18.

49. *MGA,* 1:514.

50. Ibid., p. 508.

51. Ibid., p. 514.

52. Ibid., pp. 513–14.

53. Ibid., pp. 519–20, 565–67. The Synod of Pittsburgh had made the same kind of move earlier. In 1810 it sent a petition in its own name, which did not secure the desired results. In 1811 the synod printed two hundred copies of a petition and sought signatures. Synod of Pittsburgh, *Records*, pp. 74, 77, 81.

54. *MGA,* 1:569–70.

55. *APGS,* June 1815, pp. 53–54.

56. See *MGA,* 1:577–78, 597–98, 601–02, 634; 2:182–83, 240–42.

57. Presbyterian Church, *Constitution*, pp. 92–93.

58. Alexander M'Leod, *A Scriptural View of the Character, Causes, and Ends of the Present War* (New York, 1815), p. 23.

59. Paul Eidelberg, *The Philosophy of the American Constitution: A Reinterpretation of the Intentions of the Founding Fathers* (New York: Free Press, 1968), pp. 264–71, contains a useful summary of the religious provisions of the state constitutions.

60. S. S. Smith, *Sermons*, 1:329.

61. J. Alexander, *Life of Alexander,* p. 203.

62. Romeyn, *Sermons*, 2:337–40.

63. Nott, *Miscellaneous Works*, p. 152.

64. Samuel Brown Wylie, *Memoir of Alexander McLeod* (New York, 1855), p. 309.

65. Ibid., p. 451; Glasgow, *History of the Reformed Presbyterian Church*, p. 182.

66. J. Knox, *Reformation Principles*, pp. 3–7, 17.

67. *American Christian Expositor* 2 (1832):265–68. See also *Religious Monitor* 7 (1830–1831):259.

68. *American Christian Expositor* 2 (1832):149.

69. Brodhead, *A Sermon*, p. 6.

70. George Adams Boyd, *Elias Boudinot: Patriot and Statesman, 1740–1821* (Princeton: Princeton University Press, 1952), p. 173.

71. *MGA,* 1:12.

72. Paul F. Boller, Jr., "George Washington and the Presbyterians," *Journal of the Presbyterian Historical Society* 39 (September 1961):144–45.

73. Samuel Blair, *A Discourse* ... (Philadelphia, 1798), p. 7.

74. *The Life of Ashbel Green*, ed. Joseph H. Jones (New York, 1849), pp. 270–71.

75. Pfeffer, *Church, State, and Freedom*, p. 226.

76. See *MGA,* 1:409–10; James Gray, *Present Duty* (Philadelphia, 1809), pp. 1–4; James Muir, *The Efficacy and Goodness of Providence* (Alexandria, 1809), pp. 1–6.

77. Fisher, *Two Sermons*, p. 44.

78. *APGS,* June 1812, pp. 436–40.

79. Rowan, *Sin of Insensibility*, p. 7.

80. *Christian Advocate* 1 (January 1823):48.

81. Ibid., 1 (December 1823):579.

82. Ibid., 3 (January 1825):43.

83. *Evangelical Witness* 3 (1825):313.

84. *Christian Advocate* 3 (March 1825):143.

85. Ibid., 3 (April 1825):191; 4 (January 1826):47–48.

86. *Evangelical Witness* 3 (1825): 141–43; 4 (1826):313–17.

87. John B. Romeyn, *Two Sermons . . .* (Albany, 1808), p. 60.

88. Presbytery of New Castle, *An Address to the Congregations under Their Care* (Wilmington, 1785), p. 13.

89. A. Green, *Obedience to the Laws of God*, pp. 17–18.

90. Brownlee, *Nature of a Civil Oath*, p. 2; A. Wylie, *Godliness*, p. 9; Williston, *A Fast Sermon*, p. 28.

91. Nott, *Miscellaneous Works*, p. 30.

92. Presbytery of New Brunswick, *A Pastoral Letter to the Churches under Their Care* (New Brunswick, 1801), pp. 9–15.

93. Presbytery of New Brunswick, *Rules Established by the Presbytery* (New Brunswick, 1800), p. 23.

94. Ronald W. Long, "The Presbyterians and the Whiskey Rebellion," *Journal of Presbyterian History*, 43 (March 1965):32.

95. J. Alexander, *Life of Alexander*, p. 203; McKnight, *Divine Goodness*, pp. 14–15; Dwight Raymond Guthrie, *John McMillan: The Apostle of Presbyterianism in the West, 1752–1833* (Pittsburgh: University of Pittsburgh Press, 1952), pp. 107, 158–66.

96. Long, "Presbyterians and the Whiskey Rebellion," pp. 32–36.

97. See J. Earl Thompson, Jr., "A Perilous Experiment: New England Clergymen and American Destiny, 1796–1826" (Ph.D. diss., Princeton University, 1966), pp. 117–58.

98. *MGA*, 1:425.

99. *APGS*, June 1809, p. 396.

100. Muir, *Efficacy and Goodness of Providence*, pp. 6–7.

101. Latta, *A Sermon*, 1808, p. 16.

102. *MGA*, 1:497.

103. *APGS*, June 1812, pp. 436–38.

104. *MGA*, 1:513.

105. Rowan, *Sin of Insensibility*, p. 47.

106. Perkins, *National Sins*, pp. 5, 18–19.

107. Fisher, *Two Sermons*, pp. 15, 21–22, 58.

108. Romeyn, *Two Sermons*, pp. 63–64, 80. See also M'Leod, *A Scriptural View*, p. 13.

109. Rowan, *Sin of Insensibility*, pp. 15–18; Romeyn, *Sermons*, 2:337–39; Stansbury, *God Pleading with America*, p. 23; Abercrombie, *Two Sermons*, p. 38; John Truair, *A Discourse Delivered at Sherburne, November 21, 1814* (Utica, 1815), p. 13; Fisher, *Two Sermons*, pp. 15, 21–22, 58.

110. M'Leod, *A Scriptural View*, pp. 21, 157. See also Froeligh, *A Discourse*, pp. 12–15.

111. See William Gribbin, "Covenant Transformed," pp. 297–305. Gribbin's

concentration on New England apparently led him to ignore this diversity in the middle and southern states. John R. Bodo, *The Protestant Clergy and Public Issues, 1812–1848* (Princeton: Princeton University Press, 1954), pp. 196–204, gives a better idea of this diversity.

112. M'Chord, *National Safety,* pp. 19–20.

113. Daniel A. Clark, *Independence Sermon* (Hanover, New Jersey, 1814), pp. 20–21.

114. Strong, *The Pestilence,* p. 19.

115. Williston, *A Fast Sermon,* p. 31.

116. Choules, *An Oration,* p. 3; Matthews, *Memorial of Independence,* p. 17; M'Conaughy, *Nature and Origin of Civil Liberty,* p. 17; John M. Krebs, *The Foundation of National Prosperity* (New York, 1835), pp. 7–13; M'Leod, *A Scriptural View,* pp. 10–37; Cumming, *An Oration,* pp. 19–21; *Presbyterian Magazine* 1 (December 1821):548–53.

117. Bodo, *Protestant Clergy and Public Issues,* pp. 44–52; *Christian Advocate* 1 (October 1823):484; 2 (March 1824):143; (October 1824):479; 5 (August 1827):384; 6 (November 1828):528.

118. *Christian Advocate* 6 (December 1828):570.

119. Ezra Stiles Ely, *The Duty of Christian Freemen to Elect Christian Rulers* (Philadelphia, 1828).

120. *Presbyterian Magazine* 2 (February 1822):71–72.

CHAPTER 6

1. Trinterud, *Forming An American Tradition,* p. 283; Presbyterian Church in the United States of America, *The Constitution* (Philadelphia, 1788); Reformed Dutch Church in the United States of America, *Constitution* (New York, 1793); James Brown Scouller, *A Manual of the United Presbyterian Church of North America* (Pittsburgh, 1887), pp. 12–48.

2. Presbyterian Church, *Constitution,* p. 417.

3. Church of Scotland, *The Confession of Faith* (Glasgow, 1752), pp. 507–38; Trinterud, *Forming an American Tradition,* pp. 283–91.

4. Mead, *Lively Experiment,* p. 107.

5. Presbyterian Church, *Constitution,* pp. 115–16.

6. Corwin, *Digest of Legislation,* p. 132.

7. Presbyterian Church, *Constitution,* p. 115–16.

8. *APGS,* June 1790, pp. 209–10.

9. *MGA,* 1:12. The General Synod of the Reformed Dutch Church also wrote Washington, but that letter was not recorded in the minutes. *APGS,* June 1789, p. 200; June 1790, p. 212.

10. *MGA,* 1:9–10, 46–47.

11. Presbyterian Church, *Constitution,* p. 116.

12. Ibid., p. 372.

13. Reformed Dutch Church, *Constitution,* p. 111.

14. *MGA,* 1:195–96.

15. Ibid., pp. 196–97.

16. Ibid., p. 197.

17. Ibid., pp. 206, 227, 250, 254, 257; Clifford Merrill Drury, *Presbyterian*

Panorama: One Hundred and Fifty Years of National Missions History (Philadelphia: Board of Christian Education, Presbyterian Church in the United States of America, 1952), pp. 13–17; *Acts and Proceedings of the Coetus and Synod of the German Reformed Church in the United States for 1791 to 1816,* reprinted (Allentown, Pennsylvania, 1930), p. 16.

18. Drury, *Presbyterian Panorama,* p. 27.

19. *APGS,* June 1816, pp. 7, 36; June 1817, p. 20.

20. Associate Synod of North America, *Acts and Proceedings* (n.p., 1822), pp. 19–20, 31–32.

21. [Jacob J. Janeway], *Address of the Board of Missions* (Philadelphia, 1816), pp. 21–23, 7; *MGA,* 1:633.

22. *APGS,* June 1819, pp. 8–16, 45; June 1822, pp. 18–19.

23. Ibid., June 1820, p. 52; June 1827, p. 74; Scouller, *A Manual of the United Presbyterian Church,* p. 60.

24. Presbyterian Education Society, *Report of the Board of Directors* (Newark, 1820), pp. 3–4, 17; Ezra Stiles Ely and Jacob J. Janeway, *Address of a Committee of the Board of Education* (Philadelphia, 1824), p. 10; Asa Hillyer, James Richards, Matthew LaRue Perrine, and Gardiner Spring, *A Circular on the Subject of the Education Society of the Presbyterian Church in the United States* (Newark, 1819); Samuel Miller and Archibald Alexander, *Circular Letter to Dr. Richards* (Princeton, 1819); D. W. Poor, *An Historical Sketch of the Board of Education* (Philadelphia, 1889), p. 5.

25. Charles I. Foster and Clifford S. Griffin have contributed to an understanding of the voluntary societies in nineteenth-century America by pointing to their underlying unity and their significance as social forces. While such a brief treatment fails to do justice to the complex work of these historians, especially Foster's, the study of the Reformed tradition in this period raises fundamental questions about their interpretation of the phenomenon. As a result of his emphasis on "social control," Griffin focused almost exclusively on sources for the nation societies and lay leadership, and he found "trusteeship" to be the integrating factor for the movement from 1815 to 1860. This approach fails to take into account the broader American religious life that was responsible for initiating and sustaining the societies. In addition, it fails to detect the important change in the fundamental character of the societies during the 1830s. Many of the weaknesses of Griffin's interpretation are corrected in the more complex and suggestive treatment by Foster. Foster demonstrates greater understanding of the development of religion in America by pointing to some activity prior to the establishment of the national societies and delineating the "collapse" of the united movement in the 1830s. However, his fascination with the society "machinery" and its roots in British culture places undue emphasis on a relatively short span of time. By focusing on the late 1820s and early 1830s, where there is the greatest parallel between English and American "machinery," Foster also fails adequately to take into account the nature of the American religious life that made the "machinery" seem necessary. By concentrating on this period, Foster also relied heavily on source material from the national societies for his major conclusions. Clifford S. Griffin, *Their Brothers' Keepers: Moral Stewardship in the United States, 1800–1865* (New Brunswick: Rutgers University Press, 1960), pp.

ix–xv, 9; Charles I. Foster, *An Errand of Mercy: The Evangelical United Front, 1790–1837* (Chapel Hill: University of North Carolina Press, 1960), pp. 3–27, 99.

26. *MGA*, 1:146–47, 157.

27. Ibid., p. 309.

28. Ibid., p. 402.

29. Ibid., p. 420.

30. Ibid., pp. 443, 483, 498, 529, 555.

31. Ibid., p. 502.

32. Ibid., pp. 544, 564, 575, 587, 616–17.

33. Ibid., pp. 422–23, 429–30. The Bible Society of Philadelphia, established at the same period, seriously considered the merits and disadvantages of national societies and rejected that approach for a series of state societies. Bible Society of Philadelphia, *Address to the Friends of Revealed Truth in the State of Pennsylvania* (Philadelphia, 1810), pp. 6–8.

34. *MGA*, 1:573; Spring, *Memoirs of Samuel J. Mills*, pp. 96–97. The General Assembly had for some time been concerned with the distribution of Bibles, religious books, and tracts. The success achieved through the use of the denominational resources was even more meager than that in missions and education. *MGA*, 1:12–13, 97, 123, 196, 254, 268–69, 297, 339, 346, 368, 375, 478.

35. Ibid., pp. 593–94. For similar statements on the societies on a synodical level see Synod of New York and New Jersey, *Extracts from the Minutes*, 1809, pp. 6–7; 1812, p. 54; 1814, p. 71; 1815, p. 77.

36. *APGS*, 1823, p. 36; 1826, pp. 32–36. See also *APGS*, 1834, pp. 270–72. By this latter date the American Home Missionary Society and the American Education Society were not favored and are conspicuously absent from the list. For support of the societies by the Associate Synod of North America see *Acts and Proceedings of the Associate Synod of North America*, 1822, p. 10.

37. Oliver Wendel Elsbree, *Rise of the Missionary Spirit in America* (Williamsport: Williamsport Printing and Binding Co., 1928), p. 145.

38. Lefferts A. Loetscher, "The Problem of Christian Unity in Early Nineteenth-Century America," *Church History* 32 (March 1963):3–4.

39. William Linn, *Discourse, Delivered April 18, 1800 in the Brick Presbyterian Church, Before the New York Missionary Society* (New York, 1800).

40. Romeyn, *Sermons*, 1:143–47.

41. *Christian Monitor* 1 (November 1815):151.

42. American Tract Society, *Third Annual Report* (1828), p. 40; *Ninth Annual Report*, 1834, p. 5.

43. American Sunday School Union, *Fourth Report* (Philadelphia, 1828), p. 6. See also *Evangelical Guardian* 1 (October 1817):286; Female Domestic Missionary Society, *First Annual Report*, p. 3; Edward D. Griffin, *An Address, Delivered May 26, 1829, at the Fifth Anniversary of the American Sunday School Union* (Philadelphia, 1829), p. 8; Robert Forrest, *Great Encouragement to Perseverence in Missionary Labours* (Albany, 1815), p. 22; *American Sunday School Magazine* 2 (June 1825):178.

44. Northern Missionary Society in the State of New York, *Constitution* (Schenectady, 1797), p. 14.

45. J. Mason, *Writings*, 1:151.

46. New York Missionary Society, *The Address and Constitution* (New York, 1796), pp. 13–17.

47. Gardiner Spring, *The Subjection of the Kingdoms of this World to the Kingdom of Our Lord and His Christ* (London, 1823), p. 20.

48. Bible Society of Philadelphia, *First Report* (Philadelphia, 1809), pp. 9, 12.

49. American Tract Society, *Address of the Executive Committee of the American Tract Society to the Christian Public* (New York, 1825), pp. 8–9; American Tract Society, *Third Annual Report*, p. 27; American Education Society, *Eleventh Annual Report* (Andover, 1827), p. 46.

50. Jabez Chadwick, *The Duty and Importance of Promoting the Spread of the Gospel* (Homer, New York, 1816), pp. 14–17; James Richards, *A Sermon . . .* (Newark, 1819), p. 20; John Ford, *A Sermon . . .* (Newark, 1820), pp. 6–13; George A. Baxter, "Responsibilities of the Ministry and the Church," *The National Preacher* 3 (December 1828):106.

51. Perrine, *Gospel Dispensation*, pp. 12–23.

52. Blythe, *Portrait of the Times*, pp. 38–43.

53. *APGS*, 1816, p. 20.

54. Frederick Kuhns, "Religious Rivalries in the Old Northwest," *Journal of the Presbyterian Historical Society* 36 (March 1958):19–51; Cross, *Burned-Over District*, pp. 126–37.

55. Northern Missionary Society, *Constitution*, p. 15; New York Missionary Society, *Constitution*, pp. 13–17.

56. [Gardiner Spring], *A Brief View of the Facts, Which Gave Rise to the New York Evangelical Missionary Society of Young Men* (New York, 1817), pp. 4–19.

57. John Holt Rice, *The Instrumentality of Man Employed in the Propagation of the Gospel* (Richmond, 1819), pp. 27–28.

58. New York Religious Tract Society, *Third Annual Report* (New York, 1815), pp. 3–4.

59. American Bible Society, *First Annual Report* (Philadelphia, 1817), pp. 20–21; Henry Otis Dwight, *The Centennial History of the American Bible Society*, 2 vols. (New York: MacMillan, 1916), 2:37, 62; Alexander Gunn, *Some Questions and Answers, on the Subject of the American Bible Society* (New York, 1816), pp. 28–29.

60. Philadelphia Sunday and Adult School Union, *First Report* (Philadelphia, 1818), p. 3.

61. Heman Humphrey, *The Way to Bless and Save Our Country* (Philadelphia, 1831), p. 17.

62. Lyman Beecher, *The Practicability of Suppressing Vice, by Means of Societies Instituted for that Purpose* (New London, Connecticut, 1804), pp. 14–15, 19–21.

63. Bible Society of Philadelphia, *First Report*, p. 8.

64. Prime, *An Address*, pp. 3–8.

65. Chadwick, *Duty and Importance*, pp. 14–16.

66. American Bible Society, *Constitution* (New York, 1816), pp. 13–16.

67. John Holt Rice, *Charity at Home* (New York, 1824), pp. 16–17, 25.

68. American Tract Society, *Address to the Christian Public*, p. 12.

69. American Sunday School Union, *Second Report*, 1826, p. xvii.

70. American Home Missionary Society, *Constitution* (New York, 1826), p. 47.

71. American Bible Society, *Constitution*, p. 16.

72. Society of Inquiry Respecting Missions of the Theological Seminary Established at Princeton, New Jersey, *A Statement of the Origin, Progress, and Present Design* (Trenton, 1817), p. 5.

73. Maxwell, *Memoir of Rice,* pp. 165–66.

74. Nathaniel S. Prime, *A Plan for the More Successful Management of Domestic Missions* (Albany, 1816), p. 5.

75. J. H. Rice, *Charity at Home,* p. 3; "Correspondence of the Western Foreign Missionary Society," introduction by Guy S. Klett, *Journal of the Presbyterian Historical Society* 36 (June 1958):96–97, 100.

76. American Bible Society, *Constitution,* p. 7; idem, *First Annual Report.* These were: governors William Jones of Rhode Island, Isaac Shelby of Kentucky, and Thomas Posey of Indiana Territory; lieutenant-governor William Gray of Massachusetts; and attorney general William Wirt. Congressman William Gaston of North Carolina, a Catholic, also refused to serve.

77. American Bible Society, *Proceedings of a Meeting of the Citizens of New York and Others* (New York, 1816), p. 3.

78. *Panoplist* 12 (October 1816):477; (December 1816):572.

79. Quoted in Isaac V. Brown, *Memoirs of the Rev. Robert Finley, D.D.* (New Brunswick, 1819), p. 39.

80. Ibid., pp. 75–79; P. J. Staudenraus, *The African Colonization Movement, 1816–1865* (New York: Columbia University Press, 1961), pp. 15–18.

81. Ibid., pp. 27–30; American Society for Colonizing the Free People of Colour of the United States, *First Annual Report* (Washington, D.C., 1818), p. 11.

82. American Society for Promoting the Civilization and General Improvement of the Indian Tribes in the United States, *The First Annual Report* (New Haven, 1824), pp. 7–8, 13–14.

83. Ibid., pp. 19–21.

84. Thomas E. Vermilye, *Funeral Discourse Occasioned by the Death of the Hon. Stephen Van Rensselaer* (Albany, 1839), p. 32; William Barlow, *Character and Reward of a Just Man* (Albany, 1839), p. 37; American Bible Society, *Extracts of Correspondence,* May, 1825, p. 12; *Nation* 72 (February 1901):111–12; *American Sunday School Magazine* 5 (August 1828):238.

85. William McMurray, *A Sermon Occassioned by the Death of Col. Henry Rutger* (New York, 1830), p. 31; Proudfit, *Agency of God,* pp. 7, 23; Richard S. Field, *Address on the Life and Character of the Hon. Joseph C. Hornblower* (Newark, 1865), p. 16; *Presbyterian Magazine* 2 (November 1822):490.

86. American Bible Society, *Constitution,* p. 7.

87. American Sunday School Union, *Speeches of Messrs. Webster, Frelinghuysen and Others, at the Sunday School Meeting in the City of Washington* (Philadelphia, 1831), pp. 3–24; Lee Benson, *The Concept of Jacksonian Democracy: New York as a Test Case* (New York, 1964), pp. 186–207.

88. Staudenraus, *African Colonization,* pp. vii–viii.

89. Ibid., p. 3; Brown, *Memoirs of Finley,* p. 91.

90. Staudenraus, *African Colonization,* p. 60.

91. *MGA,* 1:710. For later support of the society by the General Assembly see *MGA,* 2:154, 178–80, 365–66, 411. American Society for Colonizing, *Third Annual Report,* 1820, pp. 129–30.

92. American Society for Colonizing, *Second Annual Report,* 1819, p. 130.

93. Staudenraus, *African Colonization,* pp. 65–66.

94. Ibid., p. 187.

95. John McKnight, *Life to the Dead* (New York, 1799), p. 60.

96. *MGA,* 1:195. For further discussions of this issue see William Linn, *The Christian's Zeal for the Church* (New York, 1800), p. 14; J. Mason, *Writings,* 1:144–48; A. Alexander, *A Missionary Sermon,* p. 18; idem, *Objections Obviated,* pp. 10–13.

97. R. Pierce Beaver, *Church, State, and the American Indians: Two and a Half Centuries of Partnership in Missions between Protestant Churches and Government* (St. Louis: Concordia Publishing House, 1966).

98. Quoted in ibid., p. 64.

99. *New York Missionary Magazine and Repository of Religious Intelligence* 3 (1802):206.

100. Beaver, *Church, State, and the American Indians,* pp. 67–79.

101. *MGA,* 1:734. For the government's early support of the Assembly's Indian Missions and later refusals see *MGA,* 1:331, 355–56, 423–24, 464, 565. The Synod of Pittsburgh also received some aid from the federal government. Synod of Pittsburgh, *Records,* pp. 33–35.

102. Synod of Pittsburgh, *Records,* pp. 54, 57, 62, 71, 83.

103. *An Appeal to the Christians of America, In Behalf of the American Bible Society* (New York, 1816), p. 37. The society was generally dominated by Presbyterians and one of the most pressing criticisms of the society was that it would become solely Presbyterian in sentiment.

104. Amerian Bible Society, *Memorial of the Board of Managers* (New York, 1819), pp. 6–8.

105. Ibid., pp. 10–11.

106. Ibid., p. 10.

107. Foster, *Errand of Mercy,* pp. 29, 273–75. Others were as follows: Philadelphia Society to Aid the Magistrates in the Suppression of Vice and Immorality, 1798, sanctioned by the General Assembly; Moral Society of Easthampton, Long Island, 1803, founded by Lyman Beecher; a society in Delaware "established for the suppression of vice and immorality" in which John Latta was active; New Jersey Society for the Suppression of Vice and Immorality, 1817; Cambridge Moral Society, 1815, an "auxiliary" society in which Nathaniel Prime was a leader. See *MGA,* 1:157; Sprague, *Annals of the American Pulpit* 3:205–06; L. Beecher, *Practicability of Suppressing Vice,* pp. 25–26; Prime, *An Address,* p. 9; New Jersey Society for the Suppression of Vice and Immorality, and for the Encouragement of Virtue and Good Morals, *Constitution* (New Brunswick, 1818), pp. 3–4.

108. Samuel John Ellis Eaton, *History of the Presbytery of Erie* (New York, 1868), p. 82.

109. *MGA,* 1:648.

110. New Jersey Bible Society, *Fifth Report of the Board of Managers* (Trenton, 1815), p. 2; *Sixth Report,* 1816, p. 2.

111. New Jersey Society for the Suppression of Vice and Immorality, *Consitution,* pp. 3–4.

112. Ibid., pp. 6–12.

113. Prime, *An Address,* pp. 9, 20–21.

114. New Jersey Society for the Suppression of Vice and Immorality, *Constitution*, p. 7.

115. Quoted in Knapp, *History of the Brick Presbyterian Church*, p. 242.

116. Bertram Wyatt-Brown, "Prelude to Abolitionism: Sabbatarian Politics and the Rise of the Second Party System," *Journal of American History* 58 (September 1971):323–26.

117. Ibid., p. 327; *The Charter; Being a Plain Statement of Facts, in Relation to an Application to the Legislature of Pennsylvania, to Grant a Charter For the American Sunday School Union* (Philadelphia, 1828), pp. 3–24.

118. *Christian Advocate* 6 (June 1828):273.

119. *APGS,* 1828, p. 114.

120. *Christian Advocate* 6 (June 1828):282.

121. *Religious Monitor* 6 (1829–1830):85, 431; *Magazine of the Reformed Dutch Church* 6 (1829–1830):383; Wyatt-Brown, "Prelude to Abolitionism," p. 335.

CHAPTER 7

1. *MGA,* 1:648.

2. Samuel Blatchford, *The Excellency of the Scriptures* (Albany, 1811), p. 20.

3. Quoted in Michael McGiffert, *The Character of Americans: A Book of Readings* (Homewood: Dorsey Press, 1970), p. 62.

4. *Religious Monitor* 1 (1824–1825):74.

5. American Sunday School Union, *Eleventh Annual Report,* 1835, p. 8.

6. *Quarterly Sunday School Magazine* 8 (October 1831):236.

7. *Religious Monitor* 1 (1824–1825):74.

8. Brodhead, *A Sermon,* p. 10.

9. Philip Milledoler, *Address, Delivered to the Graduates of Rutgers College* (New York, 1831), pp. 10–11.

10. Nott, *Addresses,* p. 181.

11. American Sunday School Union, *Eleventh Annual Report,* p. 8.

12. *Religious Monitor* 1 (1824–1825):72–73.

13. American Sunday School Union, *First Report,* 1825, p. 3.

14. U.S. Bureau of the Census, *Statistical Abstract of the United States: 1971,* 92nd edition (Washington, D.C., 1971), p. 5.

15. *Panoplist* 14 (May 1818):212–13.

16. American Sunday School Union, *Eleventh Annual Report,* p. 25.

17. *Christian Advocate* 2 (January 1824):45.

18. American Education Society, *Seventeenth Report,* 1833, p. 61.

19. American Home Missionary Society, *First Report* (New York, 1826), p. 54.

20. Colin B. Goodykoontz, *Home Missions on the American Frontier: With Particular Reference to the American Home Missionary Society* (Caldwell, Indiana: Claxton Printers, 1939); Ellen Harriett Thompsen, "Protestant Westward Migration, 1830–1839," *Journal of the Presbyterian Historical Society* 26 (March 1948):44–46; William Warren Sweet, *The Story of Religion in America,* rev. ed. (New York: Harper and Brothers, 1950), pp. 243–57.

21. Everett S. Lee and Michael Lalli, "Population," in David T. Gilchrist, ed., *The Growth of the Seaport Cities, 1790–1825: Proceedings of a Conference Sponsored by*

the Eleutherian Mill-Hagley Foundation, March 17–18, 1966 (Charlottesville: University Press of Virginia, 1967), p. 43.

22. Constance McLaughlin Green, *American Cities in the Growth of the Nation,* (New York: Harper and Row, 1965), p. 2.

23. American Tract Society, *Eleventh Annual Report,* 1836, p. 3; *Christian Advocate* 5 (February 1827):55–56; 3 (May 1825):227; *Missionary Herald* 23 (May 1827):161.

24. *Panoplist* 14 (April 1818):153–54.

25. Stafford, *New Missionary Field,* pp. 9, 44; James Patterson, *A Sermon Preached for the Young Men's Missionary Society, of Philadelphia* (Philadelphia, 1826), p. 12; Young Men's Domestic Missionary Society of Philadelphia, *An Appeal to the Citizens of Philadelphia in Behalf of Domestic Missions* (Philadelphia, 1824), pp. 10–11. Charles I. Foster, "The Urban Missionary Movement, 1814–1827," *The Pennsylvania Magazine of History and Biography* 75 (January 1951):47–51.

26. Robert Bremner dated the "discovery" of poverty in the United States in the 1830s. See *From the Depths: The Discovery of Poverty in the United States* (New York: New York University Press, 1956), pp. 3–16.

27. See for example Irvin G. Wyllie, *The Self-Made Man in America: The Myth of Rags to Riches* (New York: Free Press, 1954); Stephen Thernstrom, *Poverty and Progress: Social Mobility in a Nineteenth Century City* (Cambridge: Harvard University Press, 1969).

28. Raymond Mohl, *Poverty in New York* (New York: Oxford University Press, 1971), p. 90. Figures include Almshouse, Orphan Asylum, the city hospital, the debtor's prison, Bridewell, the state prison, the penitentiary, Bellevue Hospital, and the House of Refuge.

29. Philadelphia, *Report of a Committee on Pauperism* (Philadelphia, 1827), p. 22.

30. Pennsylvania State Temperance Society, *Address to the Inhabitants of the Commonwealth* (n.t.p.), p. 11.

31. Mohl, *Poverty in New York,* p. 116.

32. Schroeder, *Plea for the Industrious Poor,* pp. 14–15.

33. Philadelphia, *Report of a Committee on Pauperism,* p. 7; Lee and Lalli, "Population," p. 36.

34. Mohl, *Poverty in New York,* pp. 34, 116, 137; Stafford, *New Missionary Field,* p. 43, makes the same estimate.

35. Edmund S. Morgan, *The Puritan Family: Religion and Domestic Relations in Seventeenth-Century New England,* rev. ed. (New York: Harper and Row, 1966), pp. 109–60.

36. David J. Rothman, *Discovery of the Asylum,* pp. 30–40.

37. Thernstrom, *Poverty and Progress,* pp. 34–41.

38. Edwin Scott Gaustad, *The Great Awakening in New England* (New York: Harper and Brothers, 1957), pp. 50–53. Gaustad does not make this particular point, but the conclusion follows logically from his data.

39. Bremner, *From the Depths,* pp. 7–10.

40. Stafford, *New Missionary Field,* pp. 10–11; *Panoplist* 13 (July 1817):315.

41. Philadelphia, *Report of a Committee on Pauperism,* p. 6.

42. A. Alexander, *Pastoral Office,* p. 20.

43. J. H. Rice, *Charity at Home,* p. 31.

44. Stafford, *New Missionary Field*, p. 6.

45. Patterson, *A Sermon*, p. 12; Young Men's Domestic Missionary Society, *An Appeal*, pp. 10–11; Foster, "Urban Missionary Movement," pp. 47–51.

46. Philadelphia City Mission, *First Quarterly Report* (Philadelphia, 1831), p. 16. For the situation in Richmond, Virginia, see J. H. Rice, *Instrumentality of Man*, pp. 32–33.

47. Maxwell, *Memoir of Rice*, pp. 54–55, 100–03.

48. Charles Grier Sellers, "John Blair Smith," *Journal of the Presbyterian Historical Society* 34 (December 1956):220.

49. Knapp, *History of the Black Presbyterian Church*, pp. 158–59.

50. Stafford, *New Missionary Field*, p. 25. See also Female Domestic Missionary Society, *Third Annual Report*, 1819, p. 3; Philadelphia City Mission, *First Quarterly Report*, p. 1.

51. *American Sunday School Magazine* 5 (January 1828):24–25; (May 1828): 129–30; 6 (April 1829):124–25.

52. Bible Society of Union College, *Constitution* (Schenectady, New York, 1815), pp. 13–14.

53. Presbyterian Society for the Promotion of Religion in the Benevolent Institutions of the City of Philadelphia, *A Plan for Establishing a Chaplain, of the Presbyterian Denomination, in the Jail, Hospital, and Bettering-House, of the City of Philadelphia* (Philadelphia, 1802), pp. 3–12.

54. Ezra Stiles Ely, *Visits of Mercy: or the Journals of Ezra Stiles Ely*, 2 vols., 6 ed. rev. (Philadelphia, 1829), pp. xiii–xv.

55. Milledoler, *A Discourse*, pp. 14–18.

56. Female Society, for the Relief of Poor and Distressed Persons in the Village of Newark, *Constitution* (Newark, 1803) pp. 3–5.

57. J. Alexander, *Life of Alexander*, pp. 209–303.

58. Bible Society of Philadelphia, *First Report*, pp. 7–10.

59. New York Bible Society, *Second Annual Report* (New York, 1811), pp. 9–11. *Christian's Magazine* 4 (January 1811):45.

60. New Jersey Bible Society, *Address to the Publick; With an Appendix, Containing the Constitutuion of the Said Society* (New Brunswick, 1810), p. 4; Bible Society of Charleston, *Second Report of the Managers* (Charleston, 1812), p. 10; Bible Society of the District of Columbia, *First Report* (n.p., 1816), p. 3; *Proceedings of Sundry Citizens of the County of Somerset, in the State of New Jersey* (New Brunswick, 1816), p. 9; Horace Galpin, *A Call, to Come Over to the Help of the Lord* (New Brunswick, 1823), p. 10; *Panoplist* 12 (July 1816):336.

61. American Tract Society, *Address to the Christian Public*, p. 3. See also *Missionary Herald* 22 (September 1826):283; *Christian Monitor* 1 (March 1816):39; *Christian Examiner and Theological Review* 1 (July 1824):250.

62. American Bible Society, *An Appeal to the Christians of America* (New York, 1816), p. 16; Dwight, *History of the American Bible Society*, 1:43; Bible Society of Frederick County, Virginia, *First Annual Report* (Winchester, Virginia, 1814), p. 10.

63. *Evangelical Guardian* 2 (June 1818):89.

64. New York Sunday School Union Society, *First Report* (New York, 1817), pp. 6, 14–16.

65. Stafford, *New Missionary Field*, p. 15.

66. *APGS,* June 1823, p. 10.

67. Bible Society of the District of Columbia, *First Report,* p. 3.

68. New York Bible Society, *Second Annual Report,* pp. 9–11.

69. J. P. K. Henshaw, *The Usefulness of Sunday Schools* (Philadelphia, 1833), p. 18.

70. Jonas King, *Report, Read, May 20, to the Female Domestic Missionary Society of Charleston, South Carolina* (Charleston, 1820), pp. 10–12.

71. *Magazine of the Reformed Dutch Church* 1 (October 1826):227.

72. Mohl, *Poverty in New York,* pp. 173–237.

73. Rothman, *Discovery of the Asylum,* pp. 193–94.

74. Brodhead, *A Plea for the Poor,* pp. 31–32.

75. Bible Society of Charleston, *Second Report of the Managers,* p. 10.

76. *Christian Advocate* 3 (March 1825):133.

77. Philadelphia City Mission, *First Quarterly Report,* p. 4.

78. American Society for the Encouragement of Domestic Manufactures, *Address to the People of the United States* (New York, 1817), pp. 12–15.

79. For an incisive contemporary criticism see Matthew Carey, *Essays on the Public Charities of Philadelphia,* 3rd ed. (Philadelphia, 1828), pp. 21–24.

80. Female Domestic Missionary Society, *Second Annual Report,* 1818, p. 6.

81. Bible Society of Philadelphia, *First Report,* pp. 7–10.

82. American Sunday School Union, *Seventh Annual Report,* 1831, p. 41.

83. Pennsylvania State Temperance Society, *Address to the Commonwealth of Pennsylvania,* p. 11; Boston Society for the Moral and Religious Instruction of the Poor, *City Missions. Seventeenth Annual Report of the Board of Directors* (Boston, 1834), p. 7.

84. *APGS,* June 1827, pp. 72–73; June 1828, p. 132. See also *Magazine of the Reformed Dutch Church* 3 (October 1828):223.

85. Presbytery of Geneva, *A Narrative of the Late Revivals of Religion, Within the Bounds of Geneva Presbytery* (Geneva, 1832), p. 6.

86. Philadelphia Society for the Establishment and Support of Charity Schools, *Constitution and Laws, With a Historical Sketch of the Institution and the Life of Christopher Ludwick* (Philadelphia, 1860), p. 19.

87. Thomas S. Grimke, *Address at a Meeting in Charleston, South Carolina, Held March 29, 1831, to Consider the Resolutions of the American Sunday School Union, Respecting Sunday Schools in the Valley of the Mississippi* (Philadelphia, 1831), p. 9; American Sunday School Union, *Seventh Annual Report,* pp. 25–26; *Eighth Annual Report,* 1832, p. 3; *American Sunday School Magazine* 4 (May 1828):144–45; Jacob Brodhead, *A Discourse on Education* (New York, 1831), pp. 16–32; Philip Lindsly, *Inaugural Address* (Nashville, 1825), pp. 17, 27, 29; William Neill, *Inaugural Address* (Philadelphia, 1824), p. 17; *Christian Monitor* 2 (June 1817):305.

88. City of Philadelphia, *The Act Incorporating the House of Refuge, and Laws Relative thereto* (Philadelphia, 1829), pp. 8–13; *An Address from the Managers of the House of Refuge to Their Fellow Citizens* (Philadelphia, 1826), pp. 5, 11; *The First Annual Report of the House of Refuge of Philadelphia* (Philadelphia, 1829), p. 17; John Sergeant, *An Address Delivered before the Citizens of Philadelphia, at the House of Refuge* (Philadelphia, 1828), p. 8; John Stanford, *A Discourse on Opening the New Building in the House of Refuge, New York; Established for the Reformation of Juvenile Delinquents* (New York, 1826). The Philadelphia materials contain extensive references to practice in New York, which was used as a model.

89. New York Society for the Prevention of Pauperism, *Report,* pp. 4–16.

90. For other examples of this see Union Benevolent Association, *Constitution;* Schroeder, *Plea for the Industrious Poor;* Philadelphia, *Report of a Committee on Pauperism.*

91. Union Benevolent Association, *Constitution,* p. 8.

92. New York Society for the Prevention of Pauperism, *Report,* p. 4.

93. Young Men's Domestic Missionary Society, *An Appeal,* p. 5.

94. Brodhead, *A Discourse on Education,* pp. 16–32.

95. New York Bible Society, *Second Annual Report,* pp. 9–11; Stafford, *New Missionary Field,* pp. 32–35; American Sunday School Union, *Fourth Report,* pp. xviii–xix.

96. Marine Bible Society of New York, *First Report* (New York, 1817), pp. 14–16.

97. Marine Bible Society of New York, *Constitution* (New York, 1817), pp. 5–14.

98. Marine Bible Society of New York, *Fifth Report,* 1821, p. 6; *Sixth Report,* 1822, pp. 4, 11–12.

99. Marine Bible Society of New York, *First Report,* pp. 7–8; *Second Report,* 1818, pp. 8–9.

100. *APGS,* June 1829, p. 212; Ichabod S. Spencer, *The Claims of Seamen* (New York, 1838), p. 17; *Missionary Herald,* February 1825, pp. 58–59; Religious Tract Society of Philadelphia, *Sailor's Address to his Seafaring Companions on the Interesting Voyage over the Ocean of Life in the Heaven of Eternity* (Philadelphia, 1819); *Magazine of the Reformed Dutch Church* 4 (1828–1829):92. The president and three of the four vice-presidents of this society were ship captains.

101. American Sunday School Union, *Eleventh Annual Report,* p. 20.

102. Estimates were Philadelphia, $120,000; New York, $80,000; Baltimore, $18,000; and Charleston, $40,000 to $60,000. See *Christian Advocate* 5 (June 1827):278; King, *Report to the Female Missionary Society,* p. 11.

103. Schroeder, *Plea for the Industrious Poor,* p. 9; Stafford, *New Missionary Field,* p. 42; New York Society for the Prevention of Pauperism, *Report,* p. 9; Female Domestic Missionary Society, *First Annual Report,* p. 6; Union Benevolent Association, *Constitution,* p. 3; Mohl, *Poverty in New York,* pp. 116–18.

104. Patterson, *A Sermon,* p. 14.

105. King, *Report to the Female Missionary Society,* pp. 10–13.

106. Stafford, *New Missionary Field,* p. 43.

107. See Richard P. McCormick, *The Second American Party System: Party Formation in the Jackson Era* (Chapel Hill: University of North Carolina Press, 1966), pp. 346–56; Edward Pessen, *Jacksonian America: Society, Personality, and Politics* (Homewood: Dorsey Press, 1969), pp. 151–59.

108. *American Sunday School Magazine* 3 (December 1826):374–75; 5 (February 1828):20.

109. Frelinghuysen, *An Oration at Princeton,* p. 9.

110. American Sunday School Union, *Eleventh Annual Report,* p. 25.

111. Leo F. Litwack, *North of Slavery: The Negro in the Free States, 1790–1869* (Chicago: University of Chicago Press, 1961), pp. 75–86.

112. I do not pretend to add to the discussion of blacks in American society, but merely attempt to illustrate the difference of the Reformed approach to the blacks and the poor whites.

113. *American Sunday School Magazine* 4 (August 1827):243.

114. Henshaw, *Usefulness of Sunday School,* p. 21.

115. Quoted in American Sunday School Union, *Speeches of Messrs. Webster, Frelinghuysen and Others,* p. 6.

116. American Bible Society, *Constitution,* pp. 13–16.

117. New York Sunday School Union Society, *First Report.*

118. Philadelphia Sunday and Adult School Union, *Sixth Report,* 1823, p. 8.

119. American Tract Society, *Address to the Christian Public,* p. 12.

120. Goodykoontz, *Home Missions on the American Frontier;* Thompsen, "Protestant Westward Migration"; Sweet, *Story of Religion in America,* pp. 243–57.

121. Mead, *Lively Experiment,* pp. 1–15.

122. *Christian Examiner and Theological Review* 1 (July and August 1824).

123. New York City Evangelical Missionary Society, *First Report* (New York, 1821), p. 106.

124. *Panoplist* 15 (May 1819):213–14.

125. American Tract Society, *Fourth Annual Report,* 1828, pp. 20–22.

126. *American Sunday School Magazine,* 6 (July 1829):213.

127. *Christian Advocate* 1 (March 1823):132–33.

128. Charles Hodge, *A Sermon, Preached in Philadelphia, at the Request of the American Sunday School Union* (Philadelphia, 1833), pp. 4–5.

129. H. Humphrey, *Way to Bless Our Country,* Philadelphia, pp. 6, 9.

130. Francis Wayland, *Encouragements to Religious Effort* (Philadelphia, 1830), p. 11.

131. American Sunday School Union, *Seventh Annual Report,* p. 24.

132. Synod of New York and New Jersey, *Proceedings, At their Late Session, in Reference to the Publications of the American Tract Society* (New York, 1845), pp. 6–7; *Review of the Tract Controversy; Being Substantially a Reprint of an Editorial Article in the New York Journal of Commerce, of April 19th, 22d, and 24th, 1845* (New York, 1845), pp. 44–45.

133. American Sunday School Union, *First Report,* pp. 32–33; *Second Report,* p. 3.

134. American Sunday School Union, *Design, Character, and Uses of the Books of the American Sunday School Union, Reprinted by Permission, from the Biblical Repertory* (n.p., n.d.), p. 9.

135. American Sunday School Union, *Sixth Report,* 1830, p. 15; *Eighth Annual Report,* p. 16.

136. American Sunday School Union, *Second Report,* p. v.

137. Willard Hall, *A Defense of the American Sunday School Union, Against the Charges of Its Opponents* (Philadelphia, 1828), p. 7.

138. American Sunday School Union, *Sixth Report,* p. 15.

139. *American Sunday School Magazine* 6 (July 1829):213.

140. Edwin Wilbur Rice, *The Sunday School Movement, 1780–1917, and the American Sunday School Union, 1817–1917* (Philadelphia: American Sunday School Union, 1917), pp. 77, 101–07.

141. *American Sunday School Magazine* 4 (May 1827):144.

142. David Hosack, *Memoir of DeWitt Clinton* (New York, 1829), pp. 173–75; *American Sunday School Magazine* 4 (July 1827):220–22; 5 (July 1828): 212–13; *Magazine of the Reformed Dutch Church* 3 (November 1828): 255.

143. *American Sunday School Magazine* 4 (January 1827):18–19.

144. American Sunday School Union, *Third Report,* 1827, p. xii; *Eighth Annual Report,* p. 14; *Ninth Report,* 1833, pp. v–vi; *Tenth Report,* 1834, p. 17.

145. *Panoplist* 13 (April 1817):158.

146. Krebs, *Foundation of National Prosperity,* p. 13.

147. Maxwell, *Memoir of Rice,* pp. 36–37; *Christian Advocate* 2 (March 1824):139.

148. New York Female Union Society for the Promotion of Sabbath Schools, *Eighth Report* (New York, 1824), pp. 39–40.

149. Samuel Bayard, *A Catechism for Youth* (New York, 1812), pp. 164–66, 177.

150. *Evangelical Guardian* 2 (May 1818):24–27. Most of the favorite stories were of English origin, but their use was distinctively American. See Foster, *Errand of Mercy,* pp. 3–27.

151. *Christian's Magazine* 3 (1810):29.

152. American Tract Society, *The Publications of the American Tract Society* (New York, n.d.), 2:2–4.

153. *Christian's Magazine* 4 (July 1811):535–64; (August 1811):409–13.

154. American Sunday School Union, *Eighth Annual Report,* p. 16.

155. Stafford, *New Missionary Field,* pp. 29–31.

156. *Christian's Magazine* 4 (July 1811):400.

157. New York Society for the Prevention of Pauperism, *Report,* p. 10.

158. Female Domestic Missionary Society, *First Annual Report,* p. 7.

159. Philadelphia City Mission, *To the Christians of Philadelphia* (n.t.p.), p. 2; Philadelphia City Mission, *First Quarterly Report,* pp. 2–4.

160. Union Benevolent Association, *Constitution,* p. 6.

161. American Tract Society, *Eleventh Annual Report,* p. 20. *Magazine of the Reformed Dutch Church* 3 (June 1828):94; American Home Missionary Society, *Eleventh Report,* 1838, p. 60; American Education Society, *Eleventh Report,* p. 10; *Quarterly Register and Journal of the American Education Society* 2 (August 1830):63; American Sunday School Union, *Ninth Annual Report,* p. 3; *Twelfth Annual Report,* 1836, pp. 23–27.

CHAPTER 8

1. Charles Grandison Finney, *Lectures on Revivals of Religion,* ed. William G. McLoughlin (Cambridge: Belknap Press of Harvard University Press, 1960), p. xix.

2. Bernard A. Weisberger, *They Gathered at the River: The Story of the Great Revivalists and Their Impact upon Religion in America* (Boston: Little, Brown and Co., 1958), pp. 3–4; Carroll Smith Rosenberg, *Religion and the Rise of the American City: The New York City Mission Movement, 1812–1870* (Ithaca: Cornell University Press, 1971), p. 47.

3. William B. Sprague, *Lectures on Revivals of Religion* (Albany, New York, 1832), p. v.

4. Ibid., pp. 3–4, 272–74.

5. Ibid., pp. 6–20.

6. Donald G. Mathews, "The Second Great Awakening as an Organizing Process, 1780–1830: an Hypothesis," *American Quarterly* 21 (Spring 1969):23–43.

7. J. Mason, *Writings,* 4:144–45.

8. *Christian Advocate* 1 (January 1823):12.

9. DeWitt, *Gospel Warbest,* p. 308.

10. Samuel Stanhope Smith, "On a Death-bed Repentance," in *The New Jersey Preacher,* ed. Woodhull and Brown, p. 299; J. Blair, *Sermons,* pp. 47–48; Kollock, *Sermons,* 4:336–39, 350–53.

11. *Missionary Herald* 19 (January 1823):15.

12. *APGS,* May 1804, p. 333.

13. *MGA,* 1:25–27, 89–91.

14. Gardiner Spring, *Personal Reminiscences of the Life and Times of Gardiner Spring,* 2 vols. (New York, 1866), 1:127.

15. *MGA,* 1:171, 431–32, 468, 474, 480, 507, 567, 589, 601, 618, 691.

16. *Christian's Magazine* 1 (1806–1807):ix.

17. Ashbel Green, *A Report to the Trustees of the College of New Jersey, Relative to a Revival of Religion* (Philadelphia, 1815).

18. *Christian Monitor* 1 (October 1815):112.

19. *Panoplist* 12 (January 1816):13–17; *APGS,* June 1816, p. 19.

20. *Christian Monitor* 1 (March 1816):291–94.

21. Ibid., 2 (March 1817):205, 231–34.

22. Ibid., p. 203.

23. William B. Sprague, *Memoirs of the Rev. John McDowell and the Rev. William A. McDowell, D.D.* (New York, 1864), pp. 53–56, 70.

24. McDowell, *Fifty Years a Pastor,* pp. 15–16.

25. William Neill, *Autobiography, With a Selection of His Sermons,* ed. Joseph H. Hones (Philadelphia, 1861), pp. 30, 39–42.

26. Robert Stuart Sanders, *The Reverend Robert Stuart, D.D., 1772–1856* (Louisville: Dunne Press, 1962), p. 37.

27. Christian Association of Washington, *Declaration and Address* (Washington, Pennsylvania, 1809), pp. 17, 36–37, 45–46.

28. John B. Frantz, "Revivalism in the Dutch Reformed Church in America to 1850 with Emphasis on the Eastern Synod" (Ph.D. diss., University of Pennsylvania, 1961), p. 86.

29. James Hall, *A Narrative of a Most Extraordinary Work of Religion in North Carolina* (Philadelphia, 1802), pp. 6–9.

30. Ibid., pp. 21–27.

31. Hurley and Eagan, *Prophet of Zion-Parnassus,* pp. 89–92.

32. John Blair Hoge, *Sketch of the Life and Character of the Rev. Moses Hoge* (Richmond: Library, Union Theological Seminary in Virginia, 1964), pp. 102–03, 122.

33. Carnahan, ed., *Autobiography of John Johnston,* p. 197.

34. Ibid., pp. 52–53, 111, 114, 197–202; Guthrie, *McMillan,* pp. 22, 60–70, 80–98; David Elliot, *The Life of the Rev. Elisha Macurdy* (Allegheny, Pennsylvania, 1848), pp. 55–103.

35. Cross, *Burned-Over District,* pp. 55–76.

36. *Panoplist* 14 (May 1818):237–40.

37. Presbytery of Oneida, *A Narrative of the Revival of Religion in the County of Oneida* (Utica, New York, 1827), pp. 14, 17.

38. Ibid., pp. 25–27.

39. Quoted in William G. McLoughlin, Jr., *Modern Revivalism: Charles Grandison Finney to Billy Graham* (New York: Ronald Press Co., 1959), p. 56.

40. Ibid.

41. *Christian Advocate* 5 (November 1827):522–24.

42. *Christian Monitor* 1 (February 1816):34.

43. *Missionary Herald* 18 (January 1822):17.

44. Smith, Handy, and Loetscher, *American Christianity*, 1:522.

45. James E. Johnson, "Charles G. Finney and a Theology of Revivalism," *Church History* 38 (September 1969):340–41.

46. McLoughlin, *Modern Revivalism*, pp. 66–67.

47. Albert Barnes, *The Way of Salvation* (New York, 1836), pp. 13–14.

48. Presbytery of Oneida, *Narrative of the Revival of Religion*.

49. Quoted in McLoughlin, *Modern Revivalism*, pp. 43–44.

50. Barnes, *Way of Salvation*, pp. 52–53.

51. *Christian Advocate* 5 (July 1827).

52. *Religious Monitor* 1 (1824–1825):145, 427–29; 3 (1826–1827):61–63, 363–66.

53. *Christian Advocate* 5 (June 1827):244–45.

54. Ibid., 5 (December 1827):538–39; A. Green, "Efficacy of Divine Truth."

55. *Magazine of the Reformed Dutch Church* 3 (June 1828):91; (October 1828):221–22; 1 (October 1826):204; 2 (July 1827):110.

56. Nathan S. S. Beman, *A Discourse Delivered at the Opening of the General Assembly of the Presbyterian Church, on the 17th of May, 1832* (n.t.p.), p. 13.

57. Albert Barnes, *The Power of Holiness in the Christian Ministry* (Philadelphia, 1834), p. 3.

58. *Evangelical Guardian* 2 (November 1818):316–19.

59. *Christian Monitor* 2 (March 1817):204.

60. Presbytery of Oneida, *Narrative of the Revival of Religion*, p. 31.

61. Ibid., p. 44.

62. Finney, *Lectures on Revivals*, pp. 110, 123, 143, 147, 154, 163, 170, 221, 272.

63. Quoted in McLoughlin, *Modern Revivalism*, p. 36.

64. Presbytery of Albany, *A Narrative of the Revival of Religion, Within the Bounds of the Presbytery of Albany, in the Year 1820* (Schenectady, New York, 1821), pp. 6–9, 30–33.

65. *Missionary Herald* 20 (April 1824):130.

66. *APGS*, June 1831, p. 353.

67. *Thoughts on Revivals* (Philadelphia, 1833), p. 8.

68. Nathaniel Porter, *A Review of a Discourse on the Soverignty of God; Delivered at Morris-town, June 21, 1829, by Albert Barnes* (Morristown, New Jersey, 1829), pp. 4–5.

69. Finney, *Lectures on Revivals*, pp. 199, 219.

70. Beman, *A Discourse*, p. 2.

71. *Panoplist* 13 (July 1817):336.

72. *Christian Monitor* 2 (December 1818):107–08. See also *Panoplist* 12 (January 1816):13–17.

73. Presbytery of Oneida, *Narrative of the Revival of Religion*, pp. 19, 25–29, 31.

74. Albert Barnes, *Sermons on Revivals* (New York, 1841), p. 22.

75. McLoughlin, *Modern Revivalism,* p. 43.

76. Ibid., p. 52.

77. Quoted in ibid., p. 59.

78. Quoted in ibid., p. 79.

79. Ibid.

80. Finney, *Lectures on Revivals,* pp. 208–10.

81. McLoughlin, *Modern Revivalism,* p. 53.

82. Cross, *Burned-Over District,* p. 168.

83. *Evangelical Guardian* 1 (February 1818):457.

84. *American Sunday School Magazine* 2 (October 1825):303–11.

85. *Evangelical Guardian* 1 (February 1818):458.

86. American Sunday School Union, *Second Report,* p. xiv; *Third Report,* p. x; *Fourth Report,* p. x.

87. Archibald Alexander, *Suggestions in Vindication of Sunday-schools, But More Especially for the Improvement of Sunday-school Books, and the Enlargement of the Plan of Instruction* (Princeton, New Jersey, 1829), p. 7.

88. *American Sunday School Magazine* 4 (January 1827):19–20.

89. Ibid., 4 (September 1827):257–60.

90. Ibid., 5 (February 1828):33–35; (March 1828):68–69; (September 1828): 275–77; (November 1828):328–29.

91. *American Sunday School Magazine* 6 (March 1829):63.

92. E. Griffin, *An Address,* p. 4.

93. American Sunday School Union, *Seventh Annual Report,* pp. 21–23.

94. American Sunday School Union, *Eighth Annual Report,* pp. 18–23; *Ninth Annual Report,* pp. 12–13, 18–20; *Tenth Annual Report,* p. 22.

95. Stephen H. Tyng, *The Connexion Between Early Religious Instruction and Mature Piety* (Philadelphia, 1837).

96. *American Sunday School Magazine* 2 (January 1825):13.

97. Ibid., 2 (February 1825):50–51.

98. Ibid., 2 (November 1825):330–34; (December 1825):355–56.

99. Ibid., 3 (February 1826):42–48.

100. Ibid., 4 (November 1826):349.

101. Ibid., 6 (May 1829):147–49.

102. American Tract Society, *Third Annual Report,* pp. 28, 38–39; *Sixth Annual Report,* 1831, p. 3.

103. American Tract Society, *Tenth Annual Report,* 1835, pp. 10–11, 34–37.

104. American Tract Society, *Eleventh Annual Report,* 1836, pp. 33–36.

105. American Home Missionary Society, *Third Report,* 1829, p. 61; *Fifth Report,* 1831, p. 3; *Sixth Report,* 1832, pp. 3, 9–10, 58–59.

106. American Education Society, *Fifteenth Report,* 1831, p. 9; *Sixteenth Report,* 1832, p. 23.

107. Presbytery of Geneva, *A Narrative of the Late Revivals of Religion,* pp. 6, 10, 16, 18, 23, 25.

108. Dwight Lowell Dumond, *Antislavery: The Crusade for Freedom in America* (Ann Arbor: University of Michigan Press, 1961), pp. 175–83.

109. "Records of the Synod of Indiana," *Journals of the Presbyterian Historical Society* 34 (December 1956):267–70.

110. *Religious Monitor* 6 (1829–1830):180–85.

111. Ibid., pp. 470–71, 483–84.

112. Ibid., 11 (1834–1835):273.

113. *Christian's Magazine* 1 (1831):85–86.

114. Ibid., 3 (1834):348–49; 5 (1836):128–29, 341, 373–81.

115. *Magazine of the Reformed Dutch Church* 3 (June 1828):95. James Fulton Maclear has dealt suggestively with the attempts of the New England Congregationalists to perpetuate their theocratic heritage. One of the results of disestablishment in New England was that it "emancipated the Puritan Tradition from its purely local reference." According to Maclear, "by the 1820's provincialism had been shed; and the Puritan heritage successfully invaded other denominations and sections." The voluntary societies were primary instruments in this movement. "Coincident with the fall of the New England establishments, an expansion of interdenominational societies was undertaken." See Maclear, "'True American Union,'" pp. 53–56. This surge of New England energy threatened Presbyterian dominance of the societies. There is a real question as to whether or not the Old School fears were justified, but they were none the less real. Whitney Cross has indicated that the Presbyterians continued to gain the most from the operation of the societies in upstate New York. The other Reformed, however, clearly had nothing to gain in their denominational capacities. See *Burned-Over District*, pp. 128–37.

116. *Magazine of the Reformed Dutch Church* 2 (July 1827):126.

117. *APGS*, June 1829, p. 206.

118. Ibid., June 1833, pp. 235–36.

119. *Magazine of the Reformed Dutch Church* 3 (December 1828):279; 4 (1829):347; Nicholas I. Marselus, *The Good Old Way* (New York, 1830).

120. *Magazine of the Reformed Dutch Church* 3 (April 1828):28–30; (May 1828):59–62; (June 1828):90.

121. *Magazine of the Reformed Dutch Church* 3 (June 1828):89,

122. Ibid., 3 (July 1828):128.

123. Ibid., 3 (September 1828):189.

124. *APGS*, June 1831, pp. 367–69; June 1832, pp. 60, 71–73, 75; June 1833, p. 207.

125. Ibid., June 1830, pp. 294–99; June 1831, pp. 375, 379, 381–84; June 1832, pp. 88, 90; June 1834, p. 327.

126. Ibid., June 1832, p. 90, 92–95; October 1832, p. 140; June 1836, pp. 525–26.

127. *MGA*, 2:235–44; *Christian Advocate* 6 (June 1828):252–63.

128. *MGA*, 2:261, 296, 301.

129. Quoted in A. Alexander, *Pastoral Office*, pp. 13–14.

130. Joshua Wilson, *Four Propositions Sustained Against the Claims of the American Home Missionary Society* (Cincinnati, 1831), pp. 4–9.

131. For minutes of the convention see R. Braden Moore, *History of Huron Presbytery* (Philadelphia, 1892), pp. 78–79.

132. Finney, *Lectures on Revivals*, pp. 306, 328.

133. Barnes, *Sermons on Revivals*, pp. 21–23.

134. Ibid., p. 37.

135. Ibid., pp. 27–31. See T. Scott Miyakawa, *Protestants and Pioneers: Individualism and Conformity on the American Frontier* (Chicago: University of Chicago Press, 1964); Yehoshua Arieli, *Individualism and Nationalism in American Ideology* (Cambridge: Harvard University Press, 1964), pp. 269–70.

136. Barnes, *Sermons on Revivals,* pp. 104–09.

137. Ibid., pp. 122–23.

Bibliographic Essay

There are a number of general works on American religious history. The massive work by Sydney E. Ahlstrom, *A Religious History of the American People* (New Haven: Yale University Press, 1972), also contains an extensive bibliography. Shorter but substantial narrative histories are provided by Winthrop S. Hudson, *Religion in America* (New York: Charles Scribner's Sons, 1965); Clifton E. Olmstead, *History of Religion in the United States* (Englewood Cliffs, N.J.: Prentice-Hall, 1960); and Edwin S. Gaustad, *A Religious History of America* (New York: Harper and Row, 1966). Several more interpretive volumes are highly suggestive. See Martin E. Marty, *Righteous Empire: The Protestant Experience in America* (New York: Dial Press, 1970); Robert T. Handy, *A Christian America: Protestant Hopes and Historical Realities* (New York: Oxford University Press, 1971); William A. Clebsch, *From Sacred to Profane America: The Role of Religion in American History* (New York: Harper and Row, 1968); and Sidney E. Mead, *The Lively Experiment: The Shaping of Christianity in America* (New York: Harper and Row, 1963). These works are complemented by several anthologies. A multivolume work edited by James W. Smith and A. Leland Jamison, *Religion in American Life*, 4 vols. (Princeton: Princeton University Press, 1961), contains two volumes of essays and two volumes of bibliography. A number of major documents with helpful introductions may be found in Hilrie Shelton Smith, Robert T. Handy, and Lefferts A. Loetscher, eds., *American Christianity: An Historical Interpretation with Representative Documents*, 2 vols. (New York: Charles Scribner's Sons, 1960–1963). The recent work edited by John M. Mulder and John F. Wilson, *Religion in American History: Interpretive Essays* (Englewood Cliffs, N.J.: Prentice-Hall, 1978), is very helpful in identifying major issues. Finally, invaluable assistance is afforded by Edwin Scott Gaustad's *Historical Atlas of Religion in America*, rev. ed. (New York: Harper and Row, 1976); the recent bibliography edited by Ernest R. Sandeen and Frederick Hale, *American Religion and Philosophy: A Guide to Information Sources* (Detroit: Gale, 1978), and Henry Warner Bowden's *Dictionary of American Religious Biography* (Westport, Connecticut: Greenwood Press, 1977).

Denominational histories serve as valuable guides to theological and institutional developments and often demonstrate the areas of most interest to members of the denomination. The various Reformed denominations considered in this treatment are covered in volumes 6, 8, and 11 of Philip Schaff et al., eds., *The American Church History Series*, 13 vols. (New York: Christian Literature Co., 1893–1898). See also George P. Hays, *Presbyterians: A Popular Narrative of their Origin, Progress, Doctrines, and Achievements* (New York: J. A. Hill and Co., 1892); Charles Augustus Briggs, *American Presbyterianism: Its Origin and Early History* (New York: Charles Scribner's Sons, 1885); Robert Lathan, *History of the Associate Reformed Synod of the South* (Harrisburg: Published for the author, 1882); David Dunn et. al., *A History of the Evangelical and Reformed Church* (Philadelphia: Christian Education Press, 1961); Joseph Henry Dubbs, *Historic Manual of the Reformed Church in the United States* (Lancaster, Pa.: Inquirer Printing Co., 1885); James Isaac Good, *History of the Reformed Church in the United States in the Nineteenth*

Century (New York: Board of Publication of the Reformed Church in America, 1911). Better than these are the more recent regional studies by Ernest T. Thompson, *Presbyterians in the South: 1607–1861* (Richmond: John Knox Press, 1963); William Warren Sweet, *Religion on the American Frontier*, Vol. 2: *The Presbyterians, 1783–1840: A Collection of Source Materials*, 4 vols. (New York: Harper and Brothers, 1936); and Walter Brownlow Posey, *The Presbyterian Church in the Old Southwest, 1778–1883* (Richmond: John Knox Press, 1952). The best treatment of colonial Presbyterianism is Leonard J. Trinterud, *The Forming of An American Tradition: A Re-examination of Colonial Presbyterianism* (Philadelphia: Westminster Press, 1949). One should also consult George M. Marsden, *The Evangelical Mind and the New School Presbyterian Experience: A Case Study of Thought and Theology in Nineteenth-Century America* (New Haven: Yale University Press, 1970).

There are several monographs on various themes written from a denominational perspective. Elwyn Allen Smith focused on the ministry in *The Presbyterian Ministry in American Culture: A Study in Changing Concepts, 1700–1900* (Philadelphia: Westminster Press, 1962). A related volume is H. Richard Niebuhr and Daniel D. Williams, eds., *The Ministry in Historical Perspectives* (New York: Harper and Brothers, 1956). Julius Melton's *Presbyterian Worship in America: Changing Patterns Since 1787* (Richmond: John Knox Press, 1967) is somewhat less relevant. Andrew E. Murray, *Presbyterians and the Negro—A History* (Philadelphia: Presbyterian Historical Society, 1966), and Noel Leo Erskine, *Black People and the Reformed Church in America* (Lansing, Illinois: Reformed Church Press, 1978), provide valuable insight into the relationship of these predominantly white denominations to black Americans.

The best treatment of the American Enlightenment is by Henry F. May, *The Enlightenment in America* (New York: Oxford University Press, 1976). Other useful volumes are Peter Gay, *The Enlightenment: An Interpretation, the Rise of Modern Paganism* (New York: Random House, 1966), and Ernst Cassirer, *The Philosophy of the Enlightenment* (Princeton: Princeton University Press, 1951). An older but still helpful treatment of the political implications is Gustav A. Koch, *Republican Religion: The American Revolution and the Cult of Reason* (New York: Henry Holt and Co., 1933). Daniel Boorstin's *The Lost World of Thomas Jefferson* (New York: Henry Holt and Co., 1948) demonstrates the kind of thinking opposed by the Reformed. The Scottish philosophy is delineated in Selwyn A. Graves, *The Scottish Philosophy of Common Sense* (Oxford: Oxford University Press, 1966), and Olin McKendra Jones, *Empiricism and Intuitionism in Reid's Common Sense Philosophy* (Princeton: Princeton University Press, 1927). Its influence on American theology is succinctly stated in Sydney E. Ahlstrom, "The Scottish Philosophy and American Theology" (*Church History* 24:257–72). The very fine recent volume by Theodore Dwight Bozeman, *Protestants in an Age of Science: The Baconian Ideal and Antebellum American Religious Thought* (Chapel Hill: University of North Carolina Press, 1977), traces developments among Old School Presbyterians.

The literature on "church and state" in America is extensive. The basic issues are most clearly defined in John F. Wilson, ed., *Church and State in American History* (Boston: D. C. Heath and Co., 1965), which contains primary documents, interpretive essays, and incisive introductions. General surveys are Anson Phelps Stokes's three-volume *Church and State in the United States* (New York: Harper and Brothers, 1950) and the shorter edition by Stokes and Leo Pfeffer, *Church, State, and Freedom* (Boston: Beacon Press, 1953). James F. Maclear's "'The True American Union' of Church and State: The Reconstruction of the Theocratic Tradition," (*Church History* 28:41–54) is a stimulating interpretive essay. A recent book by Thomas E. Buckley, *Church and State in Revolutionary Virginia, 1776– 1887* (Charlottesville: University Press of Virginia, 1977), focuses more decisively on the issues in that arena than earlier works. Several other works that deal with related cultural issues are Conrad Cherry, *God's New Israel: Religious Interpretations of American Destiny* (New York: Prentice-Hall, 1977); Paul C. Nagel, *This Sacred Trust: American Nationality, 1798–1898* (New York: Oxford University Press, 1971); and Ernest Lee Tuveson, *Redeemer Nation: The Idea of America's Millennial Role* (Chicago: University of Chicago Press, 1968).

There has been considerable discussion also of "civil religion" in the 1960s and 1970s. While some of this discussion may have been unproductive in the long range for an understanding of American religion, it has been intellectually stimulating. Russell E. Richey and Donald G. Jones, eds., *American Civil Religion* (New York: Harper and Row, 1974), include the seminal essays as well as critical appraisals of attemps to delineate an American civil religion. Much of Sidney E. Mead's work properly belongs to this discussion. His latest works, *The Nation with the Soul of a Church* (New York: Harper and Row, 1975) and *The Old Religion in the Brave New World: Reflections on the Relation Between Christendom and the Republic* (Berkeley: University of California Press, 1977), eloquently reflect his conceptualization. See also Elwyn A. Smith, ed., *The Religion of the Republic* (Philadelphia: Fortress Press, 1971), and Catherine L. Albanese, *Sons of the Fathers; Civil Religion of the American Revolution* (Philadelphia: Temple University Press, 1976). The latter, reflecting an exciting application of various history of religion methodologies, may be ultimately misleading in that Albanese does not take adequately into account the fact that orthodox Christians informed and instructed common Americans much more than the politically powerful intellectual elite on whose "civil religion" she has focused.

While Perry Miller wrote relatively little on the early national period, his thinking has been seminal. His essay, "From Covenant to the Revival" in volume one of *Religion in American Life*, edited by James Ward Smith and A. Leland Jamison as cited above, is perhaps the most important. See also his *The Life of the Mind in America* (New York: Harcourt, Brace and World, 1965). Works influenced by Miller include Alan E. Heimert, *Religion and the American Mind from the Great Awakening to the Revolution* (Cambridge: Harvard University Press, 1966) and William Gribbin, "The Covenant Transformed: The Jeremiad Tradition and the War of 1812" (*Church History* 40:297–305). This tradition of scholarship has recently been expanded provocatively by Socvan Bercovitch in two books, *The Puritan Origin of the American Self* (New Haven: Yale University Press, 1975) and *The American Jeremiad* (Madison: University of Wisconsin Press, 1978).

Southern religious history has received renewed attention in the last decade. John B. Boles, *The Great Revival, 1787–1805: Origins of the Southern Evangelical Mind* (Lexington: University Press of Kentucky, 1972) properly should be considered a narrative history of the revival since it fails to define a distinctive southern religion. Much more important and suggestive is Donald G. Mathews, *Religion in the Old South* (Chicago: University of Chicago Press, 1977), which brings into focus, among other things, the impact of southern cultural norms concerning women and blacks on southern evangelicalism. Mathews perhaps identifies the Presbyterians too much with Baptist and Methodist evangelicalism. A useful corrective is supplied by E. Brooks Holifield, *The Gentlemen Theologians: American Theology in Southern Culture, 1795–1860* (Durham: Duke University Press, 1978), whose treatment of rational, elitist southern ministers focuses significantly on Presbyterians. See also Milton C. Senett, *Black Religion and American Evangelicalism: White Protestants, Plantation Missions, and the Flowering of Negro Christianity, 1787–1865* (Metuchen, N.J.: Scarecrow Press, 1975).

There is extensive literature on the voluntary societies. The history of this type of association in Western civilization is delineated by Frederick William Bullock in *Voluntary Religious Societies, 1520–1799* (St. Leonards on Sea: Budd and Gilloth, 1963). There are a number of studies of individual societies. See Henry Otis Dwight, *The Centennial History of the American Bible Society*, 2 vols. (New York: MacMillan, 1916); Edwin Wilbur Rice, *The Sunday School Movement, 1780–1917, and the American Sunday School Union, 1817–1917* (Philadelphia: American Sunday School Union, 1917); Colin B. Goodykoontz, *Home Missions on the American Frontier: With Particular Reference to the American Home Missionary Society* (Caldwell, Indiana: Claxton Printers, 1939); and P. J. Staudenraus, *The African Colonization Movement, 1816–1865* (New York: Columbia University Press, 1961). Two important scholarly assessments of the societies appeared in 1960. They were Clifford S. Griffin, *Their Brothers' Keepers: Moral Stewardship in the United States, 1800–1865* (New Brunswick: Rutgers Unviersity Press) and Charles I. Foster, *An Errand of Mercy: The Evangelical United Front, 1790–1837* (Chapel Hill: University of North Carolina Press). See also the critical appraisal of these works by Lois W. Banner, "Religious Benevolence as Social Control: A Critique of an Interpretation" (*Journal of American History* 60:23–41). R. Pierce Beaver, *Church, State, and the American Indians: Two and a Half Centuries of Partnership in Missions between Protestant Churches and Government* (Saint Louis: Concordia Publishing House, 1966), and Robert F. Berkhofer, Jr., *Salvation and the Savage: An Analysis of Protestant Missions and American Indian Response, 1787–1862* (Lexington: University Press of Kentucky, 1965), detail the work of the societies among Indians.

The discussion of poverty in early America has developed largely in the context of urban history. Constance McLaughlin Green's *American Cities in the Growth of the Nation* (New York: Harper and Row, 1965), originally published in 1957, is still useful as a survey. Two anthologies, David T. Gilchrist, ed., *The Growth of the Seaport Cities, 1790–1825* (Charlottesville: University Press of Virginia, 1967), and Stephan Thernstrom and Richard Sennett, eds., *Nineteenth-Century Cities: Essays in the New Urban History* (New Haven: Yale University Press, 1969), demonstrate the potential of thorough research and quantitative methodologies. Edward Pessen's *Riches, Class and Power before the Civil War* (New York: Heath, 1973) is extremely helpful. Robert Bremner's *From the Depths: The Discovery of Poverty in the United States* (New York: New York University Press, 1956) is seriously flawed by his dating of the onset of poverty to the 1830s. Several works focus on the interrelatedness of poverty with religious concerns. See Raymond Mohl, *Poverty in New York* (New York: Oxford University Press, 1971); Carroll S. Rosenberg, *Religion and the Rise of the American City: The New York City Mission Movement,*

1812-1870 (Ithaca: Cornell University Press, 1971); and David J. Rothman, *The Discovery of the Asylum: Social Order and Disorder in the New Republic* (Boston: Little, Brown and Co., 1971).

Revivalism has long fascinated Americans and their historians and the litera-ture on the subject is voluminous. The most useful general narrative histories are William Warren Sweet, *Revivalism in America: Its Origin, Growth and Decline* (New York: Charles Scribner's Sons, 1944); Bernard A. Weisberger, *They Gathered at the River: The Story of the Great Revivalists and Their Impact upon Religion in America* (Boston: Little, Brown and Co., 1958); and William G. McLoughlin, *Modern Revivalism: Charles Grandison Finney to Billy Graham* (New York: Ronald Press Co., 1959). The work of Whitney R. Cross, *The Burned-Over District: The Social and Intellectual History of Enthusiastic Religion in Western New York, 1800-1850* (Ithaca, Cornell University Press, 1950), remains a most thorough and provoking study. T. Scott Miyakawa's *Protestants and Pioneers: Individualism and Conformity on the American Frontier* (Chicago: University of Chicago Press, 1964) and Timothy L. Smith's *Revivalism and Social Reform in Mid-Nineteenth Century America* (Nashville: Abingdon Press, 1957) raise questions that have never been dealt with satisfac-torily. An analysis of the literature and a promising conceptual framework are offered by Donald G. Mathews, "The Second Great Awakening as an Organizing Process, 1780-1830: an Hypothesis" (*American Quarterly* 21:23-43). See my at-tempts in "Quantitative Analysis in the Study of American Religious History" (*Journal of the American Academy of Religion* 43:287-91) and "The Restoration of Community: The Great Revival in Four Baptist Churches in Central Kentucky" (*The Quarterly Review* 39:73-82). The recent contributions to the discussion in-clude Dickson D. Bruce, *And They All Sang Hallelujah* (Knoxville: University of Tennessee Press, 1974); Sandra S. Sizer, *Gospel Hymns and Social Religion: The Rhetoric of Nineteenth Century Revivalism* (Philadelphia: Temple University Press, 1978); Richard Carwardine, *Transatlantic Revivalism: Popular Evangelicalism in Britain and America, 1790-1865* (Westport, Connecticut: Greenwood Press, 1978); and William G. McLoughlin, *Revivals, Awakenings, and Reform: An Essay on Religion and Social Change in America, 1607-1977* (Chicago: University of Chicago Press, 1978). Both Bruce and Sizer attempt to illuminate revivalism through the study of hymns while Carwardine emphasizes the similarity of British and Ameri-can Revivals. McLoughlin, who applies sociological and anthropological insights to the study of revivalism, offers a suggestive model but the work suffers from diffusion and overgeneralization.

This study rests primarily on a survey of nearly 3,000 printed documents from the period under consideration. These are reflected in the notes and include primarily books and sermons by the Reformed ministers, official church records, and publications of the voluntary societies. While I have sometimes suspected that the ministers never had an unpublished thought, I have attempted only to establish that which was of public record and I have not perused the voluminous manuscript collections. The best depositories of Reformed materials are The Presbyterian Historical Society in Philadelphia, Firestone Library of Princeton University, Speer Library of Princeton Theological Seminary, Gardner A. Sage Library of the New Brunswick Theological Seminary, and the Historical Foun-dation of the Presbyterian and Reformed Churches in Monteat, North Carolina.

Index

Adam, 75–76
Adams, John, 12, 27, 103–04, 130–32
Adams, John Quincy, 105, 131
Africa, 73, 133; African, 130–32
African Education Society, 130
African School, 63
Albany, 34–35, 97, 120, 183, 193
Alexander, Archibald, 33, 39, 43, 58, 71, 78, 102, 147, 150, 171
American Anti-Slavery Society, 191
American Bible Society, 116, 120, 123–38, 142, 151–53, 160, 168, 192
American Board of Commissioners for Foreign Missions, 116, 124–25, 192–93
American Colonization Society, 116, 124, 129, 131–32, 159
American Education Society, 116, 124, 143, 161, 190–91
American Home Missionary Society, 116, 125, 127, 143, 152, 168, 190, 194, 195
Americanism, 12
American Philosophical Society, 16
American Revolution, 8, 11–13, 21, 27, 29, 30–31, 34–35, 49–50, 55, 64, 72, 88, 113, 141, 143, 146–47, 177
American Seaman's Friend Society, 157
American Society for Promoting the Civilization and General Improvement of the Indian Tribes in the United States, 130
American Society for the Encouragement of Domestic Manufactures, 153
American Sunday School Magazine, 162, 165, 188–89
American Sunday School Union, 116, 122, 124, 127, 131–32, 138–43, 152, 154, 158, 160, 163–68, 187–88
American Temperance Society, 116, 154, 191
American Tract Society, 122, 124, 127, 150, 161–63, 166, 168, 190
"An Apology for the Associate Reformed Church," 192
Anglicans, 28
Antichrist, 69, 72–74, 83, 86
Apocalypticism, 74
Arminian, 183
Armstrong, Amzi, 70–71
Articles of Confederation, 12

Asia, 73
Associate Presbyterians, 192
Associate Reformed Church, 4, 30, 36, 54, 109, 118, 123–24, 167, 175, 192
Associate Reformed Synod of New York, 192
Associate Synod of North Carolina, 4, 117, 118, 192
"Association of Religion and Patriotism," 49, 67, 88, 100, 109

Baldwin, Eli, 193
Baltimore, 40, 135, 144–45, 152, 158, 160
Baptists, 2, 4, 28, 85, 124, 163, 167
Barnard, Daniel D., 61
Barnes, Albert, 65, 170, 179, 180–81, 196–97
Bayard, Samuel, 69
Beaver, R. Pierce, 133
Beecher, Charles, 2
Beecher, Lyman, 126, 182, 195
Beman, Nathan S. S., 181, 184
Bethune, Dixie, 150, 156
Bethune, George Washington, 61, 63, 65
Bible, 40, 44, 51, 54–61, 66, 78, 80–81, 85–86, 91–95, 101, 103, 110, 114, 116–17, 122–23, 126, 135–36, 141, 150–57, 162, 166, 168, 174, 175, 178, 180, 192, 199
Bible Society of Philadelphia, 122, 126, 150, 154
Bible Society of the District of Columbia, 152
Bible Society of Union College, 149
Bill of Rights, 92
Blacks, 63–64, 85, 97, 116–17, 130, 146, 159, 182
Blackstone, Sir William, 90, 92
Blair, John D., 65
Blatchford, Samuel, 151
Bliss, John F., 161
Blythe, James, 72–74, 85, 87, 123
Board of Education for the Reformed Dutch Church, 193
Boston, 124, 133, 144, 186
Boudinot, Elias, 69, 103, 121, 131
Bradford, John M., 35
Breckinridge, John, 49, 55